ALONE TOGETHER

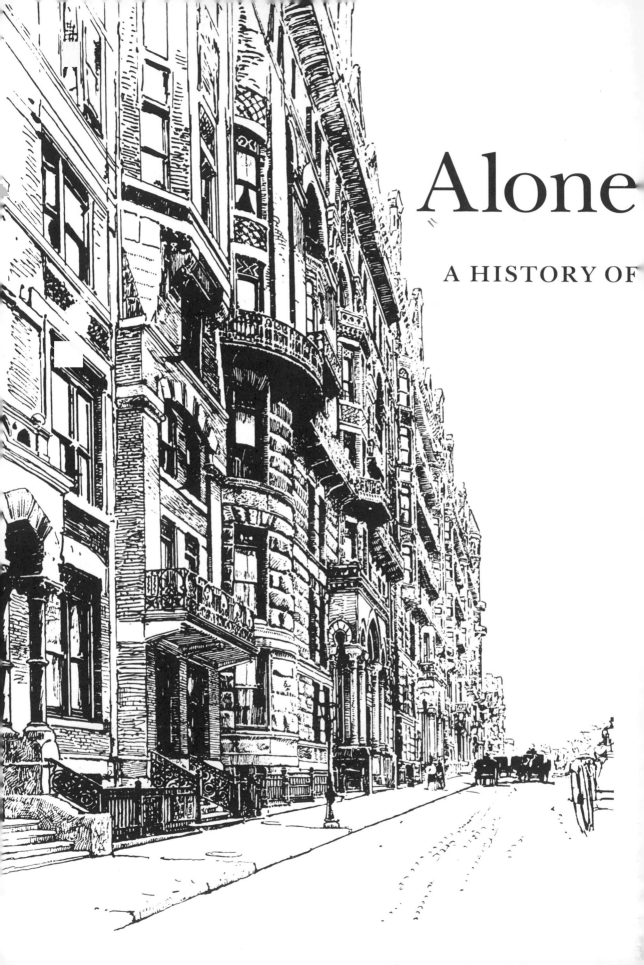

Alone

A HISTORY OF

Together:

NEW YORK'S EARLY APARTMENTS

Elizabeth Collins Cromley

CORNELL UNIVERSITY PRESS

ITHACA AND LONDON

First published 1990 by Cornell University Press.

International Standard Book Number 0-8014-2324-4
Library of Congress Catalog Card Number 89-42869

Printed in the United States of America

Librarians: Library of Congress cataloging information appears on the last page of the book.

∞ The paper used in this publication meets the minimum requirements of the American National Standard for Permanence of Paper for Printed Library Materials Z39.48–1984.

To my parents and my children

CONTENTS

ILLUSTRATIONS

PREFACE

THE apartment buildings on the Upper West Side of Manhattan provided rental homes to many young parents with small children when I first lived there in the mid-1960s. The fathers went to their paid jobs early each morning, while we mothers organized days of housekeeping, child care, and plans for the evening, when the breadwinners would return. Mothers met in the lobby in the morning to take kids to the park, ending up eating lunch together. Once or twice a week a play group met in someone's apartment, mothers taking their turns overseeing the kids one week in order to free a couple of afternoons the next week. Because there was never quite enough money, we organized a food co-op whose members all lived in the same apartment building. Every two weeks we took turns going to the wholesale markets, turning someone's apartment into a greengrocer's for the afternoon. Since going out in the evening required a baby-sitter, most evenings were spent at home, but the apartment house once again provided an expanded field. Friendships begun in the playground grew over the dinner table. Real evenings out could be managed by exchanging baby-sitting services. The apartment house served us young wives in countless essential ways: as a family home, a day-care center and play group, a mothers' network for services and information, a shopping co-op, and a social circle. With all the benefits of apartment life, why would anyone choose to live in a private house?

These virtues are not ones that architectural historians have usually identified as significant. But when I began to study the American apartment house as a specific building type with a particular architectural history, such qualities inexorably entered the picture. Indeed, the successful development of built-for-the-purpose apartment houses hinged on such issues as who the neighbors would be, how much privacy could be had under a roof sheltering many families, and what services could be gained by living with others. Thus my own experience of the 1960s and 1970s led me back to a century before that time to discover what needs inspired apartment houses and how they came to be *the* form of housing for Manhattan.

In addition to the contributions of mothers of West End Avenue and Riverside Drive, I want to acknowledge the help of many scholars, family, and friends and the support of several institutions in the preparation of this book. The City University of New York Graduate School helped with an innovative program in American art history, travel support, and sympathetic advisers: Eugene Santomasso, Jacob Landy, Jonathan Barnett, and William Gerdts.

Elizabeth Blackmar is the scholar to whom I owe the most; I learned a great deal about doing history and about New York from her dissertation and book on the housing of Manhattan in the first half of the nineteenth century. I am grateful for her readings of my manuscript, her suggestions for further research, and her hospitality. She is always an exciting thinker and a generous friend. Gwendolyn Wright made useful suggestions at the very beginning of my work on this topic. James Goode and Carroll William Westfall have provided valuable comparative pictures of apartment developments in Washington, D.C., and Chicago, and have been generous in sharing research sources.

The help of librarians in several parts of the country was indispensable. I thank especially the librarians at the New York Public Library's Local History Collection, Avery Library at Columbia University, the Henry Francis du Pont Winterthur Museum, Winterthur, Delaware, the Buffalo and Erie County Public Library, the New York City Municipal Archives, and the libraries at the University of California at Berkeley. Curators of the photograph collections at the New-York Historical Society and the Museum of the City of New York provided important assistance.

Finding good critics is hard; learning to hear what they have to say is even harder. I have been a slow learner, and I thank all my readers for putting up with my resistance at times to good suggestions. Thanks to Jennifer Cromley for comments and for pointing me to Theodore Dreiser's *Sister Carrie,* to Mia Boynton for insights into the nature of privacy, to Joseph Ernst for careful readings and candid opinions, and to Karen Franck for providing the occasion to think through the meaning of some nineteenth-century "collective" apartment ideas for late-twentieth-century households. The members of the Vernacular Architecture Forum have provided diverse models of scholarship for dealing with common architecture and continually reinforce my commitment to new kinds of architectural history by their enthusiasm and fresh perspectives. I am especially grateful to my VAF colleagues Cary Carson and Dell Upton for readings, insights, and questions. I have learned a great deal from the comments of anonymous critics to Cornell University Press and other presses about this manuscript, and I owe them all gratitude. Thanks especially to Peter Agree for infinite patience and for finding such good readers, and to Joanne S. Ainsworth for meticulous editing.

Thanks go to the institutions who have offered financial support: to the National Endowment for the Humanities for a Fellowship at the Winterthur

Museum Advanced Studies Program; to the National Endowment for the Arts for support of a study of building types in which I played a part; and to the State University of New York at Buffalo for a grant under its Faculty Development Program. Opportunities for public presentation and discussion of aspects of this research have been provided by the New-York Historical Society, the Delaware Humanities Forum, the Winterthur Museum, Columbia University's Seminar on the City, and several university departments of architecture. I have given papers on aspects of apartment history at several scholarly annual meetings and am grateful to all those who gave me the floor, and especially to those who challenged my ideas and helped me rethink the story.

I have been lucky in my own domestic history and thank the many people who, at various times, have made a home with me. Thanks to Howard and Frances for bringing me up in bungalows; to Ethan and Freda for an interim home with a chicken coop; and to Seth and Jennifer for trying out a succession of Manhattan and Brooklyn apartment and loft homes with me. Finally my gratitude to Joe Ernst for his intellectual and emotional strength, for paying half of the mortgage, and for being so swell to come home to.

ELIZABETH COLLINS CROMLEY

Buffalo, New York

ALONE TOGETHER

INTRODUCTION

Eᴠᴇʀʏʙᴏᴅʏ knows that New Yorkers live in apartment buildings. New York, famous as the city of "cliff dwellers," is piled high on an island, anomalous among American cities. Its crowds, its culture, its high prices and strange habits, have long made New York seem not quite properly American to the rest of the country. New York's mode of apartment living is especially foreign to American practices and myths of private-house ownership, where a house of one's own on one's own piece of land is the "correct" mode for family life.[1] Yet in Manhattan not many people can afford to live in a private house, and even for those of great wealth there are hardly enough private houses to go around. Since the early twentieth century nearly all Manhattanites have had to live in multiple dwellings.

This book presents a history of the "invention" of middle-class apartment buildings as an architectural form new to Manhattan in the mid-nineteenth century, a form distinct from working-class tenements and subdivided formerly private houses. It traces, over the last decades of the nineteenth and the first decade of the twentieth centuries, the emergence and maturing of apartments, both as physical, designed-and-built artifacts and as culturally defined homes. It focuses on the period when this building type began, and so reaches back to look at the dwelling conditions and expectations that encouraged the creation of apartments. The book ends at the point when architects, developers, and tenants arrived at satisfactory resolutions to the early problems in defining what apartments should be.

In 1850, Manhattan had a population of half a million people; in 1910 nearly two and one-half million. The increasing demand on land made prices rise, and individual houses became too expensive for the majority of the population. New York's tradition of privately built houses left responsibility for producing enough dwelling units in the hands of private enterprise.[2] Multiple dwellings rather than single-family houses provided the answer, in terms of both the real estate market and architecture.

When we begin to examine apartment houses within the world of architectural meaning, we find that as a building type they continually raised problems for their users. These problems can be located by a set of boundary lines, like geological "fault lines," in the conceptual formulation of later-nineteenth-century urban culture. Apartment-house architecture first straddled the line between the familiar forms of public and private buildings. Houses constituted the private architecture of the city; civic, religious, and commercial buildings made up the public world. Historically, the larger building scale for public structures and their more ambitious architectural forms made these distinctions evident. But apartment houses, incorporating features of each within a single building, challenged clear boundaries between the home as a private house and the civic and commercial, even the street, as the public realm. In an apartment house, where some public spaces and many private spaces had to coexist, the boundaries and meaning of public and private were always in negotiation.

Apartments also straddled the line between American and foreign building forms; although built on native soil, in their first decade at least they were always linked to Paris. Because of this link, early apartment buildings were called "French flats"; but because the culture behind the name was associated with certain unacceptable behaviors, apartments became morally questionable. They were also questionable in the way they crossed the line between a mature mode of dwelling in independent homes and an immature mode of dwelling in group homes. Boys in Yale colleges, girls in Lowell factory dormitories properly lived in shared housing because they were not yet adults; mature people established independent homes of their own. Such defining traits of maturity were called into question when groups of families all lived under the same apartment-house roof.

The middle class had lived in single-family houses while the working class had tenements. But apartment houses blurred the line between middle class and working class. Local tenement precedents suggested that multiple dwellings were, in their nature, lower class, an unwelcome connotation to the middle class. Could designers create an architectural vocabulary to clarify the confusing mix of classes and urban functions of nineteenth-century New York? Architectural devices might convey meanings about who lived where, improving the legibility of New York's urban face to genteel New Yorkers worried about sustaining class distinctions. In the literature of the period, writers contrast "apartment houses" for middle-class tenants to "tenement buildings" for the working class but disagree about where their differences lie. Making such distinctions and identifying shades of difference among middle-class buildings will be one of the themes this history explores.

The designers of apartment houses worked to allow genteel families and individuals to feel as much at home in multifamily dwellings as in private residences. In *Sister Carrie* the novelist Theodore Dreiser provides a sentimental definition of "home," contrasting it with the harshness of city life. "A lovely home atmosphere is one of the flowers of the world than which there is nothing more tender, nothing more delicate, nothing more calculated to make strong and just the natures cradled and nourished within it. To those who have never experienced the beneficent influence of its delightful seclusion, no words can make clear the power whereby it uplifts."[3] While homes themselves changed radically, the mythologizing of home changed much more slowly, and writers expressed a middle-class commitment to "home values" from the 1850s to 1900, although the world had not stayed the same.

In mid-century, such home values were attached to the individual private house as the protector of family privacy, morality, and identity; these meanings attached to the house took on added strength as Americans resisted the disturbing challenges of newly urbanized life. But achieving that goal of the single-family home, a safe haven in a rapidly changing world, was more and more difficult for New York City's families as the nineteenth century progressed. Could an apartment house shared with so many others also constitute a home, and would it (or should it) sustain the same kinds of values for all?

Apartments figured differently in the dwelling needs and desires of men and women. Apartment houses, just like private single-family homes, helped to affirm the boundary between the world of home and the world of paid work as spatially distinct spheres in the city for the husbands and wives of any middle-class family. However, because of their location, near transportation, apartments also meant easy access to the amusements, conveniences, and diversions of the city. Thus at a time when women were meant to be family centered, to enjoy staying at home focusing on "women's sphere," apartment buildings and their place in the city enabled women to enjoy urban choices outside the home.

Published statements indicate that the strongest protests about disruptions of symbolic "home values" in apartment houses come from male writers, while women speak most strongly in favor of the pragmatic convenience of modern housekeeping. Late-nineteenth-century life was filled with tensions over the value of modernization: industry's methods, materials, and inventions often seemed inhuman and raised resistance among thinkers who would return to a simpler life. But for women charged with keeping houses, anything that eased the burdens of housework was welcomed, and the convenient modernized housekeeping offered by apartments therefore made them appealing.[4]

Within this cultural setting, apartment buildings emerged and were slowly accepted. They appeared in various sizes and forms, in brick and in stone, constructed with masonry methods or with steel framing. There were specific moments of inventive design activity in the years when apartment houses were established, when new options were added to the architectural repertoire. In some ways, these changes can be seen as progress and improvement and can be represented by a developmental story. Part of my aim in this book, then, is to construct a chronologically organized history of apartments as a developing architectural type.[5] But as a type, the apartment house is full of variety in its characteristic size, its placement in the city, its meaning for potential tenants and for critics. In any given year or decade several architectural options are available, and within the middle-class group needing apartments, levels of income and commensurate levels of apartments vary, ranging from bare minimum to luxury.

The intended users of apartment houses were not only families but also single people. Tenants of the 1870s buildings might be nuclear families of parents and children with at least one servant, single gentlemen, widows, or childless married couples; for young, marriageable middle-class daughters, apartment living was at first less than respectable. During the decades of development choices in apartment-house offerings expanded greatly; rental costs in the early 1870's excluded all but prosperous tenants, but by the end of the 1890s those who were just making ends meet as well as the very well-off could afford an apartment. An early thin stream of executed apartment designs grew to a torrent by 1910— from about 200 apartment buildings in 1876 to more than 10,000 in the first decade of the twentieth century.

The people of the "middle class" perceived their family values and social place to be of a kind different from those of either the rich or the working class. They required dwellings designed to suit and to reinforce those values and that place. They would have preferred individual private houses; however, they were forced toward another housing form. In response to new living patterns set into motion by apartment houses, the middle-class tenants redefined some aspects of their "home values."

This redefinition can be seen as a shift from an emphasis on privacy to an emphasis on both privacy and efficiency in family dwelling units. Apartment houses satisfied many originally perceived needs and also helped to generate new "needs." Thus the experience of living in apartment houses caused a shift in attitude from the earlier nineteenth-century belief in a single-family private house as the best form. With decades of experience, New Yorkers recognized the new possibility that multifamily apartment houses could be the best settings for modern family life.

By the first decade of the twentieth-century, apartment buildings were recognized as so fully at home in Manhattan that they replaced private-house construction almost completely. Designers and developers achieved sufficient variety within the building type to provide for luxury as well as for plain and simple needs; to accommodate families with children or single people; to conform to the needs of housekeepers and to those who wanted to be free of housekeeping chores. By refining floor plans, internal circulation, and room adjacencies, designers of apartments achieved a well-developed modern dwelling plan that was flexible enough to be used at different scales. The incorporation of modern technological aids made apartment houses the exemplars of convenience. The Parisian models were reinterpreted for Americans. As a new type, the apartment house was able to straddle those cultural fault lines that had seemed so problematic: apartments made it possible for women both to run a household and to participate in city life; for a home to be both a public building and a private dwelling; and for the proliferating middle-class New Yorkers to dwell in buildings that they could define as middle class enough to make them feel socially secure.

These themes are explored in the six chapters of this book. In Chapter 1 the background for apartment houses is established in mid-nineteenth-century practices of sharing housing. A large proportion of city residents lived in two-family houses, on floors of a subdivided house, or in boardinghouses or hotels. Thus tenants and developers were already familiar with shared housing, which helped them to define the characteristics of apartment houses when their necessity became obvious.

In the second chapter, I propose that in order to create a new kind of building, designers and clients had to lean on existing models of dwellings, as examples both of good features and of what to avoid. Here we look to Paris for its history of apartment houses, to New York's private-house tradition for some ideals, and to local tenement houses for a well-established but repugnant form of multiple dwelling in New York. In Chapter 3 the first generation of purpose-built apartment houses of the 1870s is considered in both its conceptual and physical forms. What defined these buildings, where were they, what did they look like, and how did they interact with the urban environment? Chapter 4 continues with questions of the uses and meanings to tenants of the interior forms of the first-generation apartment houses.

The second generation of large, elevator apartment houses of the 1880s adds to the repertoire, and is examined in Chapter 5. Here, issues of social tension emerge with the further development of public spaces in architecturally prominent buildings; and are mediated or resolved as tenants gain greater experience in living with others. The final chapter looks at the consolidation and variation of the new building type. Here I take up many of the same themes introduced by the apartment houses of earlier decades and see how they mature. As they find a certain resolution at the turn of the century, I trace how, in the first decade of the twentieth century, architects, developers, and tenants created apartments that still accord with many of our notions of home life in the late twentieth century.

A Few Definitions

Some terms that appear frequently in this history are problematic. The term "apartment building" is a current one, as is the term "multiple dwelling"; both mean a building designed specifically to accommodate the dwelling needs of several (usually three or more) families. In mid-nineteenth-century use, "apartments" meant any set of rooms: a suite in a hotel or a set of rental rooms in a private house (also called a "floor") or a family unit in an apartment building. The terms "flats" and "French flats" were also in use in nineteenth-century New

York; a flat was an apartment unit, while a French flat building was a designed-for-the-purpose apartment house. "Apartment hotel" and "family hotel" were two other terms used, sometimes interchangeably with "apartment house," in the early years of development. I call the subjects of this work apartment buildings or apartment houses and point out nuances of meaning and name changes as the building type evolves.

New York law defined all buildings with three or more independent family dwelling units as "tenement" buildings, but in popular usage that term always implied working-class housing. The distinction between apartments and tenements was not always clear to New Yorkers, and the "necessity of new terms . . . to discriminate new things" was sometimes pressing. A property owner sued her neighbor in 1878 for erecting a tenement house, which was expressly forbidden in the deed; the neighbor defended himself, saying the building he put up was not a tenement but an apartment house because it had a restaurantlike dining room, which would never be found in a common tenement.[6] People felt the need to discriminate more finely among classes of buildings than the law did, in order to protect the boundaries of their own middle-class status.

As early as 1866, the *New York Times* identified people making $2,500 to $3,000 a year as the "middle class" and explained why they were in particular need of dwellings. Tenements for working-class residents have received all the attention, the *Times* remarked, but the middle class are equally oppressed by high costs for land, high rents, and high taxes. These are the kinds of people who now rent houses for exorbitant rents they can ill afford, or who must leave the city to find independent houses in the suburbs. The *Times* writer assumed that this class of New Yorkers shared an Anglo-Saxon heritage of love for the independent home and were resistant to any method of sharing a dwelling. The *Times* called upon readers to consider how successful flat buildings had been in European cities, to reconsider their prejudices against flats, and to see that they were the only solution to the housing problem for "people of small incomes."[7]

In the 1860s, before any major flat buildings were erected in New York, middle-class residents were known to be biased against them. And yet in very few years, flat buildings seemed to be widely accepted. The fact that apartment houses were among the appropriate dwellings for the genteel is shown in a period "self-portrait." *Phillips' Elite Directory of Private Families,* published yearly beginning in 1874, listed the addresses of individuals who lived in both grand and small apartment buildings, in hotels, and in private houses. A middle-class woman of the era might pick up this publication to take along as she made social calls. In the late 1870s and 1880s, some of these addresses identified costly houses or apartment buildings where rents were high and spaces lavish, and others named very modest French-flat buildings; nonetheless all were collected in *Phillips' Elite Directory* because all these residents stood together as the genteel. Such a diverse group of people could see themselves as a group perhaps only in opposition to those other, nonvisitable, ungenteel citizens: occupants of working-class tenements and districts.[8]

The term "middle class" is itself problematic, as anyone knows who has tried to define its meaning.[9] If apartment buildings were being designed for middle-class clients, then who precisely were they? It may be tempting to think of "class" as a container, and to consider what incomes, what educations, what occupations the people in that container should possess? But it is more helpful to think about class differences as the negotiated positions of one class in relation to another, not fixed properties. Belonging to the middle class meant negotiating a status location in the city through making "choices" (constrained or enabled by resources) in dress, behavior, education, occupation, taste and, so on, that could mark families as different from (and better than) all those others, the immigrants, the working classes.

As the social historian Michael Katz has explained, the term "class" is rightly used to point to conflict and contested terrain, not just to income stratification.[10] Areas of contested terrain in nineteenth-century New York are captured in such questions as: what is the appropriate use of streets? where can people find suitable housing? where is the edge between public and private? what are the roles of family members? For example, middle-class wives supported themselves by staying at home and producing a home for the male breadwinner; they used the street for a promenade, going visiting or shopping. For working-class women, the street was the site for a strike parade, for child rearing, indeed sometimes for earning a living.[11] Differences in family behavior, in dress, in socializing, in housing, all provided markers to distinguish working-class from middle-class life.

Definitions of middle-class values may gather around several different focal points. Mary Ryan, in *Cradle of the Middle Class*, asserts that the mid-nineteenth-century middle class identified itself with "images of private family life as [its] class insignia . . . , molded its distinctive identity around domestic values and family practices."[12] Membership in the middle class may be defined by occupation. In this emerging class, of heads of families were employed in many different occupations, but in contrast to the preceding generation they were not generally self-employed. An 1878 portrait of the class intended to make up the new group of apartment dwellers described "young business-men, professional people, artists, *literati*, employe[e]s, and others who by their education, culture and position, may fairly claim to live in seemliness and comfort." This middle class group may also be described by income, although the income range may be quite large. In 1878, "families whose advantage is theoretically contemplated in the apartment system are those with incomes of not more than three, four, or at the outside, five thousand dollars per annum," according to one observer, but others assigned different income ranges to the class in need of apartments.[13]

If membership in the middle class is defined by many characteristics (occupation, income, family strategy, lifestyle, and so on), then those wishing to be counted among the ranks of the genteel have many opportunities to enter. Dwellings were one such entry point: an apartment house instead of a boardinghouse or a tenement, well decorated, with a particularly fine parlor and perhaps the right address could help mark and secure a family's social status. From this point of view, the right kind of dwelling helped create the middle class, even as those engaged in building such dwellings meant to provide for that class. What is crucial to us is the ways that housing helped create the web of meanings portraying the middle class to itself, and particularly how apartment houses participated in the creation of those meanings. Groups of apartment houses in districts helped to establish particular parts of the city as middle-class urban space. The dwelling became for its residents a place that signified and sustained concepts of "family," or "neighborhood," or "class"—concepts of cohesion and difference—particularly significant in the nineteenth-century city.

Methods for a History of Apartment Houses

Architectural historians have written about many diverse time periods, geographical areas, building styles, architects, and building types, but they have published very little research on apartment buildings. Recent histories of apartment design include Andrew Alpern's *Apartments for the Affluent* (1975), which supplies a very useful overview, through large plans and photographs of exteriors, of what was built in New York from 1869 to 1970; and Norton and Patterson's guidebook to named New York apartments, *Living It Up* (1984), with its brief introductory historical essay. The growth of New York City understood as the history of real estate development is the subject of M. Christine Boyer's *Manhattan Manners* (1985), which lists many apartment houses and locates them in the development of Manhattan. This book is intended as a complement to these three works: where they offer catalogs of examples of apartment houses, I develop an interpretive framework for how they worked.[14]

It is not difficult to understand why apartment houses have proved an unattractive subject to most architectural historians. For those who enjoy the artistic achievements of architecture, apartment buildings offer few rewards. Great design will much more surely be found in other building types that were not so subject to the demands of a real estate market. Many historians of architecture have studied the careers and production of important American architects or firms; but most of the architects involved in late-nineteenth-century apartment-house design have not been counted among the "greats." Contemporary critics sometimes mocked the "architects" of apartment houses, suggesting that they were for the most part ill-trained, inferior talents.[15] Apartments also fulfill apparently banal functions when compared with important civic or religious architecture; indeed their programs seem in retrospect so commonsensical as to be nearly invisible. For these reasons, then, the history of apartment houses and how they came to take the forms they did is a story still in need of telling.

It is at the working class end of the housing spectrum that multiple dwellings have come in for a thorough examination—not from architectural historians but from social historians seeking connections between social life and dwelling space.[16] These writers have focused on the political and social framework of tenement buildings and tenement dwellers. While not specifically histories of architecture, books like these provide models for enlarging the scope of an architectural discussion.

In the last few years, architectural historians, learning from this contextual approach, have begun to look anew at the architecture of ordinary dwellings. David Handlin, Gwendolyn Wright, and Dolores Hayden, among others, incorporate issues of social life, trends in American culture, and meanings assigned to the concept of home into a discussion of residential architectural design.[17]

In keeping with this recent trend to broaden the concerns and interpretive abilities of architectural history, I approach this history of apartment houses on several levels: an account of the new building type in its physical form comes from factual sources and graphic documentation; an account of the mentality that stood behind the production of these built forms comes from my interpretation of the contemporary literature and the language in which apartments were discussed. Nineteenth-century participants in the creation of apartment houses range from developers to architects to tenants to critics, all of whom contributed ideas to the developing definition of apartment design. Their ideas surfaced as letters to newspapers, as architectural plans, as the reports of Buildings Department inspectors, as advice in etiquette manuals, as assertions in city guidebooks. From these many kinds of texts and many different voices, I have reconstructed the attitudes, positions, preferences, experiments, and apartment design solutions that went into creating a new American building type.

Instead of choosing buildings that are aesthetically notable, I have chosen buildings that typify the new apartment-house forms in New York, and have then asked what aesthetic properties these buildings possessed and what they might mean, speculating on how apartment designs worked for perceived client needs. I do not construct careers or oeuvres for architectural firms, but rather trace the career of a building type as it evolved. My speculations about a way to read the architectural style of these buildings, which posit additional meanings for apartment architecture, come from my conviction that architectural style may be motivated by more significant forces than simply the desire to "be in style."

Since every architectural product fulfills some set of programmatic needs (articulated or not), I have spent some time describing the shifting terms of the domestic program that these buildings were made to contain. That program, as we know from our similar experience today, is one that must take into account light and air requirements, household tasks like cooking and cleaning, bodily needs like sleeping, and spaces for sociability. But these perhaps measurable requirements are always entangled with threads of emotion, tradition, morality, and ritual, gathered in the concept of "home." Here I have tried to uncover some aspects of the concept of home as it was being created and recreated by middle-class New Yorkers, and to insist that certain features of homelife, such as the particular set of people constituting a "family" and the desire for privacy, were not innate but were created in their particular forms as part of a middle class ideology.[18]

The variety of ways of looking at buildings that I suggest here amplifies traditional modes of discussing architecture. Parts of this book are concerned with examining the visual, formal properties of buildings; other parts consider issues of planning, program, and use; and yet other sections focus on social context. I have tried to weave these elements together in ways that show architecture both reflecting and producing cultural meanings. This combination of visual, cultural, and social readings of apartments helps to explain why these buildings looked as they did and how they performed their functions for and conveyed their meanings to the tenants who first used them.

1 MAKING DO

THE creation of built-for-the-purpose apartment houses specifically for middle class tenants occurred largely after the Civil War, but the beginnings of apartment life lie in the prewar era, rooted in dwelling practices. Throughout the first half of the nineteenth century, changes in the use of houses, in the location of houses in a growing city, and in the cost of housing all contributed to the increase in the number of New Yorkers living in shared housing. People found themselves, often unwillingly, trying out a variety of types of ad hoc multiple dwellings. Their experience in these arrangements was often disappointing and led them to articulate their requirements for a proper dwelling, suited to their social station and family needs. Thus the negative responses to mid-century living arrangements helped to forge an architectural program for a workable multiple dwelling.

The old New York of 1790 had a population of only 33,131. Immigration swelled New York's population in the 1840s and 1850s, putting great pressure on scarce land and housing stock. By 1850 there were 515,547 people. Just a decade later the population had grown to 805,651—an increase of over 50 percent between 1850 and 1860.[1] In this decade of growth, many institutions of diversion and consumption began to create the cosmopolitan atmosphere for which New York is famous. The Crystal Palace behind Croton Reservoir at Forty-second Street brought a taste of World's Fair culture to New York in 1853. By 1860 there were almost sixty-two miles of passenger railroads along Second, Third, Sixth, Eighth, and Ninth avenues, giving New Yorkers access to amusements and to residential neighborhoods at a distance from their paid jobs.[2] A. T. Stewart had opened his famous department store in 1846, and Macy's, McCreery's, and Arnold Constable's followed in the next two decades, making Broadway between Union and Madison squares into a "Ladies' Mile" of shopping. Theaters, clubs, restaurants, and other entertainments proliferated, giving the fashion-conscious places to be seen, and the impecunious subjects to envy.

The construction of houses could not keep up with demand in this growing metropolis. The high costs of land in the 1860s made even small houses too expensive for artisans, clerks, and others of the "middling" class. These people were portrayed in different ways by different sources in the 1860s, but all agreed that there was a middling class and that it did suffer from a lack of housing. Families supported by breadwinners earning enough to pay $800 to $1,500 a year for their housing preferred to live in the country, the head of the household commuting a couple of hours each day. But for people who needed to live near the business part of town, there were no decent homes.[3]

A family with three children in 1863 may have claimed to have the home values of the middle class, with a "wholesome regard for . . . cleanliness, good behavior, and general rectitude of demeanor," but with an income of $1,000 a year, they could never afford a whole house. The heads of households in this class included "book-keepers, artists, editors, clerks, lawyers, copyists, mechanics, and members of other professions and trades who desire privacy and retirement." Moderate-income families like these, making between $750 and $1,250 a year, hunted for housing, but could find quarters only in shared buildings, ad hoc adaptations that tried to approximate a family home but were not well suited to the job.[4]

According to an 1866 *New York Times*, the "houseless" class comprised professional men, clergymen, shopkeepers, artists, college professors, and upper-level mechanics. This description placed the family income somewhat higher, at $2,500 to $3,000 a year, and the rents they could pay at $700 to $1,200 a year for a small house, often in a poor neighborhood. A father explained in his letter to the *New York Times* in 1869, "The love of a decent home is implanted in the heart of a man earning only 30 or 40 dollars a week quite as strongly as in that of a millionaire," but a house cost between $10,000 and $80,000. This man made only about $2,000 a year, and was better off than many. Such an income was not that of the very poor but of "those tenderly nurtured and educated," reported the *Times*.[5]

The Problem of Trickle-Down Housing

What brought genteel New Yorkers to this impasse? The many ways of sharing dwellings that developed in New York emerged from the early nineteenth century when shifts toward creating genteel residential districts separated houses from centers of commerce, and segregated workers' from owners' dwelling space.

Houses in colonial New York had often served as combined work and dwelling spaces. The houses of prosperous merchants near downtown commercial locations often included a counting room in which the head of the household transacted his business. The artisan "families" who lived in houses might include not just the nuclear family but servants and apprentice workers, all living and working together in one household. When a family was involved in furniture man-ufacture, for example, the dwelling could include a business office or counting room and sleeping rooms for nuclear family members, apprentices, and house-hold servants, with outbuildings on the site for furniture production. Appren-tices and household help often received room and board and training in ex-change for their labor, and while they may certainly have occupied the less comfortable parts of the house, nonetheless they shared the same roof.[6] In their various permutations of functions and residents, houses of the late eighteenth and early nineteenth centuries show that "workplace" was not clearly separated from "dwelling."

In the early years of the nineteenth century, however, this situation began to change in two ways. Owners of such businesses increasingly built houses for residential use only and moved their families into new neighborhoods away from the old business district of downtown Manhattan. New residential neighbor-hoods like St. John's Park, developed on Hudson Street north of Trinity Church in the 1810s, and Gramercy Park, built in the 1830s at Fourth Avenue between Twentieth and Twenty-First streets, were organized as purely residential space. Those families of the 1810s and 1820s with houses of their own were the emerg-ing middle class. Wealthy merchants could build substantial three- and four-story brick structures, while independent artisans, such as the furniture maker mentioned above, could afford wood-frame houses in lower Manhattan.

Household manners shifted to exclude servants and apprentices from their places as "family" members. Maids, once welcome at the family table, learned to eat in the kitchen alone.[7] Instead of being part of a "family," receiving training and room and board for their labor, workers received wages. No longer invited to dwell with the master and his family, apprentice workers had to find room and board outside the master's home.

As well-to-do families moved to improve their residential circumstances, they left behind buildings that could be rented to people with fewer resources; the housing, in other words, "trickled down." Many poorer families could each rent a fraction of a former single-family house, creating an ad hoc multiple dwelling. Some of the houses that trickled down to low-income workers in the 1820s and 1830s were solid, well-built houses, but others were of cheaper wood-frame construction. The poorer the quality of the original house, of course, the less likely it could withstand heavy use by several families at once. Quickly falling into disrepair, these ad hoc multifamily dwellings became New York's first slums.[8]

New Yorkers of the 1830s, looking around the city, could see that different neighborhoods and dwelling types were occupied by distinct classes. Class strat-ification was beginning to take on a visible form. The wage earners lived in rented rooms or boardinghouses; the merchants and artisans in private homes; laborers in the city's earliest tenements. Multifamily arrangements were often connected to deprivation, while a place in the respectable, middling class was signified by a single-family house—a link between class and dwelling that is still in force today outside of major urban centers.

By the 1850s a private house had become even harder to afford, and not just the poor but the artisans and merchants, who hoped for better, lacked the resources for independent homes. Within the trickle-down tradition of the earlier nineteenth century, middle-class families could have expected to have access to older housing that had been left behind by the well-to-do. Fashionable New York migrated uptown every couple of decades, leaving behind houses that could have served as single-family homes for middle-income families.[9] But New York's continual impulse to rebuild itself affected the supply of moderately priced trickle-down housing, and formerly fashionable houses were not left in single-family condition.

Constant change was the motif of the mid-century city; old buildings were demolished and new ones took their places. As an observer of the 1850s lamented: "We have no veneration for the house that saw our great-grandfather die, and if property rises in the neighborhood, we will yield to our wife's solicitations, sell it, and go to live in a hotel." Then the house would be either immediately subdivided, or torn down to make way for new stores or offices. This problem even served as the subject of a novel, published by H. C. Bunner in 1885. In his tale, the protagonist's home in St. John's Park goes through all the stages from private house to boardinghouse to tenement. He dies upon finding it demolished. A city in this state of upheaval, remarked an observer in *The Century* magazine in 1883, "cannot be an assemblage of true homes; and it must lack certain admirable and respectable traits . . . which go with stability."[10]

The ideal of having one's own home incorporated a dream of permanence in an inviolate family sanctuary, but that dream could hardly be fulfilled in New York's housing market, where few could afford new houses and older housing stock did not remain in single-family condition. For people willing to commute from out-of-town homes to Manhattan workplaces, suburban New Jersey, the Bronx, and Brooklyn provided a supply of affordable private houses. But many, then as now, wished to remain in Manhattan and partake of its cosmopolitan charms, or simply remain within reach of workplaces. What with the scarcity of houses and their expensive rents, middle-class tenants who wanted to remain were probably somewhat relieved to share dwellings. A house split among two or three families enabled them to afford a city home.

Subdivided Houses: Lodging, Boarding, and Floors for Rent

A full private house, whether priced at $10,000 or $80,000, was out of the financial reach of the New York middle class by the 1850s, and so families had to learn to make do with less. In living in subdivided houses of various sorts, New Yorkers created "multiple dwellings" long before such buildings were designed and built for the purpose. The shared house might provide either just a room or suite of rooms in which tenants took care of their own housekeeping; or it might be a boardinghouse in which housekeeping (and especially meal preparation) was centrally managed.

"Floors," "apartments," or "lodgings" in the 1850s and 1860s were all ad hoc subdivisions that revised formerly private, single-family houses into proto-apartments with newly broken-up interior spaces allocated to several individual families. Advice to wives in the 1873 *Woman's Own Book* urged that a first home ("for plain people") could just as well be four or five rented rooms as a complete private house, as long as healthfulness and convenience were the governing reasons for selection. Such subdivided houses can be traced from contemporary newspapers. Advertisements used the terms "floor" or "flat" apparently interchangeably, but the term "floor" was most common, and there were many advertisements for "parlor floor" or "second floor" as former single-family houses were fragmented into rental units.[11]

The part of a house offered for rent could consist of rooms grouped together on one or two floors, but rental quarters might equally be rooms scattered throughout the house. An advertisement from 1854 listed "Part of a house to let, consisting of front or back basement, second floor 4 rooms, folding doors. Third floor one room. Excellent pantries and sub-cellar."[12] The dispersal of these rooms throughout the house make this "apartment" sound extremely awkward. More spatially coherent rentals might have been found by answering these ads: "Apartments to let—the second floor of the new modern brick house [in the West Thirties near Ninth Avenue] . . . Furnished with Croton water and marble mantels, etc. . . . and only two families will occupy the house." Or, in the same district, "Part of a house to let—The upper part of a first-class house with modern improvements to a small genteel family." It is not surprising that in the face of these kinds of living arrangements, families felt the urgent need to have purposely designed dwelling units that guaranteed family privacy.[13]

Families who could not easily find a place to live, advertised their wants in the newspapers: "Wanted—By a Family of Adults. A small dwelling or part of a large one"; or "Wanted—By a Gentleman and Wife (no children) the lower part of a small house, parlor floor and basements, with two bedrooms in any part of the house." Another way to find housing is suggested in the advertisement run by "A lady" who wanted room and board in exchange for the use of her furniture and piano. People who were subjected to pressures from the housing market used resourcefulness and flexibility in these ads, attempting to create ad hoc solutions to their problems.[14]

Prosperous middle-class families, too, found living quarters in these ad hoc buildings, as William Dean Howells recounted in his novel *A Hazard of New Fortunes* (1890). His protagonists, Basil and Isabel March, house owners in Boston who had come to live for a while in New York, went to see an apartment in a formerly one-family house. "It was a large old mansion cut up into five or six dwellings; but it kept some traits of its former dignity. . . . The dark mahogany trim, of sufficiently ugly design, gave a rich gloom to the hallway, which was wide and paved with marble."[15] Perhaps the leftover glamour of this mansion's decoration compensated tenants for having to live in subdivided quarters.

The price range for these parts of better-quality houses ranged from $160 to $300 per year in the 1850s and up to $400 or $450 a decade later—too high for the mechanic earning $1,000 a year.[16] Disparities between income and affordable rent were a common complaint throughout the last half of the nineteenth century; they remain so in today's Manhattan. A mechanic reported in 1863 that he went to look at a third-floor family unit, rentable for just under $170 a year. Its five rooms were adequate for his family, but the peeling wallpaper, squalid halls and stairs, lack of coal bins, and absence of water supply inside the apartment unit made it uninhabitable;[17] he and others of his income level found that the affordable rooms in subdivided houses were far beneath their standards for a home.

New York's private-house architecture in the 1840s, 1850s, and later had increasingly turned into multifamily dwelling space. Surveys of all classes conducted in 1859–60 showed that 12,717 families lived in single-family houses, 7,147 families lived two families to a house, and 16,561 families lived in dwellings housing three families or more. That is, by 1860 nearly two-thirds of the New York families surveyed lived in shared quarters or multiple dwellings.[18]

From an "established" point of view this subdividing of houses threatened an architectural loss to the city. An article in the *New York Times* in 1869 was headlined "Palaces of Last Generation the Hovels of Today" and lamented the trend among wealthy families to move ever northward along the spine of Manhattan, leaving behind whole neighborhoods of single-family homes to be converted to multifamily use. The houses selected for conversion, reported the *Times*, were everything from single-lot houses and bigger double-lot houses to groups of "old style narrow houses" thrown together to make a multifamily dwelling.[19] The author regretted the loss of fine old architecture, and the infusion of not-so-fine new tenants into previously elite neighborhoods.

A special case of converting the single-family house to multifamily use was the boardinghouse—that is, rental quarters that provided both lodging and meals. These had been common in New York since colonial days. Typically someone who owned a private house resorted to taking in boarders as a way to sustain a home and also produce an income. Many boardinghouse owners were widows whose only resource was a house. In other cases, widows were hired to manage boardinghouses owned by landlords living elsewhere. But many middle-class families found themselves running a boardinghouse somewhat inadvertently: to rent a modern house with improvements in the 1870s cost between $1,500 and $3,000, but an "industrious citizen" was paid only $1,500 at his occupation so the rent gap was made up by taking in boarders.[20]

Artisans, journeymen, and laborers with modest incomes had found boardinghouses a comfortable and economical housing solution in the early years of the nineteenth century. But toward mid-century this solution was also serving clerks,

doctors, lawyers, professors, and even merchants, although they thought boarding beneath their desired middle-class status. Yet some of this housing was quite
fashionable. The broad range of boardinghouse prices in New York during the
Civil War era testified to a large range of potential tenants. Junius Browne's
1869 guidebook to New York, the somewhat melodramatic *Great Metropolis*,
described street after street of fashionable boardinghouse neighborhoods
around Union, Madison, and Stuyvesant squares, where costs ranged from $12
to $15 a week. In fancy places on Madison and Fifth avenues rates of $20 to $40
a week would buy a room and five-course meals; in poorer establishments on the
Lower East Side one could be fed and lodged for $2.50 a week.[21]

Advertisements offering boarding (or lodging) typically specified the kind of
people the proprietors would like to have in the house: "Genteel only, gentlemen
and their wives," "one or two gentlemen," "a small, respectable family," "family
must be small and of the highest respectability." Some advertisements said, "no
children"; some also specified "American families" only. Families who matched
the genteel requirements of boardinghouse owners could choose "elegant rooms
and board," or if several rooms were too many, there were plenty of single rooms
available with board. Because people wanted the most privacy they could achieve
with their available resources, would-be boarders also advertised. They an-
nounced their desire for houses where there were few or no other boarders; and
to reassure such tenants, many boardinghouses advertised how few boarders
they would take.[22]

The New York census gives a portrait of the broad cross section of occupations
that might be found among boarders, as well as their varied "family status." In
1880 the writer Horatio Alger, stating his occupation as "journalist," shared
space in a Fifth Avenue boardinghouse with two married couples and four other
single boarders. The widow Mary Mason's boardinghouse at 30 West Twenty-
seventh Street provided a home for several single men—a shipping merchant,
a hardware dealer, a bank clerk, a jeweler, and a musician; her lone female
boarder's occupation was listed as "at home." An even more diverse group of
boarders could be found at 54 West Twenty-sixth Street. There a married couple ran a boardinghouse with the help of two servants: a cook and a chambermaid. Their grown daughter who was a music professor, and their son, a printer,
also lived in the house. Seven boarders completed this household: a stockbroker
and his wife were the only married boarders. The five single boarders included
three women, an actress, an embroiderer, and a "lady"; the two single men were
employed as a singer and a printer.[23]

Boardinghouses could offer tenants a wide range of rents to accommodate
differing levels of prosperity. Locations could be fashionable and close to shopping and the theater, or more retiring on quiet city blocks. Prospective boarders
had to expect to share housing with single and married people and with people
of a great many occupations. For those who enjoyed the city for its cosmopolitan
diversity, a boardinghouse seemed to afford advantages.

At the same time that struggling middle-class families found converted houses the only feasible places to live, wealthier families demonstrated their fondness for hotel life. Hotels, historically serving visitors and transients, and built for that purpose, came to serve as ad hoc homes, appropriated as permanent quarters. In the years before the Civil War it had seemed that living in hotels could be a reasonable answer to housing shortages and expenses. "Society is rapidly tending towards hotel life," reported *Putnam's Magazine* to its general family readership in 1853, "and the advantages of a cluster of families living together under one roof, are everyday more apparent." Expensive house rents, a scarcity of servants, and the problem of upkeep and management that house owners endured were "strong inducements to take rooms at a hotel." *Putnam's* hoped that a range of new hotels would go up in the next few years providing homes to families with moderate incomes, since, in 1853, it found that the hotels available to New Yorkers were all luxury places.[24]

In other American cities, such as Boston and Washington, hotel living was also popular in the 1850s. In Washington, the fluctuating population, shifting with every election, chose hotel life as the only available form of housing for temporary residents. Boston's Hotel Pelham, built in 1857, is often called the "first apartment building" for the middle class in the United States, providing full-time homes as well as hotel services to numbers of middle-class families. It was followed by the Hotel Hamilton, the Hotel Agassiz, and the Hotel Kempton, which "housed the good society of Boston" in tastefully low-key surroundings.[25]

As anticipated, the Civil War years saw a boom in New York's hotel building as travelers moved through the city. By 1869 there were 700 to 800 hotels in town according to a contemporary guidebook, which assessed only fifty or sixty as well known, and only twenty-five or thirty as really "first class." The best were located near the fashionable shopping and residential enclaves of lower Broadway and around Madison Square. The *Times* reported in 1873 that men preferred to have a single-family house for its privacy, but women preferred hotels because they cut down on servant problems and made it possible to have lavish surroundings on a moderate budget.[26]

Hotels added luster to the existing set of attractions—the clubs, restaurants, and shops—along the Broadway of Ladies' Mile. One hotel of the era, now a historic landmark building, is the Gilsey House Hotel, designed by the architect Steven D. Hatch, at Twenty-ninth Street and Broadway in 1869. Cast-iron columns and moldings ornament an ornate seven-story facade, complemented by a billowing two-story mansard roof characteristic of public buildings of that time.[27] The elaborate Broadway Central Hotel (fig. 1), opened in 1871 on Broadway opposite Bond Street, provides another example of the quarters available to wealthier families and single gentlemen, as well as travelers. The Broadway Central was then the largest hotel in the country with a capacity of 1,500 guests in 650 rooms. The ten-story building offered its permanent boarders suites of a parlor, bedroom, and closet; families could rent contiguous suites and make themselves bigger apartments. Each floor had bathrooms for shared use with hot and cold water. Single rooms for permanent gentlemen boarders on the

FIGURE 1 In the years before apartment houses, many New Yorkers made permanent homes in hotels such as this, the Broadway Central Hotel near Bond Street, reconstructed from an earlier hotel by Henry Engelbert in 1870. (William Hutchins, "New York Hotels," *Architectural Record* 12 [October 1902]: 467)

sixth and seventh floors had superb views of the city. Public rooms included six parlors and six dining rooms richly decorated with lace, Axminster carpets, and walnut furniture. Brick and marble sculpted details on the facade signaled the luxury appointments within. The pleasures of hot-water baths, fancy food, and extensive hotel services may easily be understood as both appealing and cost-saving, since one had to pay no personal servants nor purchase any furniture or household equipment.[28]

With the increasing numbers of hotels after the Civil War came more and more families willing to try them out as a "permanent" housing solution. The diversity of residents in one of these hotels can be seen from census records of the Hotel Victoria, located at Twenty-seventh Street and Broadway.[29] In 1880 it housed 128 people, including permanent and transient residents and staff. Twelve pairs of adult residents were childless married couples; three were couples with children; three residents were single parents. Residents included a former senator, a printer, a lawyer, a ship chandler, a diamond dealer, a liquor importer, a bookkeeper, two actresses, clerks, and others. These occupations spanned the professions, the crafts, and fringe occupations such as the theater, bringing people into contact with each other who were not reliably all middle class. To bring up children among this crowd was surely to lose some control over what the child learned in his or her daily contacts. On the other hand, perhaps these unrelated adults provided single parents with company and the chance to share some child-care burdens.

The Problems with Shared Dwellings

In spite of the moderate expense, the "elegant rooms," and the "genteel families only" who were invited to live in shared dwellings, many contemporary reporters looked upon them with concern as threats to a family ideology. The idealized family, made up of husband, wife, and children, was seen as the most valuable keystone of society, requiring the support of nonpublic settings in order to thrive. Critics saw shared housing as places that threatened family life by depriving the family of its privacy from others, by weakening women's roles and morals, by encouraging questionable foods and mealtime practices, and by engaging in deceptive architecture.

The architect Calvert Vaux, who interested himself in everything from Central Park to urban tenement reform, criticized boardinghouse living: "The ceaseless publicity [that is, the absence of privacy] that ensues, the constant change, and the entire absence of all individuality in the everyday domestic arrangements, will always render this method of living distasteful as a permanent thing to heads of families who have any taste for genuine home comforts."[30] Vaux's themes identify middle-class reactions to living in multifamily arrangements: "publicity" had to be avoided, change destroyed the stability of family life, and individuality could not be stamped on the household that had to share housing with others.

Aspects of this commitment to privacy as the core of family ideology come through all the criticisms of nineteenth-century dwelling practices. For couples concerned with sustaining the moral virtues of their marriage, boardinghouses brought unwelcome contact with strangers who might not share their values. Junius Browne's 1869 guidebook to New York described a boardinghouse clientele as a mixed group of single men and women and married couples all staying together—a mixture that the author assumed readers would find offensive.[31] Single men, not obliged to get married, were understood as threatening to married couples in boardinghouse settings (perhaps through their double position as an example to the husband of "freedom" and as a potential seducer of the wife). Even in genteel boardinghouses, conversation and flirtation among strangers was common, Browne reported, and broke down the rules of propriety.

Such attitudes might be thought merely the stuff of alarmist literature if it were not for the testimony of people who reported the home ethic as their own. Tenants made their worries public through letters to their daily newspapers. A "man of moderate income" wrote a letter published in an 1869 *New York Times* complaining that the housing market had deprived him of a choice of dwelling place and he feared he would be forced into a boardinghouse. He aspired to "the dignity of housekeeping," but could not afford his own independent home. Thousands like this man seemed to agree that the "boarding house, at its best, is but a miserable mockery of a home." The census data show just what kinds of mixtures of strangers would live together: salesmen and singers, bachelors and married couples, actresses and clerks. While tenants might find boarding accommodations inside a good-looking brownstone front, according to critics they would also find: "Nothing like comfort or content anywhere, but the opposite of what you mean when you talk of home."[32]

Critics also raised doubts about the suitability of hotels as family residences: The Bible, wrote a *Harper's Weekly* columnist, shows us beautiful scenes of family life with the father protecting his wife and children; but the very essence of "the family," father's protection, mother's care, is weakened by hotel living. In hotels, "the husband is but half a husband, the wife but half a wife, the child but half a child, when all three reside in some huge caravansera in common with some hundreds of other persons, separated from them by different tastes, feelings, opinions—yet congregated with them by self-imposed necessity." While hotels may have offered the economies of a shared roof and services unavailable to any but the wealthiest private house owners, critics pointed to the publicity of hotel life, like that in a boardinghouse, as a threat to family integrity. Only "worldly and extravagant" people live this way, and their children "become spoiled, petted and ruined." Hotel living suggested immaturity and instability, and families who had no other home were "like civilized Bedouin."[33]

Shared Housing as a Threat to Women

As research on women's history has shown, nineteenth-century industrialization increasingly excluded middle-class women from the workplace and drew a firm line between the world of paid work and the world of home.[34] The work world, identified with male activities, was the place for aggressive competition. Home, the world of women, gathered into itself all the values of affection, peace, and morality that were defined as opposites to workplace values. Women became guardians of these precious values, and their charge was to protect the home and maintain its sanctity. This was understood to be possible only under conditions of family privacy.

In the home, women took up the duties of wise housekeeping, meal planning, child rearing, and setting a high moral tone for the household. This role for women was already prescribed in 1841 in Catharine Beecher's *Treatise on Domestic Economy*, where she defined women as rightly subservient to their husbands in political affairs, but "in matters pertaining to the education of their children . . . in all benevolent enterprises, and in all questions relating to morals and manners, they have superior influence."[35] The advice of housekeeping and manners books established norms for behavior; genteel families were encouraged to define themselves within this ethic of homelife and to create a private home where tender moral influences would protect family members from the industrializing city.

A columnist for an 1857 *Harper's Weekly* called for the building of flats so that single women could escape the threat to their morals inherent in boardinghouses. Single women, presumed at least until a "certain age" to be on the way to a married state, had to be protected until they were secured by a husband.[36] The flirtation and mixed company of a boardinghouse threatened to taint young women and compromise their virtue. Of course such sexual tensions are omnipresent in the public space of a city, as reflected in the complaints of a young woman writing in *Harper's* in the same year (fig. 2). She did not enjoy shopping on Broadway, she wrote, because she was not "incessantly desirous of the attentions of wandering gentlemen, as bestowed upon any well-dressed and tolerably-looking woman they may happen to meet." The city ought to provide women with "some peaceful retreat, where modest-minded and retiring women can enjoy an unmolested walk."[37] Perhaps critics were oblivious to this behavior in public, but in the "privacy" of a boardinghouse they found it dangerous.

"Little by little a certain class of lazy and fashionable women, discovering that their delicate organizations could no longer withstand what they called the drudgery of housekeeping, gravitated towards the new hotels," the *New York Times* reported in 1879.[38] The specific worry voiced by male guardians of proper family life was that women, who were supposed to perform their housekeeping duties gladly, drifted away from what was seen to be their proper roles. Women would learn from the etiquette manual *Woman's Own Book* (1873) that "Every woman instinctively wants a home of her own. There may be less work in board-

FIGURE 2   The rapidly growing city provided different experiences of urban life to men and to women, and the sexual tensions reported in the boardinghouse were repeated on the street. (*Appleton's Journal* 7 [1872]: 224)

ing, but there is also far less satisfaction."[39] Many a wife was accused of losing her housekeeping skills, and thus her very mission in life, because living in hotels gave her nothing to do but gossip and visit other wives in their rooms.

Condemnation of the leisured hotel wife did not stop with criticizing her loss of housewifcly skills; worse evils lay in wait for her. Scandals erupted at hotels, shocking the unthinking public, reported *Harper's Weekly* in 1857. If people were to reflect for a moment, they would see that

> there is a sanctity around a well-conducted household which lends an additional dignity and purity to the wife; that when in her own home the wife has aims in life which she can have in no other position; aims to accomplish, duties to fulfill which give her a healthy occupation, and keep her morally as well as physically sound. But without a home, and occupying a suite at the Bunkum House, what is she? She has no occupation but that of dress; no aim but to assassinate to-day that she may get to to-morrow more quickly. Her husband all day at his business; all the evening in the smoking or bar-room, who will wonder if she forgets him? Idle and lazy, and dyspeptic from want of exercise, . . . she loses all sense of individual responsibility, and—the atmosphere around her not being the most moral—soon loses her sense of what she owes to the world.[40]

A decade later, another male writer agreed that hotel life might be "agreeable and desirable for masculine celibates" (fig. 3), but the man who took his wife and

FIGURE 3 Hotels were found to make acceptable homes for bachelors, but to be of dubious morality for families. (*Harper's Weekly* 1 [December 26, 1857]: 825)

family to live in a hotel was asking for trouble. "How many women can trace their first infidelity to the necessarily demoralizing influences of public houses—to loneliness, leisure, need of society, interesting companions, abundance of opportunity, and potent temptation!"[41] These writers express an urgency about restoring women to the home, and the home to a private, not a public, space. They assert that hotel life, just like living in subdivided houses or boarding-houses, must threaten middle-class family ideology.

The Problem of Meals in Public

The integrity of the family in a private home was reiterated in the ritual of taking meals together, prepared in the family kitchen and served in the family dining room. Eating in boardinghouses is "unnatural, and the result of an over-crowded civilization. Everyone must pity the man with a soul above a boarding house, who is still compelled to keep his body there, with an appetite he cannot appease, and through circumstances he cannot control."[42] Likewise, restaurants "threaten at no distant date to usurp the place of the family dinner table as well as the family mansion," warned an article in the *New York Times* in 1871. If private family dinners should give way to eating in public, family values might be diminished if not lost.

But for those who rented rooms in subdivided houses without the usual house-keeping facilities, meals could very conveniently be taken in restaurants. Browne's *Great Metropolis* reported that there were 5,000 to 6,000 restaurants in New York in 1869. A large part of their clientele ("probably 150,000") were businessmen who worked far from their rooms, could not afford a hotel's meals and could not stand the unpleasant aspects of a boardinghouse. By then New York City had developed an enormous number of rooms for rent and restaurants that allowed non-family-based city living.

Another threat to family values could be found in the social life and the dining pleasures provided by clubs. Clubs had resources and often built themselves comfortable headquarters buildings near fashionable Broadway, or took over the mansions of wealthy families who had moved uptown. Elegantly furnished, serving excellent food, clubs were convenient to fashionable theaters and homes, but most did not provide lodging. In Browne's account, every club is "anti-marriage" because it provides to men the comforts of home without the burdens and ties of women and family. Warnings against life lived in too much publicity were a direct response to the availability of these alternatives to the services of the idealized family home.[43]

Shared Homes as Deceptive Architecture

Houses subdivided into apartments or made into boardinghouses for the middle class of the 1850s, 1860s, and 1870s did not show the same signs of deterioration that had marked workers' subdivided houses of the 1820s and 1830s. Those earlier wooden houses, insubstantially constructed to begin with, suffered and decayed under very crowded conditions and lack of upkeep. Mid-century converted houses for middle-class tenants usually began life as brick row houses, some with typical brownstone fronts, and were never so overcrowded as workers' housing. Thus the principal changes that turned a middle-class private house into rental floors or a boardinghouse took place only on the interior. From the street they still appeared to be solid private homes. In 1869 the New York Times speculated that 10,000 boardinghouses "polluted" the streets of New York. On the outside they looked just like private houses, but the Times believed that within were the seeds of destruction of family life. This divergence between interior use and street facade played a wicked joke on genteel city dwellers: the architectural forms—the forms of private houses—deceptively promised a single-family stronghold but contained an unknown mixture of strangers within.[44]

In hotels, surrounded by rented luxury, families pretended to a social status they had not really achieved. Elaborate services and decorations lured many a family from out of town to set themselves up like merchant princes, meanwhile escaping the demands of building, decorating, paying for, and maintaining a private house. Edith Wharton mocked such families in her novel The Custom of the Country, in which a newly rich family from the provinces, hoping to launch their pretty daughter in New York society, took permanent quarters at the "Hotel Stentorian" on West Seventy-second Street. They imagined that the elaborate decor would make a favorable impression on their daughter's suitors.[45]

Instead of seeing hotels as economical and wise alternatives to the expense of a private home, this point of view presented hotels as places where it was easy for people to deceive each other.

Some Virtues in Shared Housing

Although lodging and boardinghouses represented a theoretically unaccept-able setting for genteel life, nonetheless thousands of people did live in them, largely because of economic necessity. And for the many who included boarding in their daily city experiences, it might not have been all bad. With the extra income from boarders, families could afford higher rents on more substantial houses. Recognizing that house renters or purchasers sometimes had to make an income from the house, real estate advertisers described the houses they were trying to rent as having good potential for a boardinghouse. In this way families could turn their greatest expense, housing, into a profit. For the families who did take in boarders, it was a mixed blessing: they lost their own family privacy and saw their home generate an income for them as it "degenerated" into a multifamily dwelling filled with potentially interesting companions.[46] With the income from boarders, they could pay servants and get relief from some of the cares of housekeeping. Boardinghouse owners who were recorded in the 1880 census usually had at least a cook and a chambermaid to help run the operation. Howells's character Alma Leighton in *A Hazard of New Fortunes* finds in running her boardinghouse that she is "glad to be afflicted with a cook."[47]

The practical journalist Louise Furniss encouraged her readers to take up living in lodgings, not boardinghouses, if they had modest resources and a family to feed. The family who has to live on a thousand or two a year, she wrote in 1871, can not rent a whole house that costs two or three thousand a year. They could find space in a boardinghouse, but the food is so poor, the management so penny-pinching, the house so badly kept as a rule, that system is too depressing. Alternatively, renting a few rooms in a subdivided house with a gas fixture for cooking, where the wife does her own housekeeping and the children help, where there are a dozen food markets and restaurants within easy walking distance—that is rewarding for a young family. "It is young Paris established in the heart of New York," a jolly life for those who are willing to defy the general public opinion that the only good home is a single-family house.[48]

The loss of privacy that went with boarding proved a special, if perverse, advantage to some. Police caught a "flathouse thief" who had mastered the technique of taking a room in a boardinghouse and discovering when fellow boarders would be out for the evening. Easily breaking into their rooms, he escaped with jewels and cash, then moved on to another boardinghouse. He learned to capitalize on the loss of privacy inherent in boardinghouses. One woman in Brooklyn even found that her boardinghouse enabled her to find relief from a burdensome marriage. Having boarders in her house gave her opportunities for friendships with men that she would otherwise not have had. Her husband, however, objected that the privacy of his marriage was infringed upon. Opting for a life of fun instead of the obligations of marriage, this woman enlisted the support of her boarder friends to lock her husband out. Once he had clearly departed, she rented his room to another boarder.[49]

On a more positive note, many of these early ad hoc dwelling arrangements did afford tenants access to new, modern conveniences. During the mid-century years New York City residents lived with a number of conveniences that were part of city life. Gas lights lit first the streets, then public buildings, then the interiors of houses. Gas had been introduced to New York City in 1825, city water piped in in 1842; both were common urban conveniences. City-supplied water ran into houses and out of faucets, and city residents got used to the convenience of running water long before their country contemporaries. Central heating and elevators made public buildings such as hotels models of convenience, while horse-drawn omnibuses and street railways relieved many from long walks and instilled in them a desire for easing physical burdens if they could afford the price. The idea of convenience supported by technology as a feature of city life became part of everyday experience.

Owners and tenants in mid-century housing had to find their places within this emerging "culture of convenience." The advertisements for rentals in the better-equipped subdivided house noted the inclusion of built-in water closets, baths, laundry tubs, gas, and water. Sometimes advertisements for floors specified that rents included bathrooms and the use of tubs in the basement— facilities not yet taken for granted in the 1850s and 1860s. Thus tenants were exposed to the pleasures of modern household conveniences, but often not all tenants in a subdivided house had equal access to them. Through their mid-century experiences tenants would now include in their architectural guidelines the requirement of convenience in household arrangements, achieved by the good organization of space, by privacy, and by the inclusion of technological aids that made life easier.

First Proposals for Apartments

By the 1850s, forward-looking architects and critics were proposing apartment houses, designed to solve the difficulties of the middle class in finding suitable dwellings. Against the background of subdivided private houses, boardinghouses, and hotels, these arguments for apartment buildings tried to redress the failures of ad hoc multiple dwellings.

One of the early arguments for building middle-class multiple dwellings focused on their potential for the architectural embellishment of the city. Analyzing New York's residential architecture in 1854, *Putnam's Magazine* asserted that the city had no fine house architecture, just boring and plain little private houses that made for dull street facades; and indeed no impressive buildings at all except for railroad bridges and aqueducts. If people could be persuaded that the values of a home did not depend on being physically isolated from their neighbors, each family on a separate plot of ground, they could share a roof and live in a "virtual palace." Hotel architecture, *Putnam's* said, gave an idea of the large scale and architectural potential of the future apartment building. Twenty or thirty families together in a grand building, many such buildings around New York—if that could happen, *Putnam's* writer foresaw that New York would have a large scale and splendid domestic architecture.[50]

The excessive costs of building and maintaining individual houses was pointed out by several critics as a major reason for adopting multiple dwellings. Middle-class apartments built for the purpose would allow a young couple with a small income who could not afford a house still to find the "delights of home." The costs of land, construction, circulation space, and maintenance, all of which had to be borne individually by house owners, were shared expenses in an apartment building. By 1874, the popular magazine *Century* declared that "multiple tenancy alone can make large houses economical, and home possible to the multitude in a city like this."[51]

Fear that the city would lose its middle class motivated a related argument in favor of apartments. The *New York Times* suggested that excessively expensive housing kept "the class of professional men, clergymen, artists, college professors, shopkeepers, and upper mechanics—persons with an income, say, of $2,500 or $3,000 a year . . . the 'middle class,' if we may so call it," in constant financial trouble. Appropriate housing took too much of their modest incomes; they were drawn to cheaper suburban houses, but if they left the city it would be abandoned to "the very rich and very poor." This split along class lines, with the city inheriting only the top and bottom of society, was anathema to those planning for the city's future health. To retain that middle class the city needed apartment houses.[52]

A pragmatic argument for apartment buildings was outlined by Calvert Vaux in 1857 in a speech to the American Institute of Architects. He cited the high demand on New York land and the intolerable crowding of lower Manhattan as obvious reasons why New Yorkers would be more comfortable in multiple dwellings. Vaux accompanied his argument with plans, sections, and an elevation of a new apartment building with the characteristics he believed New Yorkers needed (fig. 4). His design was two lots (fifty feet) wide and four stories high. The elevation was symmetrical, divided by a center bay with the main entrance door at ground level. Generous windows lit the main public stair, which reached into a fifth story and culminated in an ornamental feature at the roofline. Near the cornice, the words "Parisian Buildings" were raised in relief.

Vaux's apartment units were organized as split-level spaces with ceilings that varied from nine to twelve feet high (fig. 5). He provided a high-ceilinged entrance hall, parlor, and dining room at the front; lower-ceilinged kitchen and storage rooms to the back; and raised up half a level, again with high ceilings, the bedrooms, and bathroom. One servant's room above the kitchen connected to it

FIGURE 4 Parisian Buildings, a design proposed in 1857 for an apartment building by Calvert Vaux, had huge central windows lighting the public stair. (*Harper's Weekly* 1 [December 19, 1857]: 809)

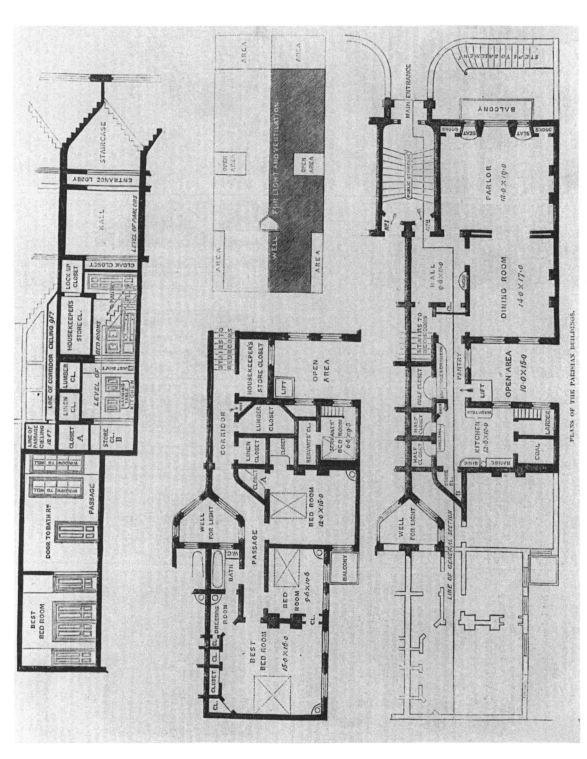

FIGURE 5 Vaux's Parisian Buildings had high-ceilinged parlors, low ceilings for service rooms, and ample built-in storage. (*Harper's Weekly* 1 [December 19, 1857]: 809)

by its own stair; a dumbwaiter opened into the pantry next to the kitchen, and there were many built-in conveniences, such as work surfaces with drawers below, coal bins, a food larder, and numerous storage closets on both levels.

Vaux attributed New York's housing shortage not just to the high price of land but also to raised expectations on the part of tenants: "The mechanic, now-a-days, shares with the millionaire his taste for the luxuries of privacy, fresh air, water and light, and the wish to occupy . . . a commodious residence, is widely spread amongst all classes." More convenience and comfort is demanded these days than ever before, he asserted, and all classes now think it necessary to have fresh air and water, sunshine, and privacy in a home. He realized that housing shortages affected all classes in New York and that multifamily dwellings would have to be devised in a range of costs and sizes to suit the wide range of middle-class tastes. His own design could be built in a quiet, respectable neighborhood, and units could be rented at a decent return to the investor, he thought, for about $400 a year.[53]

Middle-class readers perused articles like these in the popular press as they sipped their coffee at hotel and boardinghouse tables. Because of their heritage of living in boardinghouses, subdivided houses, or hotels, they often associated multiple dwellings with deprivation: they were the place one had to live when one really wanted to live in a private house. Furthermore, the only buildings constructed as multiple dwellings that were native to New York were the working-class tenements. These, by the thousands, surrounded worried middle-class families and gave them a frightening image of multiple-dwelling life. The middle class of the 1870s thus had equivocal feelings about living in apartments. But what were they to do? Being a successful American meant having one's own private home, but being middle class in New York meant that that was beyond most people's financial means. If there had been fast and cheap public transportation, the middle class could have made its home in the suburbs, but this was not to be.[54] Tenants needed, and the real estate situation required, that architects find some solution to this dilemma and design a multifamily housing type that the middle class could live in comfortably.

2 REFERENCE POINTS: GOOD AND BAD DWELLINGS

NEW YORK CITY architects, developers, and would-be tenants—those involved with advancing the new idea of multiple dwellings—looked around them for reference points. Producing a suitable dwelling required testing and judging it against other dwelling forms and practices, both good and bad, in order to arrive at a close definition of what was desired. What counted as good and bad dwelling characteristics comes through both the language and the specifics of mid- and late-nineteenth-century housing literature. Representative writings from the American press illustrate the kinds of information and evaluations of both local and foreign family dwellings that were easily available to New Yorkers. Foreign sources also supplied information for both general readers and architects. While tenants and designers identified good housing ideas, they also could begin to articulate the reasons why some ideas would not work in New York apartment houses.

These reference points were expressed through notions of the good home and its opposite: the middle-class home opposed to that of the working class, the American home versus the foreign, and the private home against the public. According to contemporaries, a set of bad ideas for shared dwellings was already evident in the local forms of tenements; this housing for the poor filled the streets of many lower Manhattan wards. Tenements offered to genteel viewers thousands of examples of the unacceptability of multiple-dwelling architecture. For good ideas about dwelling form, one had to look no further than the traditional urban private house, the heart's desire of any proper middle-class family. Private houses filled in the more prosperous streets of lower Manhattan and could be found for high rental and purchase prices on the real estate pages of daily newspapers. When designers and tenants looked beyond the city limits for reference points, it was Paris that attracted their attention. Magazine and newspaper articles and guidebook entries impressed upon the American reader the characteristics, virtues, and drawbacks of the Parisian apartment.

New York Houses

Genteel New Yorkers, during all their years of boarding and hotel life, still clung to the ideal of a separate private house. In mid-century New York, "every good Knickerbocker," wrote the architect Charles Israels, looking back from 1901, "considered it his duty to house his family within four walls where he would be the sole lord and master; and the highest reach of his ambition was a 'brownstone front.'" But middle-class house dwellers put up with inconvenience, according to the feminist reformer Charlotte Perkins Gilman, for the sake of an outmoded attachment to the single-family abode. Never mind if their private house were in a block-long row of similar structures, packed "like books on a shelf"; as long as people had their own houses, even narrow, inconvenient places did not shake their impressions that things were as they should be.[1]

As architectural forms, private row houses on New York streets subtly declared themselves separate from their neighbors and stood as a sign to the world of the individual family within (fig. 6). Although at first glance row-house blocks looked homogeneous, the individual house made use of architectural details so that it could be read as a unit distinct from its neighbors. Mid-century New York row houses had assertive front stoops rising six or eight steps above the sidewalk to a landing at the front door. These prominent stoops, often stone and wrought iron, were the site for special ornamental flourishes, as were the front doorways, window frames, and cornices. While fronts were often repetitive, the ways that stoops, door frames, and cornices marked out each house made it visually obvious that each was a separate building.

The architectural critic Montgomery Schuyler retrospectively condemned houses of the 1850s as failures of mass-market thinking: "Everybody, whether he bought his house or rented it," wrote Schuyler, "lived in a house built for somebody else, or rather for nobody else, but for the 'average man.'" Houses of that period were designed with such uniformity, he continued, that you would never guess that New York was full of diverse personalities. Schuyler observed, "The speculative builder . . . produced one elevation of a brownstone front with the conventional 'trimmings' [and] merely repeated that front in the same material as many times as he had houses to build. Unity was doubtless thus preserved, but . . . it became extremely dismal by repetition." Only on the backs of houses, where owners had added extra rooms and other kinds of extensions, was there any visible individuality.[2]

Although some critics attacked the mid-century brownstones for being too uniform in style, too undistinguished from each other, they were rarely detailed to read as a unified large building along the lines of an English terrace. The New York examples of Town and Davis's Colonnade Row of 1833, or A. J. Davis's House of Mansions of 1855, were notable as rare exceptions to the norm of individually detailed facades.[3]

The sizes, numbers, and costs of a single-family house in New York changed radically over the decades. In the 1830s and 1840s, New Yorkers who could

FIGURE 6 A block of 1850s row houses on East Fourteenth Street reveals the domain of each separate family by means of individual stairs and front doors. It was this kind of house that was later converted into floors for rent and boarding. ("New York Daguerreotyped—Private Residences," *Putnam's*

afford their own houses might have had a typical three-story house, 25 feet wide by 40 feet deep. But as land prices increased, builders of the 1850s and 1860s cut costs by making narrower houses—20, 18, 15, or even 13 feet wide. The fact that the old standard width of 25 feet had been replaced by narrower widths was charitably interpreted as a way to satisfy different-sized families and varying family needs. To make up for lost room, developers built deeper on the lot, cutting down on interior light because front and rear windows were ever more distant from the middle of a floor, and added a story, making yet more stairs to climb inside.

Finding a suitably located private house may not have been easy, even for those who could afford to spend $1,500 a year on their housing. A young couple described their troubles locating a house in 1871. Having saved up their money by living in a boardinghouse, they read all the newspaper advertisements for houses and found several in their price range. The first one they looked at, however, was next to a noisy machine shop; their second choice turned out to be surrounded by barnyard animals kept in the neighbors' backyards. After several other disappointments, they abandoned their hunt for a private house and finally advertised for apartments.[4] The piecemeal way in which houses were built, undertaken by small-scale developers, a few at a time, led to streets of mixed uses. The individual nature of a private house, so valuable in its ability to symbolize the family, was unable to control urban space beyond its meager 25-by-100-foot plot of land, leaving it prey to adjoining uses unfit to keep it company.

Interior planning in New York's urban row houses offered a model of fairly sophisticated spatial zoning—an organization of spaces separated by function and role in family life (fig. 7). In a typical New York single-family row house of the 1860s, kitchen, food storage, and family dining rooms had their place in the basement, half below ground. Work was thus kept separate from the first floor, where two handsomely furnished parlors, or a parlor and a formal dining room, provided a full-floor social zone for entertaining guests. On the second and third floors, family bedrooms had their own zone of quiet and privacy. The family members organized sitting-room functions on the bedroom floors, always out of view of guests. Servants lived in the garret, where sewing and other household work might also take place. New houses above Fourteenth Street appeared to a writer of 1854 as miracles of modern heating, lighting, water fixtures, and drainage; indeed, "it seems hardly possible that anything more compact, cozy, comfortable and elegant in the shape of a dwelling house will ever be invented."[5]

Of course, the interiors of houses could not please everyone. Some critics denigrated the New York row house as a place where residents "live, as it were, on a ladder." Tall and narrow, row houses used up far too much of their space on interior circulation (that is, spaces for people to move through). The interior space in an average house was characterized by a writer in 1874 as a "string of

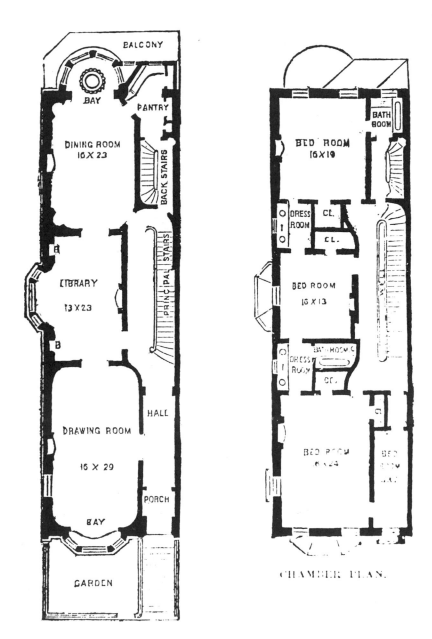

PLAN OF PRINCIPAL FLOOR.

FIGURE 7 A row-house plan by Calvert Vaux showing separated activities on different floors. (Calvert Vaux, "A Town House," *Villas and Cottages* [1867], p. 322)

36

stairs with more or less extended landings," in which the kitchen was underground and an "uninhabited parlor floor is sandwiched between the dining room and family living room." The convention of saving the parlor floor for guests made for excessive stair-climbing from the basement-level kitchen and family dining room to the second-floor family bedrooms and sitting room, an arrangement that had been repeatedly criticized since the 1840s.[6] According to an observer in the 1860s, this use of the parlor had an effect on the cityscape. Since the family was either below stairs or sitting in its private rooms above, no one used the parlor floors, which made the street look abandoned. Especially at night when house fronts ought to be lit up and inviting, New York's residential blocks seemed dead.[7]

Because the need for vertical circulation and internal hallways cut down on room sizes to the degree that one could never have a parlor of sufficient width to furnish properly, *Appleton's Home Books* advised home builders that a city row house was almost impossible to design. These parlors were described by a country couple, house hunting in New York in 1890, as looking "like steamboat saloons" because of their narrow proportions. The same couple pointed to steep stairs as making New York houses impossible places to live. To avoid this problem, *Appleton's* suggested in 1884 that, on sites outside the city, people should consider building one-floor bungalows.[8]

Private houses and the experience of living in them gave apartment designers goals for their apartment buildings plus a list of design pitfalls. Among the good features, designers kept the idea of room clusters, or zones of space, articulated as separate floors in the row house. Each zone in a house was defined according to associated uses and values, combining utilitarian and symbolic meaning. Such a zoning idea could be adapted to the single-floor plan of the flat. The relation of parlor to street in private-house plans appealed to residents' desire for participation in, yet protection from, the sidewalk and street life passing by. This link could also be retained in apartment plans. Even within blocks of relatively similar row houses, the architecture enabled the public to read the message "private family," which clients and designers would have liked to preserve.

Design pitfalls in private houses included too much space given over to hall and stair circulation, and too little consideration given to gracious room proportions or adequately sized rooms. Rooms on several floors placed extra burdens on the housekeeper: she had to oversee the work of servants on four or five floors, running up and down stairs and ruining her health, according to contemporary critics. The more rooms in the house and the more ambitious the social schedule, the more servants were required to keep it in order and the more burdensome to the mistress of the household.[9] While private houses might express their independence through separate entrance stairs and doors on the exterior, they also expressed a boring sameness from one to the next that made streetscapes undistinguished. Critics hoped for a more significant architectural style from apartment houses with which to ornament the city.

Reports from Paris

It was not unusual for New Yorkers in the 1850s and 1860s, faced with a shortage of affordable middle-class houses and disappointed with ad hoc solutions such as living in hotels and boardinghouses, to turn to Europe for ideas about urban housing. Urban Europeans had been living in apartment buildings of various kinds for generations, and the mid-nineteenth century had seen a tremendous growth in newly constructed apartments. Calvert Vaux's apartment proposal of the 1850s was called Parisian Buildings; the New York City Buildings Department recorded the new multiple dwellings of the early 1870s under names like "Parisian dwellings" and "French flats." These names acknowledged that the new housing type was linked to foreign models.

Paris was a particularly alluring capital for traveling architects, social critics, and Americans who chose to live abroad. When these people published reports in American magazines and newspapers describing the quality of Parisian apartment life, they found an eager American audience.[10] The fascination of Parisian life for Americans is evidenced by the preponderance of articles dealing with that city compared with other European centers. However, it would be a mistake to imagine that New Yorkers simply took over apartment forms from Paris, given their concern to produce housing in key with local needs.

The early reports reaching Americans in the 1850s and 1860s tended to place Parisian apartment living in a bad light. In 1853, a correspondent for *Putnam's Magazine* published his report on Paris, condemning apartment living. He felt that rented apartments existed in order to give Frenchmen as many spectators as possible: the French acted out their parts in this life, he claimed, and sought the attention of others as they ate and drank in public cafés and restaurants and then went home to "glass houses." Apartments were called glass houses because this writer thought that domestic life was completely open to observation there. Parisian apartments were watched over by a concierge, who viewed every move through his or her glass door, watched the stairs and the mail, gossiped with servants, and worst of all informed on tenants' activities to the police! In his apartment, the Frenchman and his family lived on a single floor with other residents above and below who listened to every family sound. *Putnam's* writer concluded that such a dwelling was "no home."[11]

From the point of view of the French themselves, being under the public gaze was not the same as having personal privacy violated by strangers: they maintained their privacy under the scrutiny of others, just as today's New Yorkers do. To nineteenth century American sensibilities, however, this kind of observation was intolerable and was felt as a deliberate invasion. According to this view, apartments were intimately connected to a life lived under the public eye. Walls, ceilings, and floors transmitted personal signals to the strangers who lived above and below; the concierge spied, pried, and knew too much. If Americans were to take up apartment living according to the French model, *Putnam's* writer warned, they too could lose their privacy, the very keystone of family life.

In 1869, the year of Hunt's Stuyvesant Apartments on New York's East Eighteenth Street, another condemnation of Parisian apartments appeared in the highly colored prose of the journalist James McCabe's *Paris by Sunlight and Gaslight*. Apartments in Paris were characterized as nothing but "magnificent tenements," with no features of the proper Anglo-Saxon home. McCabe reported that, except for the nobility and the very rich, everyone lived in just a few rooms on one floor with other families above and below them. The apartment buildings might be an impressive six, seven, or more stories high, with carved stone ornament, handsome roofs, and imposing gateways, but inside one had to face the predatory concierge. Furthermore, Parisian buildings rarely had any of the conveniences Americans expected in a home, such as central heating, gas lighting, and modern plumbing. It was clear to McCabe that Parisian apartments failed as a model for a decent dwelling in being so behind the times with modern conveniences. But more important, Parisian dwellings deprived their tenants "of the privacy and tender influences which surround a home organized on the English or American plan."[12] McCabe, too, felt that privacy was the heart of Anglo-Saxon home life.

If Americans were to adopt Paris apartments without making drastic changes, wrote an architect, Peter B. Wight, in an 1870 *Putnam's Magazine*, they would find themselves living with no closets or storerooms, no back stairs for servants, and no corridor circulation except the vestibule, and the "kitchen would be a dimly lighted closet." Americans are devoted to their comforts, he asserted, and any apartment worth living in in America had to have closets and storage rooms, large and fully equipped kitchens, laundry facilities, fuel storage, plumbing, and much else not to be found in the cramped Parisian apartment building.[13] Wight wanted to encourage his readers to take up apartment living, but not to imitate Parisian models that would not suit American needs for convenience in the household.

The idea that Paris was an obverse image of New York, and French family life the fascinating opposite of American ideals, was recollected in Edith Wharton's novel *The Age of Innocence* (1920), when she described the 1870s living arrangements of an elderly lady who could no longer navigate the stairs of her New York house. This woman

> with characteristic independence . . . had . . . established herself (in flagrant violation of all the New York proprieties) on the ground floor of her house so that, as you sat in her sitting room . . . you caught . . . the unexpected vista of a bedroom. . . .
>
>   Her visitors were startled and fascinated by the foreignness of this arrangement which recalled scenes in French fiction . . . and architectural incentives to immorality such as the simple American never dreamed of. That was how women with lovers lived in wicked old societies, in apartments with all the rooms on one floor, and all the indecent propinquities that their novels described.[14]

Apartments, because they were on one floor, suggested the "indecent propinquities" common in France. Wharton's characters saw Paris as a center of sensuality, and its foreign living habits could only represent dangers to New York morality. For proper New Yorkers of the 1870s, accustomed to the separation of public from private functions on the separate floors of a house, one-floor living with its vistas of the bedroom conjured up visions of unacceptable license.

While Parisian apartment life was represented in this poor light in American publications of the Civil War era, the apartments seen in their urban design context represent another set of qualities. Parisians had been living in apartmentlike quarters since the Renaissance; by the eighteenth century the majority of French middle-class families lived in flats. Neighborhoods in mid-nineteenth-century Paris, before the "urban renewal" efforts of Baron Eugène Haussmann in the 1850s and 1860s, contained a mixture of uses and social classes. Wealthy families had their homes, and their favorite expensive shops and restaurants, mixed among the dwellings and services for residents with much more modest incomes. Within a few square blocks, one could find all the social levels of the city. Multifamily dwellings in Paris shared this characteristic of containing a microcosm of society. Thus middle-class families were perfectly at home in a one-floor dwelling, whether it was subdivided from some former large house or in an apartment building constructed as such.[15]

An often-described typical French dwelling of this era had shops on the ground floor and a mezzanine level with small manufacturers, such as seamstresses. On the next level, a fine apartment would take up an entire floor and provide its residents with gilt, plate glass, carvings, marble fireplaces, and other luxuries. Ascending the stairs, one would find two more floors of well-to-do family apartments. At the top of such a building, there were one or two floors of small quarters for night lodgers, poor tenants, or servants. Sometimes the garret floor was reached by its own stairway to keep some separation between richer and poorer, but these buildings were more commonly unsegregated and have been seen as democratic mixtures in which varied classes lived comfortably under the same roof. As James McCabe reported in his *Paris by Sunlight and Gaslight*, "In seeing the inmates of one house, you see all grades of Parisian life."[16]

Baron Haussmann's reorganization of Paris in the 1850s and 1860s involved a new clarification of districts as homogeneous class quarters. Haussmann advanced a process of segmenting the city into specialized "molecules" so that urban texture became more homogenized within small "turfs" and more differentiated from turf to turf. Parallels are evident in this process to the growing division of labor and specialization of work tasks in the industrial economy. Evidence of the exclusion of lower-class tenants from their former districts is preserved in the testimony of residents from the Halles area. Forced to relocate while Haussmann's new streets and buildings were being constructed, they found they could not move back into the old *quartier* because the new buildings were designed to exclude working-class inhabitants.[17]

Like new neighborhoods, new Parisian apartment buildings, such as those designed by Haussmann's architect Jacob Ignace Hittorff and others of his generation, were intended for a more consistent middle-class occupancy. While upper floors and courtyard exposures still rented for less money, there were no poor tenants except for the servants, who typically had their rooms in the garret.

The French architect César Daly published a series of articles titled "Maisons de Paris" in 1859. In his portrait of residential life, aristocrats occupied the "hôtels," or private houses, of Paris, and the bourgeoisie lived in the entire range of apartment houses and included people from the "superior to the inferior strata of society." Distinctions among levels within the bourgeoisie were marked by levels of ornament on apartment buildings.[18] Shops still took their places at street level in many of the new apartment houses, but in the new homogeneous neighborhoods, shops in a given district would cater to a particular class level. This new homogeneity was welcomed by tenants and developers alike: the bourgeoisie was pleased by a consistent and respectable neighborhood quality, while investors felt that their capital was safest in housing whose tenancy could be expected to flourish.

For American observers, the first type of traditional apartment building in Paris with its mixture of classes stirred fears of strangers. Middle-class New Yorkers, uncertain of their social status, needed to assure themselves that they were, in fact, rising on the social ladder and could not afford to risk their new sense of social worth by mixing with people less prosperous than themselves.[19] The old Parisian neighborhoods with their mixture of all kinds of residents and services were a parallel to the conditions in antebellum New York that had represented threats to emerging middle-class sensibilities. Haussmann's clarification of districts and of individual buildings so that social classes could be kept apart from each other would seem to have presented an ideal solution to American middle-class doubts about the city's mixed social makeup. However, commentators writing for the American press did not pick up this theme of "social zoning" as a special virtue of the later Parisian model. Perhaps the results of Haussmann's work were not yet evident to visitors, or perhaps their minds were on yet more worrisome aspects of the ways they believed French families lived.

While the first reports on Paris apartments had painted a bleak picture of the loss of family life, in 1872 a champion of both women's rights and apartment living, Sarah Gilman Young, published a full analysis of Parisian apartments, giving Americans a positive point of view of multifamily living. Young, a social and literary critic, had lived abroad for several years and knew both American traditions and foreign living styles firsthand. Although well aware of American objections to the loss of privacy in apartment buildings, Young was even more aware of the difficulties of keeping a private house in the city, the exceptional amount of work involved in cleaning, cooking, and maintaining a family home, and the ways that improved dwelling design could ease these burdens on women.[20]

A French apartment house, in Young's description, was a pleasant place to come home to. One entered off the street into a paved carriageway and walked toward a courtyard at the rear, which often had flowers and a fountain (figs. 8, 9). At the point where the carriageway entered the courtyard was the concierge's office and the main staircase giving access to family apartments above. Each

FIGURE 8 The front entrance to a Parisian apartment house by the architect Dainville. ("Apartment Houses," part 2, *American Architect and Building News* 30 [November 15, 1890]: 98)

FIGURE 9 A courtyard in Dainville's Parisian apartment house provides light and air to the upper floors of apartments. ("Apartment Houses," part 2, *American Architect and Building News* 30 [November 15, 1890]: 98)

story had only two or three separate residential units at most, and each apartment was described as complete unto itself, a crucial feature for New York middle-class readers to whom privacy was all-important.

As Young described the French apartment, she argued that there were several advantages to apartment living. First, living on one floor and making use of simple furnishings meant that the household was far easier to keep in order than the several floors of a typical urban row house. Second, living under the protective eye of a concierge made it safe to leave one's apartment for holidays, knowing it would be looked after—although Young admitted that perhaps the concierge did know too much about private family affairs. The third advantage to French apartment life that Young found was the way that Paris provided services to supplement domestic work in the home, making housekeeping easier. Commercial laundries (where the efforts of laundresses were supplemented with recently invented machines) did the family wash, so that individual apartments had no need for laundry equipment nor for the space that washing and drying clothes required. Cooking establishments outside the home included not just bakeries for bread but also shops that sold all kinds of prepared foods, saving on individual family cooking. Numerous cafés and restaurants, which had dismayed earlier American reporters, were to Young additional aids to the housekeeper. Young's interpretation of housework and its support system in the city from women's point of view turned familiar analyses upside-down: the restaurant that male critics feared would break down family life here saved the health of the housekeeper.[21]

The articles in the American popular and architectural presses represented Parisian apartments to an American readership. The ways that apartments were pictured embodied writers' biases and were colored by readers' expectations. The articles described above were not, therefore, simply recording the properties of Parisian apartments, but were interpreting them. More objective sources of information on Parisian apartment design were the professional publications of French architects, available to at least some American practitioners. French architectural treatises such as César Daly's *L'Architecture privée*, which P. B. Wight had mentioned to the general readership of *Putnam's Magazine*, laid out principles for apartment design and documented the recent apartment buildings of Paris.[22]

Another such book, *Architecture de Paris*, published in London in 1871, presented many plans for apartment houses, two of which we will look at closely for comparison with the foregoing interpretations. The first example is an apartment house located on the Place de l'Etoile with its "garden front" facing the Arc de Triomphe in the center of the *place* and its street front facing onto a ring road concentric with the *place* (figs. 10, 11). Rohault de Fleury's design, with two units per floor, conformed to the concentric and radial street pattern of this district, resulting in an envelope (that is, the exterior surfaces taken as a whole) with a nonrectilinear form. Traditional Paris apartments received much of their light and air from large courtyards hidden in the middle of built-up urban blocks.

FIGURE 10 Plan of the Place de l'Etoile in Paris, where new apartment houses were going up in the 1860s and 1870s. (*Architecture de Paris: Maisons les plus remarquables de Paris* [1871], pl. 4)

45

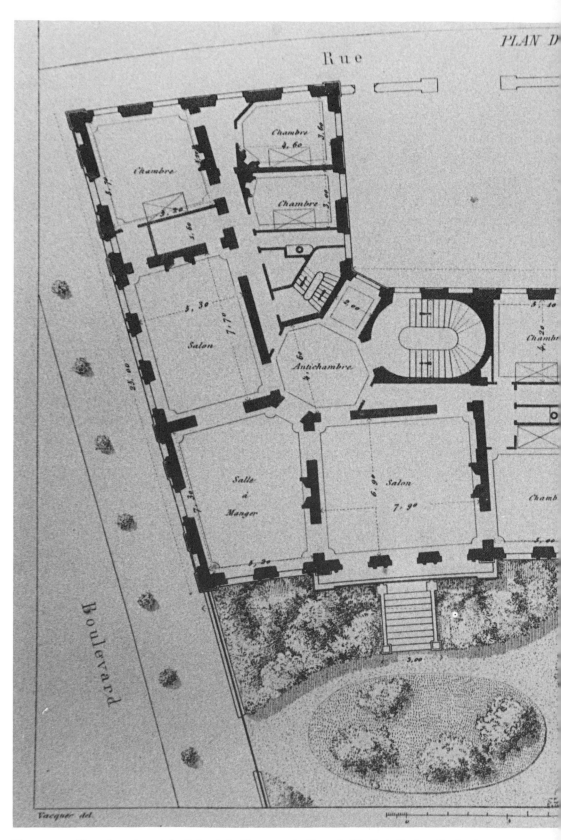

FIGURE 11 Plan of apartments by Rohault de Fleury on the Place de l'Etoile in Paris, with *chambres*, or bedrooms, grouped at either end of the floor. (*Architecture de Paris: Maisons les plus remarquables de Paris* [1871], pl. 5)

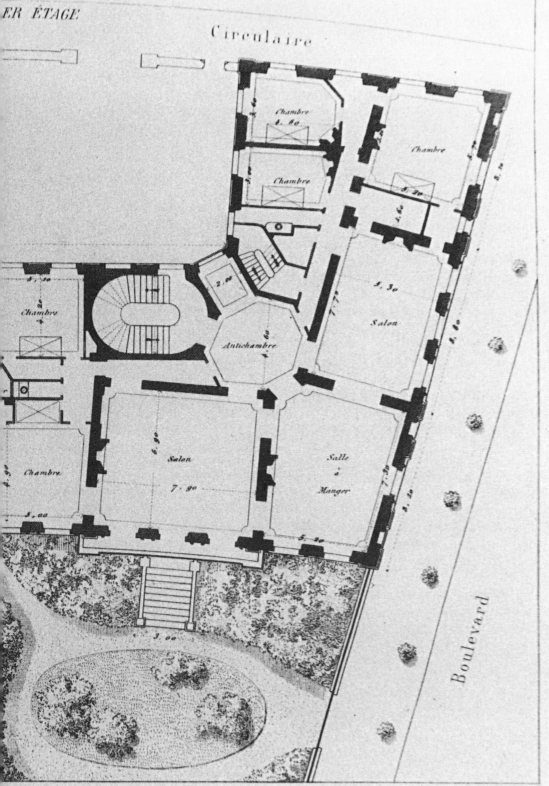

Circulaire

Chambre
4.60

Chambre

Chambre
4.30

Chambre
4.20

Chambre

2.00

7.70

Salon
5.30

Antichambre
4.60

Salon
6.90
7.90

Salle
à
Manger
7.30

Chambre
5.00

3.40

3.00

5.20

20 Mètres

Boulevard

Boullay sculp.

Although the Etoile site afforded much more light and air than could usually be expected in older Paris streets, the architect retained the characteristic Parisian courtyard as an indentation on the ring road facade.

Interior planning was based on the idea of a suite of public rooms linked to an antechamber and the entrance, and two groups of private or sleeping rooms at either end of the public suite, each with its own water closet. The kitchen and servants' rooms would have been on the floor below, a not unusual arrangement in Paris apartments, and common in private houses. Every room had a fireplace and usually several windows; most rooms were four-sided but somewhat warped off the rectangular; some had five sides, and the anteroom had eight. The principal staircase was set within walls oval in plan with windows to the exterior.

While Rohault de Fleury's design fit a symmetrical site on the radial street plan of the Etoile, M. J. Lobrot's design for an apartment house at No. 37, Avenue des Champs Elysées was sited on a typical, asymmetric lot (fig. 12). Regardless of the site, however, similar features appeared in the designs of both architects. The lot for No. 37, Avenue des Champs Elysées wrapped around the corner where Elysées meets Rue Marbeuf at an oblique angle, and extended back in an irregular five-sided shape. The architect had filled the front of the lot, and like the Etoile building, the facade and the envelope took their shapes from the street layout. At the back of the lot, a large courtyard gave light to rear rooms and contained stables and a sheltered delivery bay. Lobrot's apartment house conformed closely to the description given by Sarah Gilman Young to her American readers in the 1872 article discussed above: shops on the ground floor, a street door leading into a carriageway that opened into the rear court, and a public stair at the end of the carriageway where the concierge sat. In Lobrot's building only one apartment occupied each floor and was complete on that floor.

Room planning in the Champs Elysées apartment, similar to Rohault de Fleury's Etoile design, was organized around a central public zone comprising antechamber, *petit salon*, *grand salon*, and dining room. At each end of this group was a set of bedrooms, although apparently there was only one water closet for the whole apartment. Lobrot made use of semicircular walls to wrap his main stair, *grand salon*, and service stair; remaining rooms were all rectilinear except for the antechamber and some small storage and private hall spaces. Again every room had a fireplace and generous windows. Only the private hall and water closet were lit from a small air and light shaft in the interior of the building; all other rooms looked onto either the street or the courtyard.

These two Parisian apartment buildings show characteristic French planning features of the 1860s and 1870s. The site plan always included a sizable courtyard; lot shapes were typically irregular, which often led to nonrectilinear building envelopes and room shapes; good light and air were achieved without the use of air shafts for more than one or two rooms: all the principal rooms, including bedrooms, looked onto the open light and air of streets and courtyards. Social or public spaces were grouped in the center of the apartment next to the entrance. These rooms had many openings into each other in the

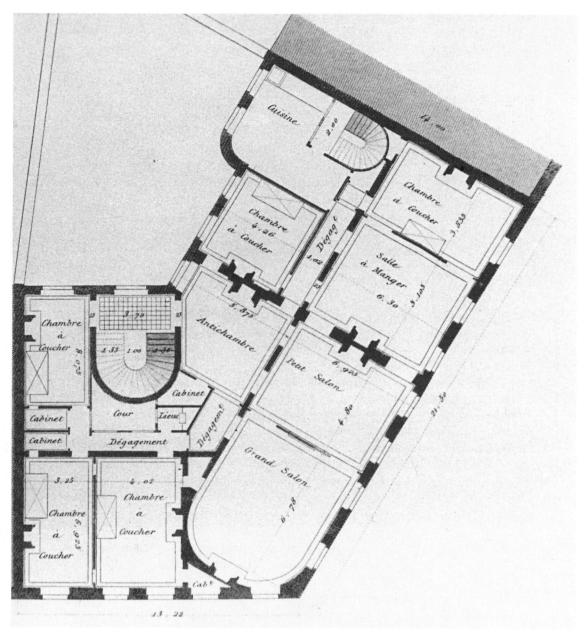

Cuisine

Chambre
à Coucher

Chambre
à Coucher

Dégag.t

Salle
à Manger

Chambre
à
Coucher

Antichambre

Petit Salon

Cabinet

Cour   Lieux

Cabinet

Dégagement

Dégagement

Cabinet

Grand Salon

Chambre
à
Coucher

Chambre
à
Coucher

Cab.t

FIGURE 12   Plan of an apartment at No. 37, Avenue des Champs Elysées and Rue Marbeuf in Paris on a characteristically irregular lot. (*Architecture de Paris: Maisons les plus remarquables de Paris* [1871], pl. 62)

49

form of wide pairs of doors, or doors on each side of a fireplace, leading into the adjoining spaces. In this way the antechamber, large and small salons, and dining room could easily be used as a grand, continuous suite for entertaining.

The typical pair of bedrooms accessible from this public zone of the house were those of the master and mistress of the house. In Lobrot's building one of the bedrooms had two doors opening into the dining room and another to the passage: this bedroom was available to be used as a social room too. The other bedroom at the social end of the house opened directly into the antechamber and the passage so it too could operate as a social space. The remaining bedrooms, clustered at the opposite end of the apartment, each had two doors also—two bedrooms had a communicating door between them plus a door to the passage, while the third had both a door to the passage and one leading directly to the main stair. Thus while there were, in both apartments, separate circulation paths through halls and corridors, the architects also made the rooms "permeable" by numerous communicating doors between them.

American readers could easily become familiar with French apartment design through the publications mentioned, both popular and professional. In the 1850s and 1860s they would have received a bad impression of apartment life as a system seemingly geared to destroy the privacy they held dear. At the same time, publications such as Daly's *L'Architecture privée* and the *Architecture de Paris* gave specific and detailed architectural plans and elevations from which Americans could learn, while articles such as Sarah Gilman Young's showed advantages to apartment life, illustrating that housekeeping on one floor could make life easier and more economical.

As New Yorkers saw hundreds of "French flats" erected on their own city's streets in the late 1870s, and larger and larger ones during the early 1880s, they continued to feed their imaginations and hone their critical faculties on reports from Paris. The early doubts expressed in articles during the 1860s and 1870s faded. By the 1890s, articles on Parisian apartments published for American readers stressed the advantages of apartment living more than the drawbacks. A plan published by the *American Architect and Building News* in 1890 for a small Paris apartment house (fig. 13) was selected to match lot sizes and shapes common in New York. It showed apartments that had fewer permeable rooms and more well-developed corridor circulation than those of the 1860s and 1870s. This professional magazine reported that "curiously enough, the first inspiration for the improvement" of American apartment houses came from Paris, suggesting that by 1890 it no longer seemed a French building type. By then it was clear that New Yorkers were both committed to and restricted to apartment life. Pressured by high land values and spiraling population, developers slowed, and by 1900 nearly stopped, the construction of individual private houses. Positive views of apartment life in Paris could give valuable lessons to New York designers, and by the turn of the century, negative views were beside the point.[23]

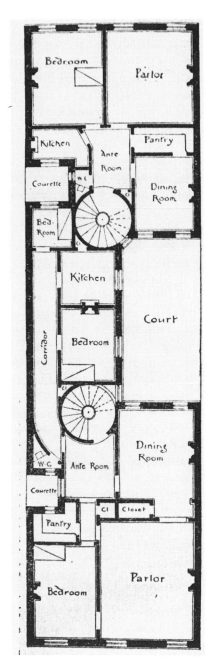

FIGURE 13 A small apartment in Paris that would easily fit on a New York rectangular lot. Design by Monsieur Bailly from Caillat's *Parallele* ("Apartment Houses," *American Architect and Building News* 29 [September 27, 1890]: 194)

Tenements: Multiple Dwellings for the Working Class

Throughout the historic development of apartment houses, participants made reference to another kind of opposite pole, the tenement. The legal term "tenement" neutrally named a multiple dwelling with three or more families living independently of each other. But images of illness and death, immorality and filth, swarmed around the realities of tenement life and held power over middle-class imaginations. In the 1870s, property owners fought in court over whether a particular building was a "tenement" or an "apartment"; they continued to do so over the next several decades, while judges were forced to recognize the heavy cultural weight attached to housing differences. Tenements raised questions about how health could be preserved in a city setting, and where lines should be drawn between public and private terrain when people lived together in multiple dwellings. As New York's architects and tenants worked to identify the proper features of an apartment house, they reacted against many of the characteristics present in tenement design.

Workers and their families had had to make do with subdivided houses, one family to a room, as early as 1795. With the population escalating every decade, creating ever more crowded conditions in Manhattan, subdivided houses could not come near to supplying the housing needed by working-class families, so developers began to erect built-for-the-purpose tenements. One source suggests that the first such building was built in 1824. By the mid-nineteenth century, the great numbers of immigrants settling in the Five Points district and the Lower East Side had given identity to that part of town as the working-class center, made visible by its tenements.[24]

Immigrants had been pouring into New York over the previous decade— 156,844 people in 1863 alone (fig. 14). By 1863 there were 15,369 tenement houses in New York to house the new arrivals, more than 9,000 of them below Fourteenth Street and most on the Lower East Side, housing about 500,000 people. The tenement buildings were typically laid out on lots 25 feet wide by 100 feet deep and were four to six stories high. They were built side by side like row houses, so along both flanks most of a tenement's rooms had no windows. Sometimes tiny air shafts allowed some ventilation of internal rooms. Access to individual rooms in a tenement unit was always a problem because circulation in separate corridors could easily be seen as wasted space, a luxury. Without separate circulation spaces, however, rooms opened directly one into the next, destroying the possibility of privacy and opening up charges that tenements destroyed the morality of the home.[25]

By the late 1870s the physical planning of tenements took two general configurations. One form, the narrow 25-foot-wide building, was reinforced by typically long and narrow lot shapes. These small tenement buildings were most commonly erected by speculative developers who were reputed to make up to 25 percent a year on their investment, so tenement development was a popular and

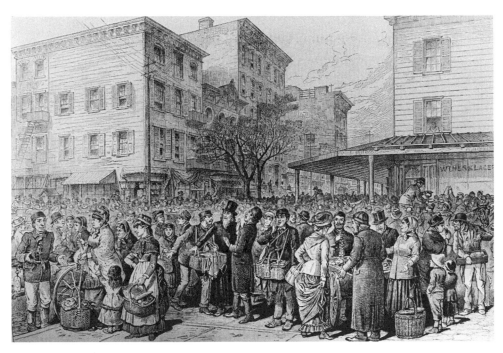

FIGURE 14 In a tenement district, Polish immigrants hold a street market. Such working-class uses of the street were antagonistic to a middle-class sense of propriety. ("A Polish Trading Post in New York," *Harper's Weekly* 28 [April 19, 1884]: 280; drawing by A. Berghaus)

profitable form of real estate practice. The other tenement form was designed as a big block of housing around a courtyard. Because more land was required to erect a courtyard building, returns on investments were more likely to be about 5 percent, making the courtyard tenement far less desirable to investors.[26]

In order to encourage improved architectural solutions to the tenement problem, the *Plumber and Sanitary Engineer*, a magazine founded in 1877 to improve sanitary awareness, held a competition in 1878 for better tenement designs. Competitors were to design a 25-foot-wide building following the suggested provisions of a new tenement law (enacted the following year) that would require every room to have direct exposure to outside light and air, outside light in halls and stairs, water closets inside the building, and a rear yard (fig. 15). While the 25-by-100-foot lot was limiting, nonetheless some inventive tenement designs emerged. Instead of too-narrow light shafts, some designers pushed all their light-shaft space to one side of the lot to make a bigger, courtyard type of light well. Some built external fireproof stairways on the facade and in the courtyard for airy and self-cleaning vertical circulation. One design even managed a tiny balcony for each apartment unit.

Improved architectural solutions suggested by the entries in the *Plumber and Sanitary Engineer* competition, however, did not go far to improve housing for the poor. The winning design was James Ware's unimaginative plan, often called

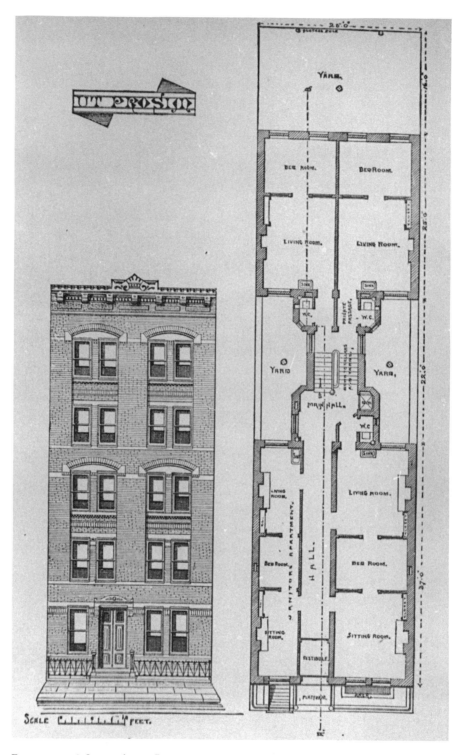

FIGURE 15 A four-unit-per-floor tenement entry to the *Plumber and Sanitary Engineer* competition for a better tenement, 1878. (Charles Frederick Chandler Scrapbooks, Avery Architectural and Fine Arts Library, Columbia University in the City of New York)

the "dumbbell" type, variations of which were built by the hundreds through the last two decades of the century. Although Ware's design met the criteria of the improved 1879 tenement law, public halls remained dark and narrow, stairs too steep, and yards too small. Air shafts only twenty-eight inches wide meant that a neighbor's windows were within easy reach and privacy was still hard to maintain.

Indoor plumbing was a great improvement over the shared backyard privy, but there were normally only two water closets on a floor shared by four families. Ten out of the typical fourteen rooms on a floor still remained dark and poorly ventilated. Contemporary critics asserted that innovations in tenement planning were discouraged by adhering to the 25-by-100-foot lot size. This system "says to the architect, the builder, the physician, the sanitarian, the philanthropist: 'Expand yourselves. Let us see what you can do.' The cook might as well say to the dough in the waffle-iron: . . . 'let us see what you can do.'"[27]

Nonetheless, thousands of these tenements were erected under the 1879 law. By 1900 there were 13,600 new tenement buildings in the area below Fourteenth Street and nearly 28,000 above it. "The overcrowding of the tenement houses renders them nurseries of vice and crime," asserted a middle-class observer of 1886. "Children of all kinds are thrown together, and learn vicious ways, which develop as they grow older into worse traits. Privacy is impossible, and the various families may be said to live almost in common." The occupation of tenement districts by immigrants incited a xenophobic panic in middle-class observers, to whom tenements became a symbol of all that was opposite to a proper home.[28]

Some philanthropic tenement-building efforts created large-scale multiple dwellings with greater concern for tenants' comfort and health (fig. 16). These reform tenements featured various collective spaces and shared facilities, but such sharing was problematic, pointing up the disputed boundaries between genteel and working-class definitions of public and private. In the 1878 Warren Street Buildings in Brooklyn, the philanthropist Alfred Treadway White and the Field Brothers, architects, gave tenants a courtyard for both service uses and recreation. The even larger courtyard of White's 1890 Riverside Buildings, also in Brooklyn, was planned to hold a fountain, plantings, and a bandstand for free concerts (fig. 17). These buildings covered less than 50 percent of the twenty-four city lots that made up the site. Shops, a common reading room on the ground floor, and a bathtub room in the basement with hot water courtesy of the management were part of White's efforts to expand communal facilities and encourage the cultural growth of his tenants.[29]

Family units at the Riverside Buildings were two rooms deep and faced both the street and the courtyard, assuring cross-ventilation. Units were modestly sized with three or four rooms per family; the three-room unit averaged 486 square feet. But each had its own water closet and washing sinks, built-in storage shelves, and direct sunlight. Instead of interior corridors for circulation, White and the Field Brothers adopted balcony circulation. Balconies were self-cleaning

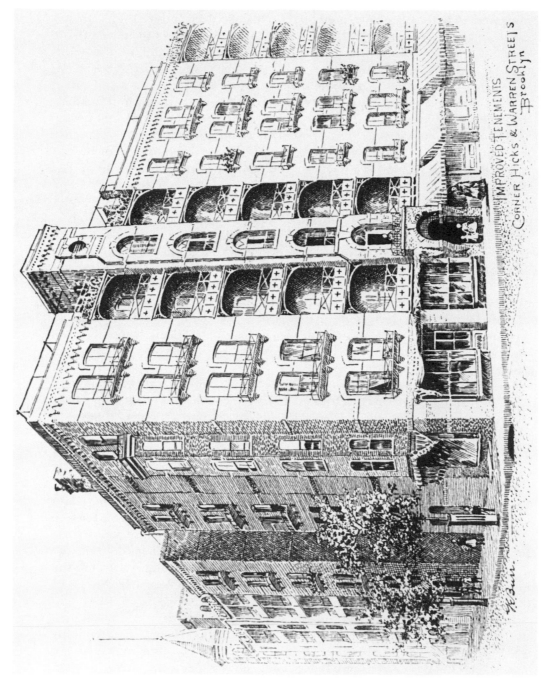

IMPROVED TENEMENTS
CORNER HICKS & WARREN STREETS
Brooklyn

FIGURE 16 The philanthropist Alfred Treadway White's reform tenements at the corner of Hicks and Warren streets, Brooklyn, New York, stand out because of their balconies. (Elizabeth Bisland, "Co-operative Housekeeping in Tenements," *Cosmopolitan* 8 [November 1889]: 35)

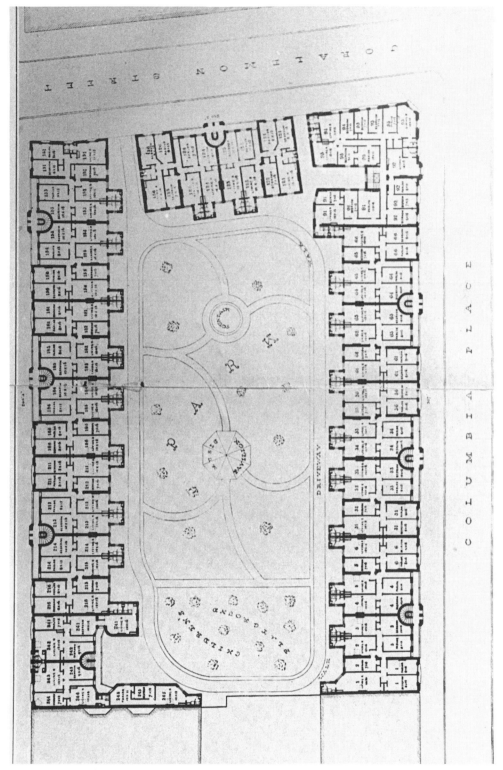

FIGURE 17 At Alfred Treadway White's Riverside Buildings, reform tenements built in Brooklyn in 1890, all the apartment units wrap around a huge courtyard. (*Sunlighted Tenements* [1912])

and served as fire escapes. Disapproving middle-class critics, however, claimed that these balconies, pleasant in theory, were "in practice, liable to be hung with clothes and bedding, to say nothing of the promenading of the tenants, [and] are apt to give a frowzy look to the front, not inviting the better class of applicants for rooms."[30]

Similar to White's buildings, the Astral Apartments were erected in Brooklyn's Greenpoint section in 1885 (figs. 18, 19). Sponsored by Charles Pratt, founder of the Pratt Institute in Brooklyn, this large building provided six floors of two-, three-, and four-room apartments for $10 to $25 per month. Tenants had the shared use of a large lecture room, basement bathtubs with free hot and cold water, and an 8,000-square-foot rear yard for children to play. Each family had individual rights to a coal bin in the basement and a place on the roof or in the yard for clothes drying. Some units provided just sleeping rooms and a living room, but the larger ones also gave tenants a sitting room, indicative of middle-class notions of sociability in a room specifically set aside for that purpose. Also within the apartment unit, tenants got the conveniences of a scullery with hot and cold water, a private water closet, and a window in every room.[31]

Who lived in tenement houses? Family makeup reported in the 1880 census indicates the variety of people and occupations in tenement households on the Lower East Side. While some buildings contained desperately poor individuals, many housed families of apparently hard-working and respectable parents and children. In a tenement house in the Eleventh Ward, at 654 East Twelfth Street, most of the thirteen families had two parents in the household; many of the mothers contributed in-house labor (child care, for example) to family success rather than earning a living outside the home. Those with outside occupations included two washerwomen, a wet nurse, and two shirt finishers. Most of the children were in school at least until their teens. The fathers were employed in occupations such as laborer, butcher, silver gilder, carpenter, and coal peddler.[32]

Another tenement building, at 16 Chrystie Street, held twenty families, mainly with German and Irish names. The male heads of household held jobs such as porter, bookbinder, teamster, carpenter, confectioner, machinist, and barber. Nearly every household had both husband and wife in residence and from one to three children.[33] This population hardly matches the middle-class image of filthy and immoral tenement life. Such reports indicate that cramped quarters, and an alternative distribution of public and private functions in these multiple dwellings, did not necessarily generate family collapse.

Yet for clients and designers of middle-class apartment houses, tenements often represented a way to define multiple dwellings as unacceptable. The list of qualities that the middle class rejected was long. Too many families together in one building forced people to mix socially to a far greater extent than genteel standards allowed. Children learned too much too soon; they played in the street, exposed to rough language and habits. Interior spaces set out questionable boundaries for privacy: water closets in the public hall shared with other families and bathtubs in basement bathing rooms deprived residents of proper

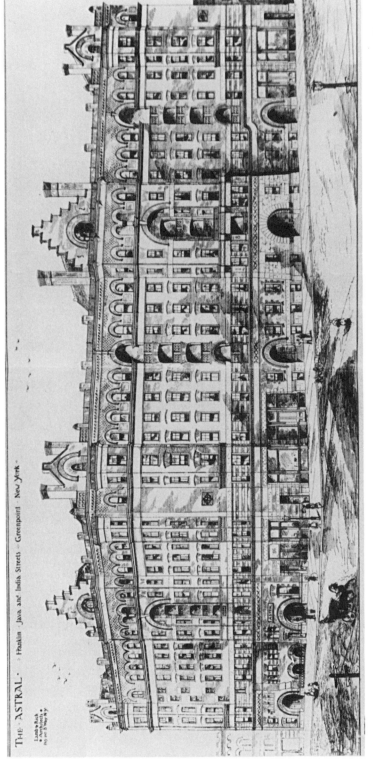

FIGURE 18 The Astral Apartments, a reform tenement by the architectural firm Lamb and Rich, still standing in Brooklyn, New York. (*American Architect and Building News* 20 [November 13, 1886]: pl. 568)

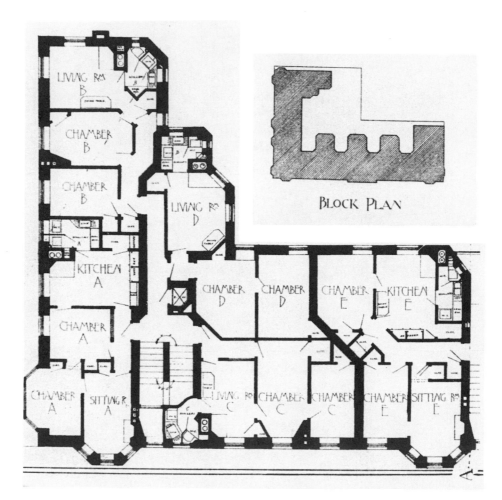

FIGURE 19 Plans for the Astral Apartments showing the layout of the block and some individual units. (*American Architect and Building News* 20 [November 13, 1886]: pl. 568)

levels of privacy. Lack of completely separate corridor circulation within a family unit meant residents walked through each other's sleeping space—spaces that *must* be private, yet were not—compromising the morals of children. Common spaces designed for tenants to share or benefit from collectively, such as courtyards, reading rooms, or bandstands, also raised fears about exposure to the public eye.

These opposite reference points—the private house, the foreign apartment, the working-class tenement—proved invaluable to New York designers, developers, and tenants as they mulled over their housing problems. A private-house tradition supplied them with models of spatial organization that kept the various functions of family life spatially discrete. It also provided them with an equivocal image of the house as a sign of family independence: houses were clearly individual, independent family dwellings, yet were so repetitive that they created a homogeneous impression that seemed architecturally tedious. The apartments of Paris provided models of urbane architecture, creating streetscapes of tasteful harmony and variety. The planning of Parisian apartment houses was admired for its spacious courtyards and successful public circulation system. However, within a family unit, many felt that Parisians failed to create clear circulation that would keep activities suitably discrete, and all agreed that in the area of technological innovations, Paris lagged behind America. Closer to home, the tenement tradition reminded designers that light and air were crucial factors in creating a successful apartment house—a lesson often compromised by the exigencies of site and budget. A tenement's allocation of such facilities as bathtubs or water closets, or the provision of bandstands or reading rooms, threw into relief the question of what should be public and what private in apartment houses. All of these examples of residential design remained available as designers set about creating the first generation of full-blown middle-class apartments.

3 THE FIRST GENERATION OF NEW YORK APARTMENTS

THE New York City of 1870 had survived its Civil War disruptions, and the population had grown by perhaps 150,000 since the end of the conflict. By 1870 there were nearly a million people with just under half of the population foreign-born. The East Side near Central Park had become the center of wealthy residential development. Street railways advanced during the 1870s to reach 125th Street and farther north, transporting people beyond the built-up areas south of Forty-second Street. Central Park had been in use for a decade, and Riverside Park and its carriage drive were already under way. These amenities were planned to make the undeveloped northern and western areas of Manhattan Island appealing for new, especially residential, real estate development.[1]

Urban life and the fine points of city conduct became a topic for etiquette books of the early 1870s (fig. 20). Such books instructed women on the correct way to take an omnibus (be sure to have change ready), proper shopping behavior (don't stare at the shop windows: it looks "countrified"), and attending the theater (never go alone with a gentleman who is not a relative or fiancé).[2] New York's first telephone exchange opened in 1879 with 252 subscribers, beginning the era of modern communications technology. New York in the 1870s gained a consciousness of itself as an urban center, and an awareness that housing its enormous population needed special attention.

The first generation of apartment buildings expressly designed to house middle-class New Yorkers appeared on city streets at the end of the 1860s and the first years of the 1870s. These apartments were often called "French flats," and usually had five or six stories and no passenger elevators. Occasional exceptions such as the 1870–71 Stevens House (fig. 21), with its eight stories and an elevator, only point up the preponderance of typical walk-up buildings. In 1870s Manhattan the new apartment houses first concentrated near the old commercial and hotel strip along Broadway from Union to Madison squares. A recession in 1873 put a damper on real estate development, but economic recovery was in

FIGURE 20 Women as travelers on public transportation are mocked because their skirts take up all the room. ("Habits of Good Society," *Appleton's Journal* 7 [1872]: 196)

view at the end of the decade as both apartment and private-house building experienced a resurgence and expanded into the east and west sides of mid-town Fifth Avenue and the south side of Central Park.

The First Apartment House

Any history of New York apartment houses ought to begin with the first example of this new type. That first example, however, is elusive. The claim that 1869 or 1870 is the moment of the "first" apartment house should be viewed skeptically. I have already suggested that dwelling practices established a culture of shared housing, a sharing that was concretized in the purposeful design of apartment buildings. From that point of view the "first" multiple dwelling is thrown into question. Both nineteenth-century sources and twentieth-century historians have named several different apartment buildings as the historic "first."

Two early "first" apartment buildings erected in the mid-1850s were identified in an 1874 article on New York residential architecture. One of these, on Wooster Street, was attributed to Richard Morris Hunt and described as a "small but handsome apartment house." The other, on Hudson Street, also offered "complete facilities for modest housekeeping on separate floors." Another candidate for "first apartment" was Stuyvesant House, built by Dr. Valentine Mott

FIGURE 21 At eight stories, the Stevens House apartments at Broadway and Twenty-seventh Street looked very much like a contemporary hotel, and indeed became the Hotel Victoria by the end of the 1870s. (*Appleton's Journal* 6 [November 18, 1871]: 561)

in the mid-1850s on Bleecker Street, looking like a collective dwelling on the exterior but working more like a set of row houses within.[3]

These buildings of the 1850s are quite a bit earlier than the apartment house that is very often cited as New York's first: Richard Morris Hunt's 1869 Stuyvesant Apartments on East Eighteenth Street. Montgomery Schuyler wrote in the 1890s that Hunt's Stuyvesant was "first of the elevator [meaning dumbwaiter?] apartment houses." The Real Estate Record's 1898 *History of Real Estate, Building, and Architecture in New York City* called the Stuyvesant "the first flats in New York City. . . . they were the first embodiment of new ideas." The Record, however, maintained (erroneously) that the Stuyvesant flats were a renovation job, not a fully conceived new building, so they called another building, the Jardine, New York's first built-from-scratch apartment house. Most modern historians have followed Schuyler and given Hunt credit for introducing the middle-class apartment to New York in the form of the Stuyvesant Apartments.[4]

This disagreement about the first apartment building for middle-class tenants does not represent a failure of historians to track down the original. Instead it may be fruitfully traced to confusion over the definition of the building type "middle-class apartment" itself, which was only then being formulated. If apartment houses are all multiple dwellings that are not working-class tenements, then the apartment category will include all the "second-class" dwellings built to be rented in floors, as well as the subdivided houses and other dwellings with rental units that were common places to live in mid-nineteenth-century New York. If, on the other hand, the stress is placed on "middle class," and not on "apartment," then the 1850s buildings with independent family units on several floors cited above may not have been perceived as genteel enough by later reporters looking for the landmark "first" apartments. The attribution of the "first" prize to the Stuyvesant Apartments by Hunt has been reinforced by the tendency of architectural historians to focus on well-known architects and to neglect anonymous works; but if the fame of the architect were the determining factor, surely the 1850s Hunt apartment building on Wooster Street should have emerged more strongly as the first.

The aim to identify one particular building as the first apartment house leads to disappointment, since even 1870s observers were not clear as to which one should be honored. But when the history of dwelling practices is placed in the foreground, there is no need for one clearly identifiable "first apartment building." The focus shifts rather to an ever-growing trend among non-working-class people to live in multifamily settings, a trend that by the end of the 1860s gave rise to purposely designed apartment houses.[5]

Early Names for Housing

The New York City Buildings Department required that plans for new buildings be filed with the city before it would issue building permits. Inspectors recorded residential plans from 1866 to 1874 under the categories printed in the department's "New Buildings Docket" books: "first class dwellings," "second class dwellings," and "third class dwellings or tenements."[6] But until 1875 there was no Buildings Department category for apartment buildings; in their record books, such a building type did not exist. Begun in 1866, these docket books preserve, in handwritten entries, the terminology used by people confronted with new dwelling types. Their language and the changes in their terminology are significant indicators of how the Buildings Department defined dwelling options and when they saw changes entering the picture.

The first-class dwelling is almost always a single-family private house—significant exceptions will be noted later. This type provided the most expensive kind of residential space per occupant, and was usually a three-, four-, or five-story building on a narrow lot of no more than 25 by 100 feet. Under this category fell the familiar New York brownstone row houses of the middle and later nineteenth century.

The second-class dwelling was usually a three- or four-story, two- or three-family dwelling, often with a ground-floor store, and a whole floor for each family above. These were clearly multifamily dwellings and thus might be expected to come under the category established for multifamily dwellings: that of "tenement." But in fact, second-class dwellings were given their own category by the Buildings Department, which recognized a major difference between a house for two or three families and one for eight to twenty or more.

In 1865, 167 of these second-class dwellings were begun. The superintendent of buildings, James MacGregor, reported, "The demand for second-class houses has, for the past three years, greatly exceeded the supply . . . the need of which is of serious importance to hundreds of families who can ill afford more expensive accommodations." The numbers were down slightly in the following year, then up again in 1867. The superintendent remarked that many families, happy to live two or three to a house, have welcomed the opportunity offered by second-class dwellings "of obtaining apartments in comparatively private and well-arranged houses."[7]

A row of four second-class dwelling units was described by the admiring superintendent of buildings in 1867. The houses, on the south side of Thirty-fifth Street between Ninth and Tenth avenues, had 25-foot-wide fronts. In four stories, they each housed three or four families. The apartments had a parlor, dining room, kitchen, three bedrooms, a bathroom, and a water closet, and included the water and gas fixtures, perfect for an "ordinary family of moderate means and desires."[8]

Hundreds of these second-class buildings were listed in the late 1860s and early 1870s docket books. Their average value of $10,000 apiece places them at the low end of housing construction costs, so they must have been intended for renters whose payments had to be low. Nevertheless, these tenants must have had incomes above those of the usual tenement dwellers, because each family could afford a full floor, which was more generous space than the quarter of a floor common for poorer tenement families.

A typical example from the 1869 docket book is a plan for ten second-class dwellings filed for the east side of Second Avenue, filling the block between Forty-second and Forty-third streets. All the houses had four stories and were forty-three feet high. Each building, of brick construction with a brownstone facade and a metal cornice, held three families above a ground-level store. In another example from 1869, plans were filed for a four-story dwelling with three apartments: a two-floor unit for the first and second stories, and two single-floor units above.[9]

While tenants in second-class dwellings had a reasonable amount of space, they often lived over stores, still not quite respectable. In earlier centuries, Roman, medieval, Renaissance, and colonial American merchants and artisans had lived above their own street-level workplaces. But the separation of home from workplace in early-nineteenth-century New York had given an ambivalent meaning to houses that combined domestic and commercial functions. The owners of the Albany and of the Stevens apartments in the early 1870s found tenants who were happy to live above a ground floor of Broadway shops. But when expensive apartment buildings caught on in the 1880s, they rarely included shops on the ground floor: upper-middle-class notions about the sanctity of home did not like to admit this common mixture of uses seen in second-class dwellings.[10] Once apartment living had become acceptable, however, middle-class sensibilities about mixing commerce with residence were often enough adjusted to accommodate the shops, and later, apartment hotels made a virtue of the convenience provided by shops inside the building.

The mixtures of use in second-class buildings is suggested in an advertisement of 1871 for renting floors above Dunlap and Company's men's store on Fifth Avenue and Twenty-third Street at the north end of the old Ladies' Mile district. The second floor was advertised for rent to tailors or other suitable "first class business"; the floors above were available for milliners or dressmakers, "or will be rented in flats." Another advertisement of 1875 suggests the same flexible attitude: "To Lease, No. 25 E. 21st Street . . . 5 story 70' deep on each floor, brownstone basement house suitable for doctors, milliners, boarding or renting rooms." The owners mention no special facilities such as kitchens or plumbing fixtures that might make a floor suitable to be used as a dwelling.[11]

The Buildings Department's third-class dwelling category was the tenement. This type has been seen in retrospect as fairly standard: endless instances of 25-by-100-foot buildings, five stories high with four units per floor. While this may be a fair characterization of tenements erected after the 1879 law (the "old law" dumbbell type, where each floor had two apartments in front, two in back, and a narrowed center with stairs and water closets), there is a surprising amount of variety of size and numbers of families in 1860s and 1870s tenements. The docket books record many tenement-class buildings of four stories containing units for only four families, one per floor (fig. 22). At the same time many tenements of the same dimensions were built to house eight, nine, or ten families. Sometimes the differences between a second-class and a third-class dwelling are obscure, suggesting that the Buildings Department inspectors were, themselves, grappling with problems in their own categorizing system. Second-class dwellings commonly had three family units over a store, but there are multiple dwellings listed as third-class tenements in the docket books with exactly the same arrangement.[12]

These three categories of dwelling types—first, second, and third class—were

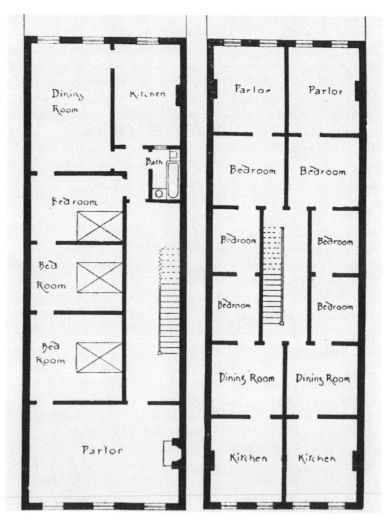

FIGURE 22   Two kinds of New York tenements before 1879, with one unit per floor and two units per floor—spacious when compared with the four units per floor that became the norm. (*American Architect and Building News* 29 [September 27, 1890]: 195)

intended to contain all the housing variety in New York of the 1860s. Some kinds of dwellings, however, slipped through category boundaries. The most significant exceptions to these categories occur in the case of first-class dwellings. Because almost all first-class dwellings are private single-family houses, it is surprising to see in the 1869 docket books a "first-class" entry listed as "Parisian dwellings" designed for "four families."[13] The architect was Richard Morris Hunt, the owner Rutherford Stuyvesant, and the building, the Stuyvesant Apartments (fig. 23). The listing is a striking anomaly among first-class dwellings, since the building inspector listed a multifamily building under "first-class dwellings," breaking the pattern of single-family designations in that category. The superintendent of buildings remarked, "this set of plans does not legitimately belong to what I have designated as first-class dwellings," since it contained more than one family, but he decided to include it anyway because of "its vast dimensions, the novelty of its construction, its elaborate finish and great cost."[14]

The next first-class anomaly in the docket books was another building by Hunt, the enormous Stevens House, built for the hotel developer Paran Stevens (fig. 21). Plans were filed in 1870 for this eight-story brick building with a Nova Scotia freestone front, a mansarded slate roof, shops on the ground floor, and apartments for eighteen families.[15] The Stevens apartments were located on the south side of Twenty-seventh Street, filling the 247-foot-long block between Fifth Avenue and Broadway. After recording the building under the first-class dwelling category, the buildings inspector noted that it was a "Parisian Dwelling Building."[16]

George B. Post's design for the six-story, all brick Black Apartment Building was filed with the Buildings Department in 1872. Classified as a "first-class" dwelling and budgeted at $150,000, the Black building was designated in the Remarks column as "French flats."[17]

As these examples illustrate, neither multiple families nor mixed uses kept buildings inspectors from calling a building "first class." Substantial budgets, architectural ambitions, or the promise of a significantly stylish building persuaded inspectors to list these new dwelling forms under the category formerly reserved for a single-family house. With Hunt's Stuyvesant Apartments, buildings inspectors for the first time began to categorize multiple dwellings as "first class," recognizing a problem with the old second-class and tenement categories that was due to a shift in the class of intended tenants and the architectural ambitions of the building.

Buildings Department inspectors adopted the name "French flat" in the early 1870s as a way to make social class distinctions between kinds of multifamily dwellings. This was not at first a formal category in the docket books, but appears in "Remarks" handwritten after a docket entry.

By 1874 this handwritten French-flat designation became common in the third-class-dwelling category as well as in the first-class. Plans filed in January of 1874 for a building on West Sixty-first Street west of the Boulevard (now Broadway) proposed four buildings housing four families per building. The build-

FIGURE 23 The Stuyvesant Apartments, by Richard Morris Hunt, completed in 1870, stood at 142 East Eighteenth Street. (Photo courtesy of Photo Library, Museum of the City of New York)

ings were sixty feet high, making higher-ceilinged rooms than contemporary second- or third-class buildings usually had. Their brownstone fronts made them look more like single-family row houses than cheap, brick-faced tenements. The cost of each was estimated at $20,000, implying better materials and craftsmanship than comparably sized tenement houses. But these flats were still listed under the "third-class or tenement" category, so the inspector had to make a note after the entry calling the buildings "French flats."[18]

Plans for another French-flat building were filed in February 1874, again entered under the third-class category. It was to house four families over a ground-floor store, just like most second-class dwellings and some tenements before it. Located at Eighty-eighth Street and Third Avenue, and valued at $15,000, this building was probably not very different from second-class dwellings in previous years, but inspectors were now alert to quality differences among multiple dwellings, so they chose to categorize it under third class, indicating a multiple dwelling, and to note by "French flat" after the entry that it (or its projected tenants) was better than the usual tenement found in the third-class category.[19]

Increasingly through the 1874 docket book, more and more entries have "French flat" written into the record. In various locations—on Fifty-eighth Street between Second and Third avenues, on Fiftieth Street between First and Second, on West Forty-seventh and Forty-eighth streets—third-class buildings were going up which inspectors called French flats. An average size for a French-flat building in 1874 was 20 to 30 feet wide and 60 to 75 feet deep. Most of these flat buildings were intended to house three or four families in four stories, and some included a shop on the ground floor. They often had brownstone fronts instead of cheaper brick, though that is not a determining factor for a French-flat designation.

Throughout 1874 the need for a new Buildings Department category for multifamily buildings was making itself obvious. Inspectors needed a formal designation that was neither first class with its usual implication of single family, nor third class with its usual meaning of working-class tenement. "First class" could have been useful as a quality designation but was misleading on size; "tenement" pointed to the size but was wrong for quality. In 1875 the "New Buildings Docket" came out with a new set of printed categories that tried to resolve the problem of how to classify the new apartment buildings going up in greater numbers every month. The new categories that inspectors began to use in January of 1875 were "first class dwelling," "second class dwelling," "French flats," "hotels and boarding houses," and "tenements." Three categories replaced the one multiple-dwelling type in the old "third class"; French flats and tenements expanded the types included, while hotels were brought into the multiple-dwelling category from their former designation as public buildings, reflecting the fact that many people used hotels as permanent residences.

The first-class-dwelling category was now restored as the category for purely single-family houses. Second-class dwellings remained two-, three-, or four-family units over a store; the difference between these and small French flats was thus obscured.[20] "French flat" was now a category to take in all multiple dwellings of a quality above tenements, a quality claimed by the owners and attested to by buildings inspectors. That included the $150,000 Black apartments as well as the $20,000 flats at Sixty-first Street and the Boulevard. The "French flat" classification also contained all the entries for the large and glamorous apartment houses like the Dakota, the Central Park, or the Osborne, which started to appear in significant numbers in the early 1880s.

A set of plans filed in 1880 shows the difficulty of maintaining the distinction between "tenement" and "French flat" classifications. The architects Vaux and Radford filed plans for a set of thirteen buildings, designed as a reform courtyard tenement. The buildings wrapped around three sides of a courtyard, were each six stories high and were planned to hold twenty-four families each. The buildings' sponsorship by the Improved Dwellings Association, and their generous common outdoor spaces, put them in the class of "model" tenements, but still, in plan, numbers of units, and numbers of tenants, they were the same as the typical tenements of the moment. Nonetheless buildings inspectors listed the project as "French flats."[21]

It is hard to find consistent physical differences between tenement and French-flat entries in the docket books. One might expect that estimated cost, number of floors, number of separate units within the building, height, or materials used would be significantly different between the categories of "tenement" and "French flat," but some or all of these features are often the same. Bathroom and toilet facilities may have been a deciding factor in making distinctions between them—privies in the rear yard or water closets in the common halls for tenements, and bathrooms within the unit for French flats—but this information is not recorded in the docket books. Testimony from one inspector in 1880 verifies that the distinctions between the tenement and French-flat types were "meagre" and usually rested on plumbing arrangements. French-flat tenants usually had a private water supply and tenement tenants usually did not, but this was not a consistent distinction.[22] Specific guidelines for the buildings inspectors' classification of multiple dwellings must have existed, but no such rules have been found.

Instead of specific physical differences between these two types, the distinction drawn between French flats and tenements is better explained as differences in naming and classifying as they changed over time. In May 1872, before the "French-flat" name entered buildings inspectors' vocabularies for third-class dwellings, plans were filed for 126 third-class dwellings, all designated as tenements. After the hiatus in building starts due to the financial panic of 1873, the building industry began to recover. In May 1882 plans were filed for forty-nine third-class tenements and forty third-class French flats. What had been one category was now two, and the numbers of new multiple dwellings were divided between them. On the evidence provided by the buildings inspectors, it does seem likely that inspectors themselves made personal assessments of building quality based on some combination of neighborhood, costs, architect, building sizes, plumbing arrangements, numbers of units, interior space, and intended class of occupants in order to decide which category to file building plans under—French flat or tenement.[23]

Although it is clear that the exact elements that constituted a first-, second- or third-class multiple dwelling were contested, still the new name "French flat" for the genteel type acquired significance for middle-class tenants. In 1872 the authors of *The American Home Book* recommended living in the new flats, reminding readers unfamiliar with the type that "a French flat house and a tenement house are as different as a gentleman and a bootblack." In the 1878 *Phillips' Directory*, headings grouped tenants' names under the name of their multiple dwellings, and then explained what kind of building it was: "'Rockingham' (Hotel)"; "'The Adelphi' (French Flats)." This visiting guide for respectable families was especially useful for those paying calls because it was organized alphabetically by address. The inclusion of these apartment houses in *Phillips' Directory* indicates that the apartments listed were recognized as genteel multiple dwellings, not seen as socially debasing to their residents, which they would have been if the association with tenements were as strong as some critics feared.[24]

French-Flat Buildings from the Street

If the new flat buildings presented a categorization problem to buildings inspectors, what would they have looked like to the ordinary passerby? Three actual buildings (only one of which is still extant) will serve as examples, amplified by some comparative published buildings and plans. The three examples are Richard Morris Hunt's 1869–70 Stuyvesant Apartments on East Eighteenth Street, Bruce Price's 1878 French-flat building, still standing at 21 East Twenty-first Street, and the Albany, designed in 1874 by John C. Babcock, on Broadway between Fifty-first and Fifty-second streets. These three buildings illustrate the norms and variations within the size range of typical walk-up French flats of the first generation.[25]

These three typify the size range of buildings in the first decade of apartment construction. Price's flat building, representative of hundreds of this size recorded in Buildings Department records, is a 25-foot-wide building, comparable in its outside dimensions to private houses as well as to most tenements and to second-class dwellings. Hunt's Stuyvesant buildings occupied four contiguous lots with a frontage of 112 feet, preserving something of the scale of a set of row houses; Babcock's Albany occupied ten contiguous house-sized lots, or the full end of a block (approximately 200 feet of frontage on Broadway).[26]

The Stuyvesant Apartments, described by a contemporary as "somewhat grotesque but highly picturesque," was a seventy-foot-high building of five stories—four floors of family units and the mansarded fifth floor of artists' studios (fig. 23).[27] Although the building was as long as four row houses, and therefore massive in context, in height the Stuyvesant conformed to familiar private house sizes. Its materials of brick and stone were not unusual for residential architecture in New York, but its ornament and wrought-iron balconies, combined with its somewhat over-scaled mansard roof, probably suggested Parisian style to contemporary viewers. Through its incomplete match with ordinary private houses and other familiar dwelling forms, the building's style hinted at unusual uses within.

Another notably early apartment building near the Stuyvesant that passersby might have stopped to stare at in 1871 when it opened was the Haight House, an example of a conversion, rather than new construction, on Fifth Avenue at Fifteenth Street. The *Times* described Haight House under a headline that read "French Apartment Houses," while a writer for *Appleton's Journal*, a general-interest magazine, called it "Parisian flats." On a plot of land measuring 80 by 150 feet, a former private house (or perhaps two) was completely rebuilt to create an apartment building containing twenty apartments on the lower four floors and fifteen bachelor suites on the fifth floor. The exterior, stretching along Fifteenth Street for 130 feet, seemed "imposing" with its "Palladian" facade and mansard roof.[28] Its street front was even longer than the Stuyvesant's and its height about the same.

Of the same period and neighborhood was the Stevens House, by Richard Morris Hunt (fig. 21), noted in *Appleton's* in 1871 as an example of "so-called Parisian flats." Brick walls, stone trim, and a stupendous mansard roof of iron, slate, and tin gave it a strong presence; *Appleton's* writer called it "splendid . . . bold and unique . . . a striking picture" and suggested that it would have been even more effective if sited on an open square. The ground floor had five stores, and above there were eighteen suites of rooms reached by a steam elevator.[29] The Stevens did not even pretend to sustain a homelike image, but at eight stories looked frankly like a hotel, and indeed it was converted and renamed Hotel Victoria shortly after completion. Anomalous in the 1870s, it did, however, have progeny in the grand apartment blocks of the 1880s.

Price's flat building at 21 East Twenty-first Street had five floors, one complete unit to a floor, with a steeply roofed top floor for servants and a basement for the janitor (fig. 24). The building was on a house-sized 25-foot-wide lot and fitted in rather inconspicuously with its neighboring five-story houses on the block. Each floor was somewhat lower than those in the four-story house next door, so its height did not make the building appreciably taller than others nearby. The front was brick with stone trim, terra-cotta foliated ornament, and tiles. Because the delicate scale of its ornament, oriel, porch, and dormer preserved a strongly domestic flavor, Price's French-flat building was less likely to arouse suspicions of unusual uses, although the attentive viewer would guess from its having more floors than the usual row house that this was a flat building. It should, however, not have been mistaken for a tenement house. Although it shared overall dimensions with common tenement forms, it was located in a finer district and its design was too individualized to be misread.

FIGURE 24 Looking like a private house in size, this apartment house at 21 East Twenty-first Street was designed by Bruce Price. (*American Architect and Building News* 3 [May 4, 1878]: pl. 123)

The four-story Albany (fig. 25) begun in 1874 filled a whole block along Broadway. Initially the architect had filed plans for a set of ten individual French-flat buildings on the same site, but plans were changed to make a single, large apartment block instead. The Albany's identity at first glance seems equivocal. Because the entire site's ten building lots were occupied by a single mass, viewers might have read it as a commercial block, or perhaps have seen in it kinship to a hotel. Along the Broadway facade a series of eight shop-fronts at ground level made the building fit into neighboring blocks of commercial development. Its brick facade with sandstone trim had simple ornamental details to give it character, and over the raised center of the Broadway facade its own name was presented in relief. This name was probably chosen to preserve the name of a unique early nineteenth-century apartment house in Piccadilly, London.[30]

The Albany's street image changed from the commercial Broadway front to the residential side-street facades. Around the corners on Fifty-first and Fifty-second streets each entrance facade gave the building a unified presence at a scale well beyond the domestic, four stories high and 110 feet wide. To critics looking for imposing city architecture, the Albany would have made a positive impression through this unity, when compared with the small disjunctive 25-foot-wide French-flat and tenement buildings and private houses nearby. John Babcock's choice of imagery came from diverse sources: through reference to historically larger buildings, such as hotels; to second-class dwellings with their inclusions of storefronts; and to a foreign source with literary associations, London's Albany. None of these sources refers obviously to "homes" with which the local middle class could identify.

At first glance, then, these buildings might have raised questions in the minds of contemporary viewers about what kinds of buildings they were. While Price's flat building might pass for a single-family house, or at least rested comfortably within the imagery of a house, Hunt's Stuyvesant and the Haight were both too big for a single house, and entrance designs showed them to be something else than the four row houses that their massing might suggest. The image the Stuyvesant presented even created confusion in the mind of the buildings inspector, who mistakenly recorded it as having four family units inside. The Albany's image was hardly domestic at all, because it rested on a ground floor of solidly commercial, street-oriented shops, and only revealed itself as residential around the corners, where its main entrances were. The Stevens too had ground-floor shops and the glamorous mansard roof of a period public building. The variety of architectural imagery suggested by only five of the early apartment buildings is characteristic of this early stage in apartment development. Later generations of apartment designers and tenants agreed upon increasingly clear-cut formal requirements, but even so there were always rival possibilities for the most satisfactory apartment styles.

The first advertisements for family dwelling units in built-for-the-purpose middle-class flat buildings appeared in newspapers in 1870 and 1871. Sometimes these apartments were listed under "Dwellings to Let," the heading where

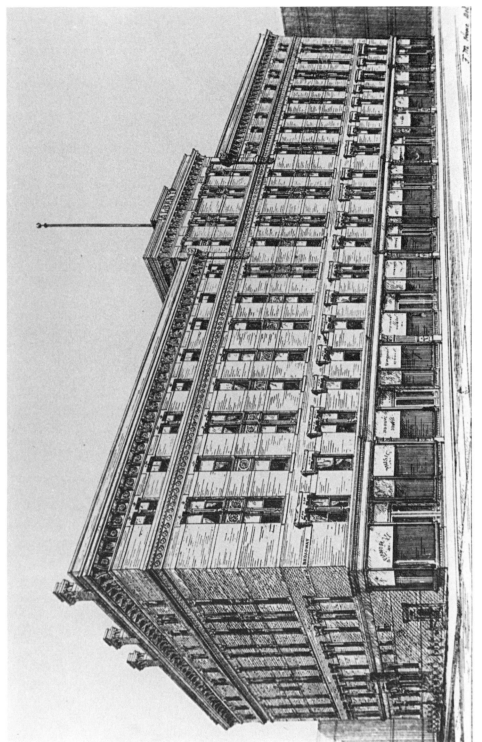

FIGURE 25 The Albany at Broadway between Fifty-first and Fifty-second Streets, by John Babcock, had shops on the ground floor and apartments above. (*American Architect and Building News* 1 [December 23, 1876]: following p. 412)

single-family houses would have traditionally been advertised, rather than the category of "Boarding and Lodging," which had always been the heading for subdivided houses. Searching for a rental home in 1871, would-be tenants could find an apartment like this: "First-Class Floors to Rent to private families in the four new and improved buildings . . . each floor separate and complete, containing water, gas, bath, range, wash trays, etc. with separate coal vaults and elevator from cellar."[31] The stress on each floor's completeness as a whole unit, and the list of modern conveniences available to tenants make evident the differences between this flat and the fragments of subdivided houses available in the preceding generation.

Building Lots and French-Flat Layouts

The common New York building-lot size of 25 feet wide and 100 feet deep often influenced designers' thinking about the forms that new flat buildings could take, as Hunt's Stuyvesant and Price's Twenty-first Street buildings both show. Designers of apartment buildings arrived at their first architectural solutions for multiple dwellings in a landscape that had been divided up by the Commissioners' Plan of 1811, which had platted the undeveloped area of Manhattan in regular rectangular blocks of streets and had based the standard lot size on the simplest unit for sales and development.

Published theoretical plans for many French-flat buildings of the 1870s and 1880s used as a basic starting point the standard house-sized 25-by-100-foot dimensions, which were also used for the 1878 improved tenement competition held by the *Plumber and Sanitary Engineer*.[32] Although Buildings Department records show that lot proportions varied considerably, long, narrow lots were the rule through the 1870s and 1880s both for smaller middle-class apartment houses and for the lower end of the rental market.[33]

Developers with greater resources could assemble several small lots and erect a large apartment house, such as the Albany, where ten lots were put together and the apartment house filled the whole block front. Lots were advertised in the newspapers of the early 1870s either singly, or in groups of a few or a dozen or more contiguous lots. Such larger sites gradually replaced 25-foot-wide building lots as the preferred size. By the time the new tenement law of 1901 was passed, it was rare to find a multiple dwelling going up on a single lot; developers chose at least a double lot, 50 feet wide, in order to comply with the new law's light and air provisions and still make a profit.[34]

Having selected the lot or lots for a new apartment house, designers and developers then needed to establish the ways the new building would sit on its plot of land and relate to the street. Richard Morris Hunt, at the Stuyvesant Apartments, erected a building whose facade reinforced the street wall, picking up the line of existing buildings on the block to help create an urbane street facade (fig. 26). When Price designed his little flat building on Twenty-first

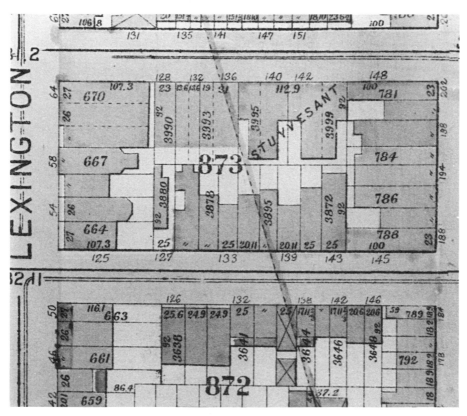

FIGURE 26 This "footprint" of the Stuyvesant Apartments in its street context shows the facade lined up in the same plane as neighboring buildings to make a consistent street wall. (*Atlas of the Borough of Manhattan* [Brooklyn: E. B. Hyde, 1907])

Street, he located its facade nearly in line with contiguous buildings. The Albany filled its site out to the edge of the sidewalk along Broadway and Fifty-first and Fifty-second streets. Broadway does not meet the side streets at right angles, so the Albany's facade did not meet its side walls at right angles either (fig. 27). In all three buildings, the designers left no gaps in the street wall, but aimed to establish regularity by adding their facades to others on the block for a clearly stated urban face.

Filling the lot in this way was common practice for both apartment- and private-house designers at mid-century. In the early nineteenth century, building patterns tended to produce irregular street-wall configurations. Restrictive covenants on real estate were sometimes used to force house builders to make their houses fill the front of the site from lot line to lot line, and to meet a standard setback line in order to ensure an orderly and attractive street wall in residential neighborhoods.[35] European designers too were especially concerned to enhance urban space by bringing the facades of their apartment houses out to the street edge. In Paris this concern was amplified by regulations controlling

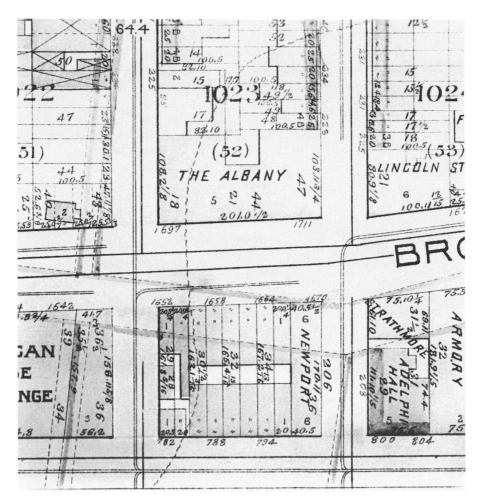

FIGURE 27 The Albany fills its plot out to the edge of Broadway and the side streets, with an indentation on the rear for light and air. (*Atlas of the City of New York* [New York: Robinson and Pidgeon, 1880–86])

cornice height as well, making for a regular appearance even on the most odd-shaped lots. In Vienna, as the American architect John Niernsee informed American readers in an 1870s publication, several developers might join together to build a uniform facade enclosing three or four separately owned apartment houses, in order to develop a clear and beautiful public face for the city. In 1870s New York, individual designers, while not willing to subsume their apartment houses within a Vienna-style larger envelope, nonetheless followed the tradition of bringing their buildings up to the lot line on the street side and reinforcing the street wall.[36]

The apartment house whose facade met the edge of the street had one wall in place; the location of its remaining exterior walls was determined by the struggle between maximizing the rentable interior space, which required that the entire plot be filled, and the need for fresh air and light for all the interior rooms, which required courtyards, light wells, and other kinds of indentations in the envelope. As early as the 1830s, observers of crowded city neighborhoods had reported close links between disease and death rates and the lack of fresh air and sunlight. Apartment-building designers, working to produce genteel dwellings in dense urban settings, had to be especially careful to design for sufficient light and air.[37]

Designers of apartment buildings on the typical narrow lot adopted some fairly standard configurations. One popular plan type filled the lot at the street side, then narrowed the building with a series of small indentations or one large one toward the rear (figures 4, 5, and 6 in fig. 28). Rooms at the front were lit from windows facing onto the street, but party walls prohibited any light along the side walls of the building, unless those side walls were moved away from their neighbors. Rear rooms could face both the backyard, if there was one, and the

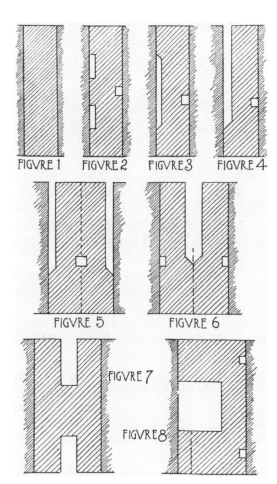

FIGURE 28 Typical apartment-building "footprints" show the relation of building mass to light wells, light courts, air shafts, and courtyards—all ways of bringing ventilation and light to interior rooms. (Irving Pond, "The Architecture of Apartment Buildings," *Brickbuilder* 7 [1898]: 116)

side light court, while rooms in the middle of the apartment looked out only onto the court. Another popular plan used a series of small indentations in the flank walls to create light wells (figures 2, 3, 4, 6, and 8 in fig. 28); rooms would look out onto the street, the light wells, and the backyard.

Richard Morris Hunt treated his Stuyvesant Apartments almost as if it were four narrow row houses with party walls, rather than one large building on a bigger site (figs. 26, 29). He broke down that division by giving the center pair of buildings a shared light court twice the size that a single building could have on a narrow lot. When such narrow apartments were erected one by one, only the single light court was possible, such as we see in the plan for a three-unit-per-floor "cheap flat" (fig. 30) published in 1874.[38] The cheap flat had the same floor configuration as one of Hunt's four Stuyvesant units: the front rooms filled the width of the lot while the rear rooms were against the party wall on one side, and faced a long, narrow light court on the other side. In the cheap flat, the building was so deep on its lot that it had no backyard, and one rear corner was angled off to allow a window in a rear bedroom.

Price gave his floors the same shape—wide at the street side, narrow in the rear, with only the light court lighting all the central rooms—in his flats on East Twenty-first Street (fig. 31). He too extended the building as far back on the lot as it could go and gave light to his rear corner room with a small indentation for a pair of windows. In addition, Price added a small light shaft toward the front of the apartment for additional light in the anteroom and private hall.

This kind of single-lot-sized apartment was described by Howells's character Mr. March, flat hunting with his wife, in *A Hazard of New Fortunes*: "The New York ideal of a flat . . . was inflexibly seven rooms and a bath. One or two rooms might be at the front, the rest crooked and cornered backward through increasing and then decreasing darkness til they reached a light bedroom or kitchen at the rear." A disbelieving March demanded of the janitor why such apartments were advertised as having "all light rooms," and found that that only meant all rooms had windows to the open air—no matter if that open air were merely a light well or air shaft.[39]

The larger Albany apartment house got its light and air from extensive street fronts, from a major light court incorporated in the center rear of the building as an indentation measuring about 30 feet on each side, and from shafts that penetrated the body of the building from cellar to roof in several locations (fig. 32). At the Albany the smallest of these were called "air and light shafts" and measured about 8 feet on a side, while the largest ones were called "open courts" and were 12 by 41 feet.

From these examples it is evident that both cheap and expensive apartments on single narrow lots exhibited similar perimeter wall configurations to get light and air. As a writer of 1879 skeptically observed, "sunlight . . . is considered a mere luxury in most of the rooms, and even direct light and air are treated as being of very little importance."[40] In single-lot-sized buildings such as Price's French flat, the lot itself prevented other building shapes: it was simply too

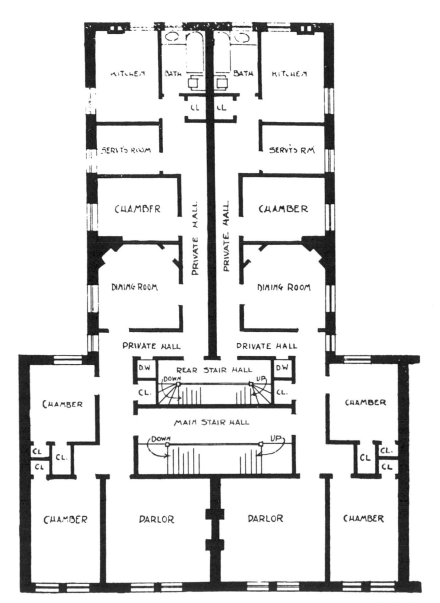

FIGURE 29 Half of the plan for the Stuyvesant Apartments, by Richard Morris Hunt, shows two of the four row-house-like divisions of the plan. Each unit has a long, narrow light court at the rear. (*Architectural Record* 11 [July 1901]: 479)

narrow for experiment. While the amount of light and air was clearly greater than what tenements got, because budgets were higher and numbers of units were lower, such plans were still not satisfactory. One might have expected those apartment buildings erected on bigger pieces of land like the Albany and the Stuyvesant to arrive at configurations that would guarantee more light and air,

FIGURE 30 The 25-foot-wide "cheap flat" gets ventilation and light from rear and street windows and a narrow light court. The middle apartment is ventilated only by the court. (James Richardson, "The New Homes of New York," *Scribner's Monthly* 8 [1874]: 64)

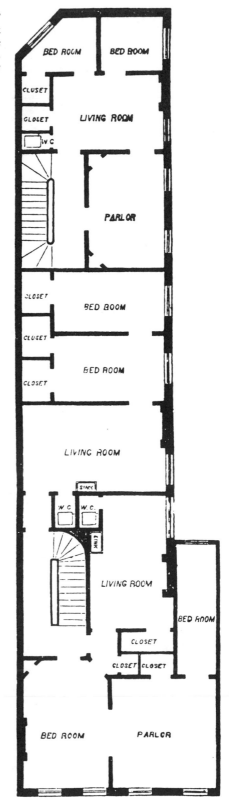

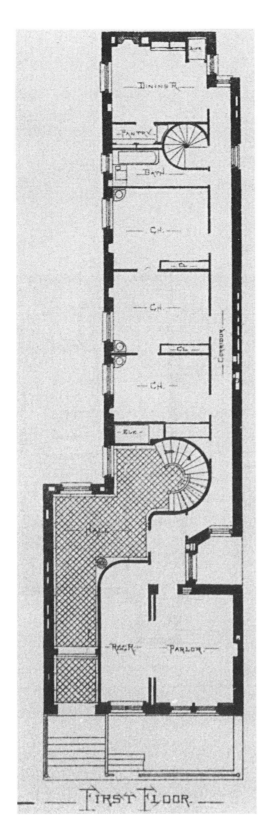

FIGURE 31 A floor plan of the ground floor of 21 East Twenty-first Street by Bruce Price shows a long, narrow light court plus a small, squarish air shaft for ventilation. (*American Architect and Building News* [May 4, 1878]: pl. 123)

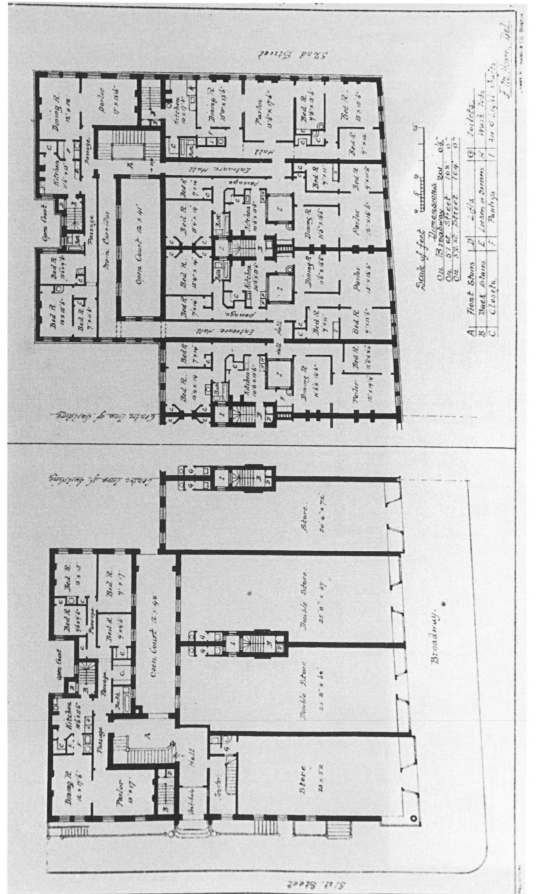

FIGURE 32 An indentation on the rear, two large and two small open courts, additional light shafts, plus extensive street facades all brought light and air to Albany tenants (*American Architect and Building News* 1 [December 23, 1876]: following p. 412)

but their designs relied on the same small courts and shafts used in single-lot buildings. Improvements in light and air had to wait until the next decade and even then were not widespread.[41]

Public Circulation in French-Flat Buildings

The circulation of people and goods in a building is a critical issue for the architect. For apartment-house designers, circulation questions split into two kinds—public paths of movement (for tenants, guests, and servants), and movement inside the private apartment unit. Problems of public circulation in apartment buildings involved the arrangement of stairways, elevators, lobbies, corridors, and dumbwaiters. The smaller buildings on narrow lots of the first generation (and on into the 1890s) cut down on this complexity by rarely having elevators for passenger use, so the only vertical circulation was stairs. Both large and small apartment houses made distinctions between service-circulation paths and those for tenants and their guests.

The first circulation element to greet the visitor or tenant is the front entrance. Since front doors on houses had historically been the locus of extra architectural attention, those on apartment houses received the same. The major difference is that doors of private houses serve only family members, whereas front doors of apartment buildings serve all the tenants. If a door projects images to passersby of family taste, for example, apartment-house group doors can make such a statement only in broad terms through style choices that may well not represent tenants' individual tastes.

Hunt emphasized the front entrance of the Stuyvesant with a pair of doors, framed in lighter-colored stone, ornamented and raised three steps above the street. These low steps preserved New York's earlier house tradition of entrances raised up above the sidewalk by a stoop with several steps. It was important to make a good impression on visitors, who might, like the journalist Charles Carroll, doubt the social tone of an apartment house. Carroll reported his relief at seeing the "handsome portal with its polished granite columns and tasteful architecture" when he arrived to visit at an unfamiliar middle-class apartment building. "Clearly there is nothing of the tenement-house to be feared here."[42]

Price's front door at 21 East Twenty-first Street, raised well above the sidewalk by six steps, was detailed with small-scale ornament in keeping with that on the oriel, dormer, and other parts of the facade. Price's projecting three-story oriel, or curved bay, overhangs the side of his front door, giving it a sheltering presence and lending its supporting column to ornament the doorway. Babcock raised the entrance doors of the Albany up three steps and ornamented them with collonettes supporting a small masonry hood, similar to those above the windows on the second floor. None of these doorways is exaggeratedly tall— they stay within the height of the first story—and none extends out onto the sidewalk with porte cocheres, awnings, or other devices.[43]

A "family hotel" proposed by the architect Henry Hudson Holly takes the idea of front stoops to its extreme (fig. 33). In his apartment house he created a street front with seven front doors reached by seven high sets of stairs. Six of these led into private family abodes. The seventh led into the building's main lobby and gave access to the rest of the apartments above and behind the private units with their street access. He hoped to create the impression of a row of houses, comforting to families made uneasy by multiple dwellings.[44]

Once through the front door, visitors surveyed the lobby, one of the features that marked out the new French flat from earlier, second-class, multifamily dwellings. When tenants at the Stuyvesant Apartments entered their building, they arrived first in a sparely decorated lobby where the concierge's office was located. In narrow buildings like Bruce Price's French flat, the street entrance and the public lobby were usually at the side rather than in the center of the facade, allowing a somewhat curtailed apartment on the ground floor to be fitted in beside the entrance. The public lobby, however, would not be any larger than necessary and was not expected to serve for anything more than access.

From the lobby tenants went to the public staircase, which permitted access to their floors. At the Stuyvesant, Hunt clustered all his vertical circulation together in one core, away from the apartments' windows. Tenants walked up a "grand" stairway and reached their own front doors from either end of a public landing.[45] Only two family units opened off each landing, but the tenants from all four floors, plus the tenants of the attic studios, shared the stairs (fig. 29). This stair design contrasts with Calvert Vaux's in his 1850s Parisian Buildings (fig. 5), where he gave public circulation spaces the best light and an enticing atmosphere. Back to back with the Stuyvesant's main stair was a service stairway that opened into the private hall of each unit. Adjoining that stairway was a dumbwaiter for each apartment, located toward the front of the apartment and not adjoining the kitchen as was more commonly done.

For its principal vertical circulation paths, Bruce Price's design (fig. 31) included a main stair and service stair—both circular. The main stairway toward the front of the building rose around a circular open well in the center, while the service stairway in the rear was a tight spiral. These curved stairwells were reminiscent of typical features of Parisian apartment design. An additional circulation element was the dumbwaiter provided for servants' use. It connected apartment units to the basement with its storage areas and to the roof with its laundry facilities, often opening into the kitchen. In a lively description of 1890s apartment life in a flat building with two units per floor, Theodore Dreiser uses the dumbwaiter as a space for social contact. His heroine Carrie meets her next-door neighbor when both women open their dumbwaiter doors at the same moment to retrieve the cream and the morning paper, and see each other across the open shaft.[46] This begins a welcome friendship for the two women that expands to include jaunts together out into the city.

In the 1874 "cheap flat" (fig. 30), three apartments per floor necessitated two stairways, one to serve the front and middle apartments and one for the rear

FIGURE 33 Henry Hudson Holly's proposed "family hotel" had seven front doors and stoops; the center one led to several upper-floor apartment units, while the three on each side led directly from the street to private houselike units. (James Richardson, "The New Homes of New York," *Scribner's Monthly* 8 [1874]: 64)

unit. Giving over square footage to public space is expensive, and small budgets did not allow for central public stairs, lobby, and corridors. Because this flat was not for well-to-do families there were no service stairs, nor was there a dumbwaiter. Both of the stairways were placed against the party wall so as not to use up precious windows; these stairs, like those in Paris apartments, may have been skylit.

The Albany's circulation included two main stairways but no passenger elevators, as was typical at the time in New York for buildings up to five or six stories, just as it was in European cities (fig. 32). Each main stairway was reached through a lobby off a side-street entrance around the corner from Broadway, one on Fifty-second Street and one on Fifty-third. Because the apartment house was large, with ten separate apartment units on each upper floor, circulation economies were possible by centralizing access to the floors in two main stairways, one for each end of the building.

To get to the center apartment, tenants had to walk about eighty feet of public hall. This was a long distance for a corridor, but windows opening onto both the open court and the rear indentation provided light and changing views. At one point the Albany's corridor even had windows on both sides looking onto both courtyards, rather like an internal bridge, and would not have seemed nearly so grim as many windowless modern apartment corridors. This corridor with its light on two sides seems to be an unusual feature, not repeated in later New York apartment plans. While older Viennese buildings sometimes had the public corridor placed along a courtyard wall with light along all its length, New York designers generally preferred to save all exterior wall windows for the private rooms themselves and did not worry too much about good light for circulation spaces. Parisian designers avoided long corridors altogether by using skylit stairway access limited to only two or three apartments per floor.

Service stairs were also provided for every one or two apartments in the Albany. These stairs led directly from an individual unit to both basement and roof, so servants could accept deliveries, hang the laundry, or get to their own attic rooms without using the main stairs. The service stairways, buried within the building, were lit only from the air and light shafts. Dumbwaiters were also provided to the Albany's tenants, adjacent to the kitchen and opening onto the service-stair landings.[47]

An interesting variant on the stair and hall circulation system for small apartment houses was proposed in 1876 by the Brooklyn firm of the Parfitt Brothers in a design called "A New System of Apartment Houses" (fig. 34). They suggested a building with a central light court, and instead of the usual stairs and internal public corridors, a system of external stairs and access balconies. In the Parfitts' projected middle-class apartment design, each unit had its own service stairs, and two family units on each floor shared external front stairs as well as a service lift, which opened onto a balcony in the central light shaft.[48] An interior public corridor normally cuts a building apart, separating its front from its back and preventing through ventilation. But with an external circulation system like this one, each unit had fresh air and good light from both front and back exposures.

Although balconies had been successfully used by Alfred Treadway White in Brooklyn model tenement buildings from the 1870s to the 1890s, their use in tenements made access balconies seem too closely associated with buildings for the poor and therefore undesirable from a middle-class point of view. Balcony or gallery entrances, according to an 1879 article in *American Architect and Building News*, were embarrassing because of their "publicity." In the following year, the same journal praised recent tenement proposals for avoiding the balconies used by White.[49] For the Parfitt Brothers, then, to propose balcony access for middle-class apartments was seriously to risk making their building socially unacceptable because of its association with working-class housing. Balcony access does not seem to have been a feature of executed middle-class apartments in the later nineteenth century, and reappeared as a successful device only in the years after World War II. Such buildings as Moshe Safdie's 1967 Habitat apartment house in Montreal make use of external corridors and stairs for public circulation, but by that time the "publicity" and social interchange among neighbors that takes place on these circulation paths was seen not as a problem but as a great virtue.[50]

Interiors of the First-Generation Apartments

Lot sizes and building layouts determined the overall shape of an apartment block, but the tenants' special concern was the individual family apartment unit, for there a home had to be created. The contents of that unit were a set of rooms related to each other along private circulation paths in ways that could satisfy contemporary values. For the middle-class family, the values of privacy and the sanctity of homelife influenced plans for individual units.

The names of rooms and the choices among possible rooms in any nineteenth-century multiple-dwelling unit indicated the class of building and the class of occupants. Just as the names "French flat," and "tenement" designated class-related categories within the multiple-dwelling type, so too the names "parlor," "sitting room," or "living room" could all be used to designate the room used by families of different classes for their common social activities and entertainment of guests. Published plans of the 1870s and 1880s made use of these different room designations to distinguish between classes of potential tenants.[51] The numbers of rooms included in a family unit were also class related. A tenement unit had two to four rooms, while a flat had four to ten, according to a writer in 1880 introducing New York housing to a public uninformed about multiple dwellings.[52]

The principal room in tenement units was called a "living room," as seen, for example, in Vaux and Radford's 1880 model tenement on First Avenue (fig. 35). An illustration published by White showed a woman in the living room of the

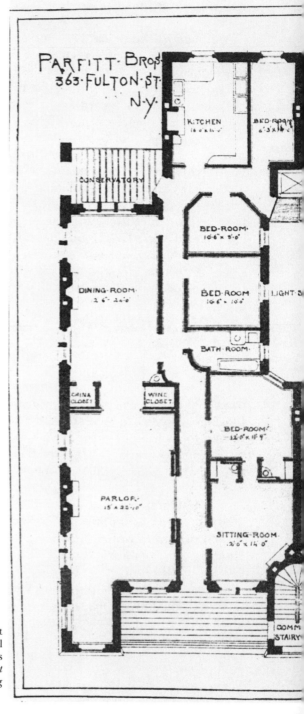

FIGURE 34 "A New System of Apartment Houses," by the Parfitt Brothers, utilized external access balconies more often found in tenements than in middle-class buildings. (*American Architect and Building News* 1 [October 21, 1876]: following p. 340)

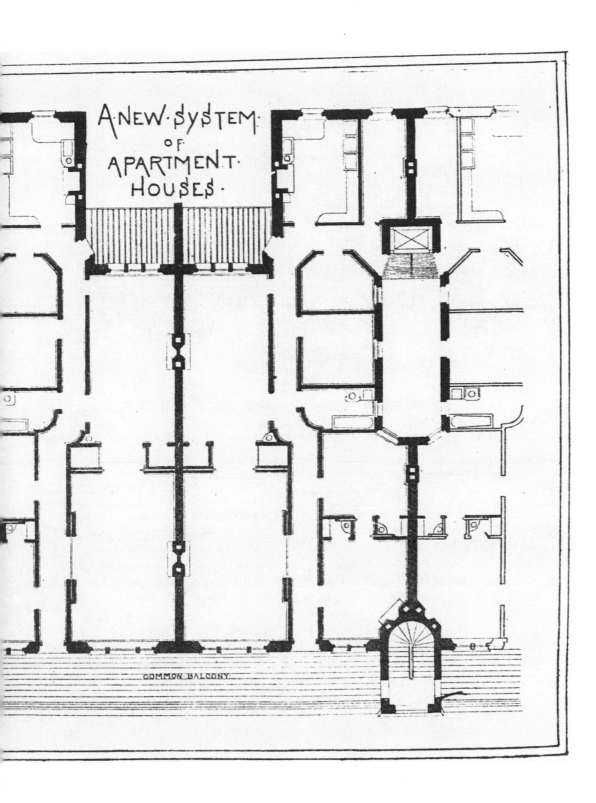

A NEW SYSTEM OF APARTMENT HOUSES

COMMON BALCONY

FIGURE 35   A "living room" that includes the kitchen facilities in Vaux and Radford's 1881 tenements for the Improved Dwelling Association on First Avenue between Seventy-first and Seventy-second streets (Elizabeth Bisland, "Co-operative Housekeeping in Tenements," *Cosmopolitan* 8 [November 1889]: 36)

Riverside Buildings cooking at the range. An activity such as cooking may seem out of place to modern observers who are used to living rooms as nonwork spaces. But for tenements of the period, the living room was the place for cooking, eating, family socializing, washing the clothes, and anything else that needed to be done. Tenement living rooms even became sweat shops for families doing piecework at home for the garment trades or preparing tobacco for cigar makers.[53]

For tenants aspiring to middle-class status, the plan (fig. 30) published in 1874 for a floor of a "cheap flat" shows both "living room" and "parlor" as the names of the principal rooms in both the front and the back units. This plan represents a bridge between tenement and middle-class room designations, keeping the living room as the common family-kitchen-work room, and then trying to rise above the tenement with a purely social parlor. The parlor, of course, was a certificate of gentility, because there one's guests would be saved from glimpsing the inner workings of the household.

In better middle-class apartments a designer would choose the names "parlor" and "library" for the principal reception rooms, usually providing at least two such purely social spaces for receiving guests. Sometimes "parlor" and "music room" were the names of this pair. Middle-class tenants expected work to be completely removed from social spaces like the parlor and allocated to the kitchen and other service rooms. When the social room was given the name "sitting room," it was usually in a hotel or bachelor flat and not in a better-quality family unit.[54]

Sleeping rooms also had names associated with social rank. Tenement dwellers usually slept in bedrooms, whereas the middle class slept in chambers (although the perfectly respectable tenants at the Albany had "bedrooms" and the much poorer ones in the Astral had "chambers"). Even circulation spaces had socially determined names: tenement occupants moved through halls, servants used passages, but middle-class tenants and their guests entered through a foyer or anteroom.

Bathing facilities and water closets (toilets) were usual in middle-class apartment buildings from the first, and in tenements water closets were required by law after 1879. The widespread concern with health in the mid-nineteenth century had made indoor toilets a contested domestic feature: did they enhance cleanliness or did they introduce germs into the home? By the time apartment buildings were finding their places in the urban housing market, interior plumbing had been accepted as a part of the middle-class city home. Improvements in toilet technology had calmed worries about contaminating the house with escaped sewer gas.

The distribution of toilet facilities was different from that familiar today. Today's toilet was named "water closet" for all classes of buildings. Tenement dwellers typically found the water closet outside the family unit in the hall and would have shared it with at least one other family. Middle-class tenants had their water closet inside the unit, but one such fixture was considered adequate for even such large units as the twelve- to twenty-room apartments at the Dakota. Rather than being combined with the washing functions of the sink or bathtub, the water closet often had its own little room.[55]

Bathtubs in the earlier part of the nineteenth century had taken the form of movable washing containers—anything from a large basin to a full-size tub—filled with water from a separate source. Fixed bathtubs with their own water supply became common in the 1870s and were always supplied in middle-class apartment houses. Tenement buildings did not have regular bathing facilities at first; White's model tenements were especially progressive in that they included a basement room with fixed bathtubs and hot and cold water. For those without a bathtub, public baths were an alternative. As late as 1917, one writer stated that bathtubs were still a luxury, and other ways of keeping clean should be found by tenants who had to economize on housing.[56]

Although by the 1870s many middle-class tenants had a unified bathroom enclosing bathtub, water closet, and lavatory basin all in one room, they also had separate sinks in bedrooms. It was common to have a water pitcher and basin for washing supplied to sleeping rooms in the era before fixed plumbing, and a small sink in the bedroom continued this tradition in early apartments such as the Albany.

Planning the One-Floor Family Unit

The several rooms just considered had to be put together to make a middle-class apartment unit, a planning job that proved difficult for designers. Rooms had to find their places within the building envelope, where space was always restricted by lot size, circulation requirements, and exposures. How rooms should be grouped and related to each other—the question of what architects call "adjacencies"—was a question not easily answered. The first logical model for planning a domestic unit was the private house, as described in the last chapter. The way that houses had their various functions clustered together created a full-floor basement service zone and a separate parlor floor social zone for entertaining guests. On the second and third floors, family bedrooms had their own zone, and servants lived in the garret, where sewing and other household service might be accomplished.[57]

When considering a one-floor arrangement for family dwellings, architects were unable to find precise models. In hotels too many domestic functions such as dining and receiving guests were carried on in public spaces, and by people whom critics found frivolous. Hotels, therefore, failed as a model for one-floor private family units, which had to be both self-contained and respectable. The other one-floor dwelling unit established in New York was the tenement unit, built by the thousands since the 1820s. But of course that was completely unacceptable for a middle-class clientele, because it was for the poor, whose culture and income marked them out as representing the opposite of decent family life. Second-class flats over shops did not provide a satisfactory model either, perhaps because their room relationships were not well-enough articulated to afford the spatial zoning that middle-class families desired.

A well-established tradition of middle-class apartment living in Paris offered examples for American architects to study, but there, too, characteristics of family life and social conduct made Parisian apartments less than perfect precedents. The Parisian grouping of rooms *en suite* gave advantages for entertaining that American designers and clients found very impressive.[58] Yet many American commentators represented French apartment plans as irrational: kitchens were located far from dining rooms, while bedrooms actually opened onto the parlor—the "indecent propinquity" that shocked Edith Wharton's characters. Americans preserved their sense of privacy by insisting on independent corridor access to each room, while the French were content to use the rooms themselves (in addition to corridors) as circulation paths from one room to the next. Where Americans thought of public and private spaces as clear and distinct, the French conceived of a continuum from public to private space.

American designers, therefore, used these sources in the 1870s only as reference points to help define what was and was not wanted in American apartments. Representative plans of the small French-flat type illustrate how designers thought about internal planning problems in smaller flat buildings. For the placement of rooms for receiving guests in the family apartment, Richard Morris Hunt's Stuyvesant Apartments on Eighteenth Street is a good early example. Visitors entered from the main stair hall into a private hall that gave onto the parlor, adjoining chamber (on some plans identified as a library), and contiguous second chamber (fig. 29). The dining room, also near the entrance to the Stuyvesant apartment unit but not directly joined to the parlor, was another reception space for entertaining guests. Located toward the middle of the floor, it was reached by a hall that continued back to additional bedrooms. Hunt's design met New York expectations for a parlor that both had a street view and was located near to the entrance, in keeping with traditional row-house arrangements. Calvert Vaux, as early as 1857, had advised apartment designers always to have the main street outside the parlor window to satisfy American tastes.[59] Yet Hunt's public-room grouping included only the parlor and optional library; later practitioners would agree that the dining room ought properly to be part of the public group.

Hunt's dining room at the Stuyvesant was easily accessible from the main entrance, yet at some distance from the parlor, where dinner guests might be expected to be entertained. More awkward, the dining room was at some distance from the kitchen, where food would be prepared and from which the servant would carry dishes to dinner guests. Unlike more mature apartment planning, Hunt's apartment had no pantry and no direct link of kitchen to dining room, nor was the dumbwaiter linked to the kitchen for greatest convenience. On the other hand, the kitchen's location at a corner of the house with windows on two sides gave it ample ventilation, a feature that enabled cooking smells to disperse. All agreed that the management of kitchen heat and odors was essential to the survival of apartments.

The location of bedrooms for the middle-class household also presented problems to designers. When Hunt, at the Stuyvesant, interspersed his chambers with public rooms, he may have been referring back to private suburban or rural house designs of the pre–Civil War era, where bedrooms were often included on the main floor.[60] Hunt's linking of chambers with reception rooms was in keeping with French precedents, not surprisingly, since Hunt was trained in France. His placement of chambers linked with the reception rooms and separated from another cluster of chambers was also common in other early flats of New York. At the same time, Edith Wharton's characters, perhaps overly fastidious, reported that they were offended at the thought of guests glimpsing such a private space as a bedroom.

It seems clear that designers of this generation were not organizing room adjacencies according to strictly utilitarian descriptions. If so, all sleeping rooms would be clustered together. Instead, symbolic meanings seem to have been attached to the ways rooms were grouped. The group of reception rooms in the

Stuyvesant and other apartment houses of its era constituted the "master" suite, to which a principal bedroom could attach itself. Master and mistress of the household laid claim to the set of rooms grouped together at the apartment's front. Other bedrooms, belonging to lesser members of the family, were placed off together in a group of sleeping rooms. A decade or two later, apartment designers found that this kind of intermingling of rooms violated a newly clarified way to categorize rooms—by their use. Functional definitions tended to prevail in room groupings by the end of the century, leading architects to group all bedrooms together.

Bruce Price's 21 East Twenty-first Street apartment-house plan also interspersed sleeping and social spaces. Its plan was called "essentially that of the French Flat" by the *American Architect and Building News* when it published Price's scheme in 1878. The principal stairway opened into an anteroom toward the front of the building, while at the rear, servants had their own separate stairway (fig. 36). Price gave each of his flats a dining room and a parlor, entered from the anteroom. Also off that reception space, Price located a major chamber, or "master bedroom." Three more chambers, and a kitchen, a pantry, and a bathroom were located along a hallway that reached back from the main stairway toward the rear. Like Hunt at the Stuyvesant, Price allowed the possibility that the front chamber might be used in conjunction with the parlor. Its placement suggests potential uses defined along a French-style continuum of privacy, rather than strictly categorized uses that were either public or private.

The kitchen at 21 East Twenty-first Street was placed against the building's rear wall and had for ventilation a window onto the main light court to the west and a tiny light court window on the east for cross-ventilation. Price supplied a pantry off the kitchen, but located both at a great distance from the dining room. After having made the full connection of parlor to dining, creating a public or social ensemble of rooms, Price could not find a way to link the kitchen to this ensemble.

At the Albany, the ten apartments per floor had different configurations, but all of them had more clearly functional, less symbolic, room zoning than either the Stuyvesant or Price's French-flat building (fig. 37). In the Albany's northeast-corner apartment, the parlor was located directly opposite the entrance, and was one of the larger rooms. Opening into both parlor and hall was the dining room. A third, service, doorway connected dining room to kitchen through a storage-pantry area. The three bedrooms occupied the corner space in a group. All three opened into each other; two had doors into the corridor as well. The remaining bedroom, like the Stuyvesant's front chamber, opened into the parlor, as happened with one bedroom in every apartment at the Albany. As at Price's flat building, no servants' rooms were located within the apartment unit but instead were in the attic or basement, reached by service stairs near the kitchen.

Ventilation was an unsolved problem at the Albany. While the corner apartment afforded windows to the outside street from every room, the other apartments at the Albany had to use light courts or air shafts for several rooms'

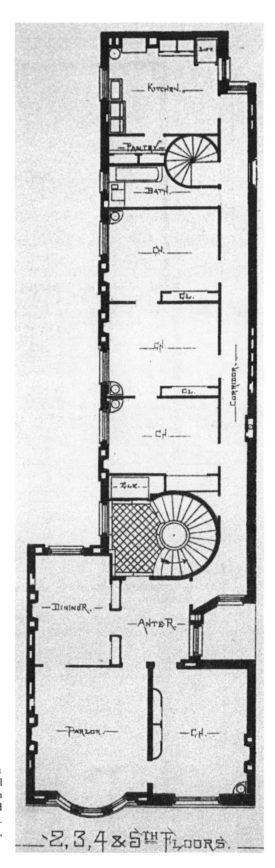

KITCHEN.

PANTRY.

BATH.

CH.

CL.

CH.

CL.

CH.

CORRIDOR.

CL.

DINING.

ANTER.

PARLOR.

CH.

2, 3, 4 & 5TH FLOORS.

FIGURE 36 The plan of an upper floor at 21 East Twenty-first Street shows the typical rooms of the period: chambers (ch), anteroom (anter), parlor, dining room, kitchen, and bath. One chamber opens into the parlor. (*American Architect and Building News* [May 4, 1878]: pl. 123)

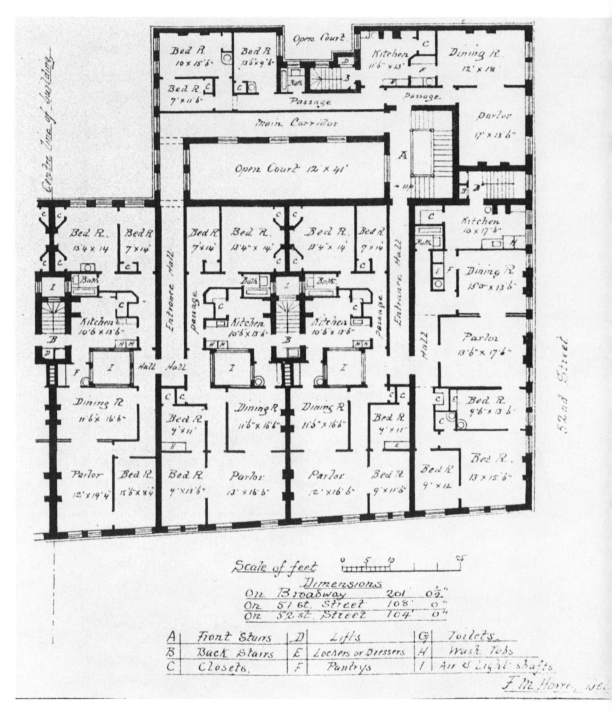

FIGURE 37 The plan of an upper floor at the Albany shows that most parlors are linked to a bedroom. Some bedrooms are unventilated. (*American Architect and Building News* 1 [December 23, 1876]: following p. 412)

ventilation. Two of the street-facing apartments had four bedrooms each: two looked onto the open court, one onto the street, and one had no windows at all. In these apartments, the kitchens, bathrooms, and dining rooms were all ventilated only by air shafts. Such planning did not create especially livable apartments and left plenty of room for improvement.

There was an apparent lack of fixed rules about room relationships in the 1860s and 1870s. The early apartment designers seem to have been most concerned with achieving family units suitably distinct from each other, building envelopes that could provide healthful light and air, and acceptable imagery along the street. Greater refinements of interior planning had to await another generation of designers and tenants whose concerns went beyond the first generation's worries over family privacy. Once the individual family unit was established as protected from others, then tenants and designers developed more concern for the details of interior privacy. Later observers would scoff at the attempt to build a decent apartment building on a small lot, where light, air, and space were never generous enough and room planning seemed naive.[61] In the next generation, issues of family members' privacy from each other, or the privacy of family from servants would be added to the list of planning concerns.

Flats Proliferate

By the end of the 1870s, several hundred new middle-class apartment houses, known by names as well as addresses, had established this new building type as a feature of New York life. French flats had captured everybody's attention—the capitalists who hoped they would be a good investment, the architects who worried over their design, the builders who erected them, and the thousands of families who paid exorbitant rents for narrow single-family houses or were stuck in a long commute and longed for better housing.[62] The *Real Estate Record* projected an increasing number of apartment houses based on the growing population of New York. In 1875 builders had erected 112 apartment buildings; in 1879, 253; and in 1880, 516.[63] And the new apartment houses began to reach out to new levels of potential tenants, both more and less prosperous, still members of the middle class.

Soon there would be many less-expensive flat buildings, the *Record* predicted in 1880. The Bedford, built in that year on the corner of Eighty-second Street and Tenth Avenue, was an innovative flat building because it was built for lower-income genteel families. Brick fronted, trimmed in stone, and near an elevated rail station, it charged rents in the range suitable for a merchant's clerk and his family, respectable and comfortable. Monthly rents were $28 to $34 for the front units, $20 to $26 for rear units. Two stores fronted on the avenue and two basement stores were underneath; its main entrance for tenants was on Eighty-second Street with a janitor's apartment near the door. Stairs led to two flats on each of the three upper floors. The flats had a parlor, a dining room, a kitchen, three bedrooms, a bathroom, closets, a dumbwaiter accessible to all, and modern plumbing and heating systems. Such buildings, reported the *Record*, were eagerly awaited by salesmen and clerks, and gave "ample return for the money invested."[64]

This type of small flat building, designed for the lower ranges of income in the middle class, filled many of the side streets of the West Side and was described by Charles Carroll for the readers of *Appleton's Journal*. The tenants expected were the "better class of artisans, master-workmen, and small shopkeepers." Typically the buildings had service lifts but no passenger elevators, and instead of a concierge to let in visitors, they had an electric bell system and sometimes a device for opening the door "by a wire from the apartment above." The construction of such a building may be shoddy, Carroll warned, and the decorations minimal. Many rooms were lit only from air and light shafts, so apartments tended to be dark inside. But people with only $1,500 or $2,000 a year to cover all their expenses could make do in houses like this.[65]

Variety in tenancy was possible as designers introduced more variations in their apartment plans. The Florence, on the northeast corner of Fourth Avenue and Eighteenth Street was planned with rooms for three kinds of people: "First, for the family, that adheres to the old style of housekeeping, next, for the young married, who desire to keep house without being burdened with any of its cares and troubles, and last but not least, for the old bachelor class." Hence there would be suites with kitchens, suites without kitchens, and a tenants' restaurant on the ground floor. On each floor there would be at least two bachelor suites made up of just a bedroom, a parlor, and a dressing room.[66]

Apartment houses had come to represent a "revolution in living," according to an 1878 *New York Times*. In the second half of the 1870s, the article stated, flat buildings had been constructed at a rapid rate in the "best quarters of the town," and were occupied equally by the well-to-do and the not-rich. Hotels were standing half-empty and boardinghouses had closed, as flats had become the popular new way to live.[67] In 1880 the *Times* reported a fresh addition of fine flat buildings to the city's repertoire, with apartments ranging from twelve to eighteen rooms, renting for $2,500 to $5,000 a year. Apartments had become so favored that "Families, especially women, who have occupied them any time, grow greatly attached to them, and are frequently unwilling to live out of them."[68]

The social prominence of apartment buildings had been secured by the willingness of well-to-do families to choose them for principal residences. "The number of rich people who want to live in elegant apartments and yet not be hampered with a whole house is steadily increasing," reported an 1881 *Real Estate Record*, "while families from abroad will prefer apartment houses as it gives them a sense of luxury and comfort which they cannot get at the public hotel or private lodgings in an ordinary family house."[69] Their luxury and comfort were to increase with their size in the 1880s. Hunt's Stuyvesant or Babcock's Albany were no higher than contemporary private houses, but apartment buildings soon began to rise much higher. Hardenbergh's Van Corlear of the late 1870s had six stories, and the Windermere and the Florence rose to seven stories before the end of the decade.[70] The physical prominence of these buildings asserted that they were to be taken seriously.

4 AT HOME IN THE FIRST APARTMENT HOUSES

FAMILIES searching for appropriately genteel housing must have been happy indeed to see the first apartment houses go up on the streets of New York. Yet as tenants they had a lot to become accustomed to. The acceptability of the first apartments depended upon both practical, utilitarian concerns and associational, symbolic meanings. How could the idea of "home" be attached to a large building shared with numerous others? What were the practical daily life and housekeeping implications of this new kind of home? What kinds of people in addition to the nuclear family deserved special consideration from those who were designing apartment houses? And how could an apartment house affect the tone of the city around it? By the end of the 1870s a whole new set of living patterns had been installed in New York, taken up by thousands of middle-class people. The fact that they did take to apartment life suggests that the new housing form offered many advantages.

Meanings of Home

Among the problems presented by apartments was their relation to already held images of "home." Residential hotels, French flats, boardinghouses, parts of houses, tenements, and specialized clublike buildings for bachelors or hotels for working people each represented a changed image and a potential new definition of what "homelife" must mean. Yet images of "home" did not accommodate comfortably to changed customs and circumstances. How did apartment residents construct their images of "home," and how did architects design to convey homelike messages?[1]

The words "home" and "homelife" occurred in the 1860s and 1870s in a context of warnings explaining how easily home values might be lost. Those who went to live in hotels would see "an utter upsetting of all home habits, an entire disregard of old-fashioned domesticity and comfort." Should they live in a boardinghouse, they would be "forced into a manner of living which violates the very first requirements of the life we most affect, namely, individual privacy and family seclusion." When several families lived together in a boardinghouse, the "privacy of the home is invaded," and "*'home'* [becomes] an empty name."[2]

Privacy appears to be the very keystone of successful Victorian family life. Descriptions of "home" pointed to the "beneficent influence of its delightful seclusion," where the family members could thrive because they lived separate from others. This prized privacy, it should be noted, was sought for the family unit; it was not a question of assuring individuals within the family privacy from each other. The ordinarily understood family consisted of husband and wife, children, and servants; this group required complete privacy for their own family activities. Bachelors too, even though their commitments to "home" were not secured by marital bonds, regretted the loss of privacy and individuality in boardinghouses and hotels.[3]

Beyond its ability to guarantee precious privacy, a true home also was the place where individuality could be established. The private expression of individuality took place inside: a married couple would decide upon and act on their own rules of decorum and bring up their children to follow their principles. In the home they could also surround themselves with the furniture, books, and pictures that asserted their individual taste. In the home, as a family established its individuality from other families, it also built up its own coherence.

Home, wrote a New England minister, John Ware, was above all a moral place where true values could be maintained, usually through the dedication of women, in the face of the world's darker aspects. Home, believed Ware, is "an anchor by which he [the male house owner] holds amid the tossing temptations of life,— a place of refuge and of love, whose charms, whose solid, pure delights, prevail against all that pleasure offers or appetite suggests."[4] Home as a refuge suggests both a moral quality and a location away from all temptation, but such a locational refuge could never be part of the apartment-dweller's home.

Apartments might harbor within themselves dangers to familial success. Howells's protagonists Mr. and Mrs. March discussed their feelings about "family consciousness" as they reflected on apartment buildings. They condemned the show that went into fancy lobbies and was reiterated in the social pretenses of drawing rooms where middle-class apartment dwellers were expected to entertain and impress their guests. Such pretensions were absurd when apartments did not have a single family room for quiet togetherness, nowhere "where the family can all come together and feel the sweetness of being a family." Mr. March felt that even tenement dwellers had a better family life in their rental quarters, because at least there, there was a true "living" room. "There the whole family lives in the kitchen and has its consciousness of being; but the flat abolishes the family consciousness."[5]

The idea of the home as a valued family center has been characterized by the cultural geographer David Sopher as the "domicentric" view. This view poses home values as good, in opposition to "rootlessness," which is bad. Sopher quotes both nineteenth- and twentieth-century sources to show persistent associations between homelessness, understood as rootlessness, and criminal behavior. Sopher also points out that a "domifugal," or home-leaving, myth has a central position, but usually not for families. Frontiersmen, cowpokes, and other adventurers characteristically enacted the male myth of leaving the "confines" of home, striking out into the "freedom" of the wilderness.

In the mid-nineteenth century, movement from one home to another was endemic, and everyone in New York City was reputed to move every May 1. Immigrants from many countries, families of pioneers, and upwardly mobile middle-class families in the nineteenth-century city left home to improve, or at least change, their circumstances. They left not "home," but specific homes in order to find others more fitting. Apparently, then, Americans held domicentric and domifugal myths at the same time. If these myths were legitimized, then apartment buildings would provide the ideal home, a home both permanent and transient. Once settled in, a family could easily move; rented quarters are perfect for departures and quick landings and that was, in fact, how tenants behaved. However, the literature on apartment life did not admit this paradox; instead it always supported domicentric aims. Socially established people regarded flats, Howells wrote in *April Hopes*, "as makeshifts, the resorts of people of small means, or the defiances or errors of people who had lived too much abroad. They stamped their occupants as of a transitory and fluctuant character."[6]

If these dimensions of home were credible to first-generation apartment dwellers, then they must have felt some tension between the home ideal and the facts that their new dwelling presented to them. No apartment home was secluded from all others except by its front door in a public hallway. Wives waiting at home could be envisioned as the anchor saving drifting men from the world's temptation, but such temptation might live just down the hall and might tempt the wife just as easily. The solidity and stability linked to home images was permanently undercut by short leases and annual moving day in apartments.[7]

Built Images of Home

"A house to be a true home must be strictly adapted to the owner's position in society," asserted John Ware in his 1866 book on the home. The home, because it had to be an appropriate representation of a family's social status, needed to be separate and individualized. Since the private house had been the only kind of architecture that provided mid-century New Yorkers with the image of home, designers of apartments were faced with serious problems. How were they to make larger-than-house-size multiple dwellings fit that image? Smaller apartment houses might be more in scale with a private house idea, but even there the building was clearly no longer private.[8]

Transferring signs of individuality to an apartment building was full of difficulties. For small, single-lot buildings such as Bruce Price's French flat (fig. 24), the architect relied upon the houselike scale of the building and its ornament to give tenants a feeling that these flats were homelike. The building sat comfortably with neighboring houses on Twenty-first Street. Its roof began at the same height as its neighbors' cornices, and while the roof rose above adjoining houses, its gable shape and dormer kept it within the realm of domestic imagery. In a French-flat building such as Price's, where a full floor belonged to each individual family, identification of that family's quarters from the exterior was easy for every tenant. While they may not have had the resources to rent or purchase a full building of their own, at least tenants could identify with a full floor, their own territory in a shared building. But of course they lost the capacity of a private house to declare to the public its owner's social standing.

For a larger French-flat building such as the Stuyvesant (fig. 23), houselike heights were maintained, but other elements of individuation had to be reinterpreted. The top of the Stuyvesant was given a prominent mansard roof and four overscaled studio windows to supply light to the artists' studios on the top floor. This roof both unifies the whole, through its imposing size, and reiterates the four-part division of the interior seen in plan, four parts representing four family units per floor. Hunt does indicate, by means of window changes and ornamental details, that there are breaks between individual family units on each floor, but the first-time viewer might easily find the image ambiguous. There are no clear clues by which residents could identify the extent of their individual domains from the exterior. It is very difficult to think of this building's features as representing any one family's status—only a generic social status for all the tenants at once.

The architect Henry Hudson Holly tried to remedy the loss of individuality by creating a "family hotel," which had apartments reached by public corridors on the upper floors but private apartments with their own front entrances from the street on the first floor (fig. 33). He thought that the series of front doors and high stoops would convincingly represent familiar private houses with their reassuring individuality. A central entrance for all the other tenants led to the upper stories of the large building where concealed apartments lay behind this screen of private-house imagery.

Tenement designers and reformers subscribed to the same values as the tenants and designers of middle-class apartments. They believed that individuation was good for working-class tenants and would give them a sense of self-worth. Even the standard 25-foot-wide tenement house tended to follow the individuating model of private row-house facades with a side or center stoop, and a strong cornice cut short of the party walls on each side. Often these tenement buildings further emphasized their "individual" nature with a central decorative feature on the cornice carrying the name of the building (fig. 38). A large tenement block like White's Riverside or the Astral represented "dangerous communal tendencies," but a house-sized building maintained the proper image of home.[9]

For all these new buildings in the city, creating an image of home was difficult

FIGURE 38 In working-class flats at 16 St. Mark's Place, the building's name, Manhattan, still decorates the top of the facade. (Courtesy of United States History, Local History and Genealogy Division, New York Public Library, Astor, Lenox and Tilden Foundations)

because buildings that had initially established that image for city dwellers were so much smaller than the new, large multiple dwellings. On the positive side, the repetitive brownstone fronts, the landscapes of urban architecture that had seemed so homogeneous, were now being supplanted with variety. The new streets of flats had more diversity, and the new types of flats ranged through many styles, many sizes, many strata of tenants. City residents could create new images of home for themselves from these architectural offerings, replacing seclusion, for example, with stylishness as a desired home quality.

Social Rank and Strangers

Throughout the 1870s, New Yorkers saw apartment houses erected in ever-increasing numbers, and many families whose backgrounds and social position would have led them to private houses in an earlier generation now lived in apartments. Given the beliefs in privacy and individuality attached to ideas of home, how could an apartment house allow a family the opportunity to declare its social rank, and how could family members sustain their privacy while brought into daily and close proximity to others?

Imagine tenants who were attempting apartment life for the first time moving into the Bella Flats, a small French-flat building that opened in the 1870s on the corner of Twenty-sixth Street at 358 Fourth Avenue.[10] The people who found themselves living together in this building comprised fourteen household units and included married couples with and without children, a widower, single men sharing a "bachelor flat," a janitor, and servants. Among the male heads of households living at the Bella, three were lawyers, two were in banking, and one was a physician, one a clergyman, one a stockbroker, one a bookkeeper, and one a gentleman at leisure. In addition there were several businessmen engaged in wine importing, silks, and produce. Of the married women tenants, all but one listed their occupations as "housekeeping"; the remaining one was an artist. The children living in the Bella Flats ranged in age from infancy to twenty-two years. Most of the families with children had one, two, or three children, but one family, headed by a widower, had six.

Every Bella household but one had at least one live-in servant, several had two, and one family had three; all the servants at the Bella were Irish. Four of the households also had lodgers living with them; a single lodger in two cases, and three lodgers in two other cases. The last family in residence was the janitor with his wife, son, and daughter. They lodged two servants who worked at the general upkeep of the Bella Flats.[11]

This cross section of genteel occupations and a fairly homogeneous tenancy of mostly small families would have characterized "the neighbors" for anyone moving into the Bella Flats. Living among clergymen, physicians, stockbrokers, and lawyers could be socially comfortable for these tenants; yet nonetheless every other family was still made up of "strangers." Did the married people find their bachelor neighbors a problem? Was it comfortable for families of related individuals to live with "families" of couples with lodgers? Did the clergyman have doubts about the morals of the wine importer? How did all those "housekeeping" wives treat the one woman pursuing her own career? Confronting unknown neighbors was only one of the several novelties that tenants encountered when they chose to try apartment life.

Living among strangers was a frequently mentioned difficulty of apartment life. Social rank could be irremediably compromised by choosing the wrong apartment building, the writer of a letter to the *New York Times* explained in 1873. He and his wife had many church and community acquaintances who were friendly to them while they lived in a boardinghouse. However, their family budget would only allow them to afford an independent apartment in a tenement building. Even though such a move would give him the privacy he valued, he could not make it because his friends would "cut" him socially for living in the wrong kind of building. Apparently desiring the clarity of social relations that well-defined classes implied, Americans also wanted the fluidity that allowed potential rising on the social ladder. But in a city full of recent arrivals, as Karen Halttunen has shown, no one's social rank was clear, and people feared to be brought down in rank by living in the wrong sort of apartment building and associating with others who might be "below" them.[12]

The form of the apartment house increased exposure to strangers. Certain spaces were used in common by all the tenants—"collective" space. Usually apartment buildings had one front door shared by all, one main lobby, shared staircases and elevators, and on the upper floors, shared public corridors. While the numbers of tenants sharing these public spaces could be limited by planning decisions, there always remained some collective space. In a large building one lived one's life in "publicity"—the opposite of privacy—which exposed the family to view and to gossip. Private houses allowed residents to shut the street door, "excluding all strangers from the building, while in the apartment house there are always some portions of the interior . . . which are open, if not to all the world, at least to all the tenants of the building and to their visitors."[13] Contact with strangers in such a setting was sure to breed dangerous familiarity, critics warned, and, by cutting down on privacy, could destroy the family.

In America "there are no distinct classes," Catharine Beecher had written in 1841, but "all are thrown into promiscuous masses." She observed that Americans constantly compared themselves with others and were prey to the temptation to imitate those with large means, a tendency later traced in detail in Veblen's analysis of conspicuous consumption at the end of the century. Living under the same roof with others could only exacerbate people's tendency to engage in consumption rivalry.

Because there was no "natural limit" to Americans' ascent in social status, they tried to outspend their neighbors to get ahead. The desire for a fine house with a showy exterior was particularly American, Sarah Gilman Young asserted in 1881. Europeans were born to their social positions and were therefore content with modest dwellings, she said, but Americans had to purchase their distinction through material display, and looked upon a fine house as a mark of social success. The house in question might be elaborate and showy or subdued and tasteful, depending on how the owners wished to present themselves; still, it remained the place where monetary success could be exhibited. This tendency to purchase the signs of social rank resulted in a pervasive feeling that people's "true" social rank was always hidden, that people were passing themselves off as "better than they really were," and that social intercourse was fraught with risk.[14] Of course, for those who counted on signaling their success though their houses, apartment buildings seemed to defeat their ambitions.

American writers looked to Europe for a way to deal with the social mixture in apartment houses, but found that there apartment dwellers got along without the same anxieties. Sarah Gilman Young claimed that Europeans were oblivious to who lived over or under them in an apartment building, because Europeans, born into a social rank, were never threatened by contiguous living arrangements. Parisians lived happily with the well-to-do on the lower floors and the poor in the garret. But mixing classes in one building in America, reported the French-trained architect Philip Hubert, was thought to be impossible because of "jealousy from the bottom and exclusivity from the top."[15]

European apartments, of course, had the same mixture of people who were strangers, yet given their years of experience of living in apartments, strangers did not seem a problem. "It may be urged as an objection to living on floors," wrote Sarah Gilman Young, "that it is not pleasant to meet people one does not know in the halls." But she felt it not particularly different from meeting such people on the street. In any case one did not often meet one's neighbors on the stairs, and if one did, "courteous salutations, which give no right to recognition elsewhere" were exchanged and that was the end of it. Parisians were used to regarding the halls and stairs of apartment houses "as a continuation of the public street . . . used for generations by all manner of people," but to Americans it made no sense to allow interior spaces to be called "public" and given over to outsiders.[16]

Many middle-class families resisted the move to apartments for such reasons of social rank, according to a reporter who was enthusiastic about apartment houses. It was not until a few successful buildings for the rich "demonstrated to those of moderate means the possibility of multiple tenancy without the risk of social debasement," he asserted in 1874, that large numbers of middle-class families felt comfortable in apartment buildings. The success of the Stuyvesant Apartments demonstrated "how the most respectable people can live upon flats precisely as the gentry and even the nobility do in many of the leading capitals of Europe," asserted a real estate spokesman, who urged capitalists to understand the value of such buildings and invest in them.[17]

These responses to the social acceptability of multiple dwellings reflected the diversity of standards held by the several strata of the middle class. For one person, moving into a tenement implied the risk of losing his social standing; for another, moving into an apartment of any kind carried social risk. In spite of doubts about losing social rank, however, New Yorkers by the mid–1870s seemed happy to move into multiple dwellings and only wished there were more of them to choose from.

Who Can Make a Home?

As the design of physical settings for "home" expanded beyond the single-family house, attention was directed beyond the nuclear family to the variety of persons who constituted "households," leading designers to produce alternatives to the full family apartment. The people who shared an apartment house could be seen not just as an accidental gathering of tenants but as a group that shared a common social status or lifestyle. This was the way developers pictured them when they established the income level of prospective tenants or when they determined rents, building location, and elaboration of design. It was also a choice of tenants who selected buildings to live in on the basis of congenial neighborhoods and culturally familiar fellow tenants.

A collective dwelling that housed large numbers of people with related interests or circumstances was not a new idea. Earlier in the nineteenth century philanthropists and social reformers had created some dwellings for special tenant groups such as the Working Women's Home of the 1850s, created out of rehabilitated tenement buildings at 45 Elizabeth Street. There some 500 women were provided with a bed in a dormitory setting, with curtains rather than walls for privacy. On the main floor were parlors, a reading room, a laundry, and a common dining room, which served meals paid for by the week along with the rent. In the basement were a common kitchen and the bathrooms. The age range of these tenants was eighteen to thirty-five, and they made $6 to $7 a week. For $1.25 women could get a bed and their laundry done; for another $1.75 to $3.25 they could get meals. For an extra $0.25, tenants could be let in after 11 P.M.[18]

A group home without real walls was hardly acceptable to working women who could afford to maintain a middle-class style of life. For them, the department-store owner A. T. Stewart and the architect John Kellum planned a "hotel for women of modest means" on Park Avenue, begun in 1869 (figs. 39, 40). The "hotel," intended for sales clerks, included bedrooms of 16 by 18 feet for two women to share, and rooms for single women of 8 by 9 feet.[19] A grand entrance portico with columns, a marble floor, and elevators added elegance and convenience to Stewart's hotel; interiors were to be enhanced with good-quality furniture and even fine paintings.

Shared facilities such as parlors and reading rooms made Stewart's similar to an ordinary hotel, as did a central dining room and kitchen. Since it was just for women, however, it would have escaped the moral criticism leveled at hotels where both sexes lived. Stewart had planned a duplicate building for young men

FIGURE 39 Stewart's Home for Working Women on Fourth (Park) Avenue between Thirty-second and Thirty-third streets was designed by John Kellum in 1869 as a multiple dwelling for department store employees and other single women who wanted genteel, yet economical, homes. (*Appleton's Journal* 1 [July 3, 1869]: 417)

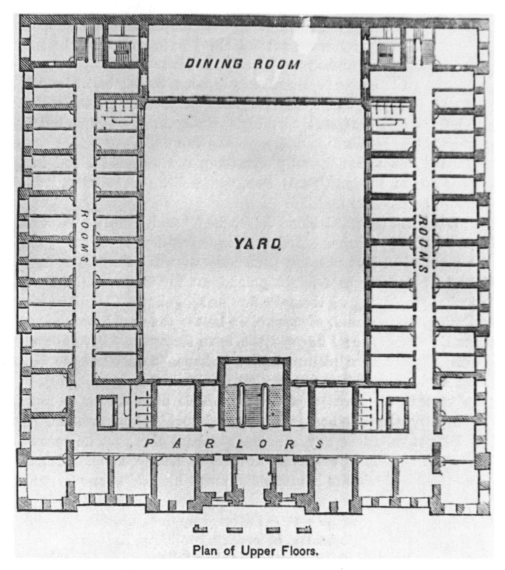

Plan of Upper Floors.

FIGURE 40   Small single and double rooms at Stewart's Home were rented by working women who shared parlors and bathrooms and ate collectively in the group dining room. (*Appleton's Journal* 1 [July 3, 1869]: 418–19)

that was never built. Unfortunately the hotel for women did not fulfill its original aims; construction lagged and the hotel did not actually open until 1877. By then the set rents were too high for store clerks, and the intended tenants were also beleaguered by too many rules and regulations. The experimental was converted to the conventional: the women's home became the Park Avenue Hotel. A greater impediment to producing a good apartment building for single women was the fact that in the 1870s, young, respectable women did not have society's blessing to make independent homes of their own.[20]

In contrast to young working women, men alone in the city endured no social stigma for their marital abstinence. Bachelors, some 125,000 strong in the New York of 1870, constituted a group acknowledged to have more active social lives than the traditional family, but like the women, they did lack suitable housing. Hotels were available to bachelors, but critics complained that only the wealthy could afford them, while boardinghouses were an unacceptable alternative for those who valued privacy.[21]

Solving the bachelor's housing problem required a suite of rooms scaled to the needs of a single person, perhaps consisting only of a parlor, a bedroom, a bath, and closets. The architect E. T. Littell proposed in 1876 that developers create a bachelor dwelling unit with a parlor, 14 by 16 feet; a bedroom, 8 by 10 feet; a bathroom, 5.5 by 8 feet (with perhaps a bigger parlor for those who wished to "chum together"). Some suites could be connected so two friends could share quarters if desired. Bachelors usually took their meals in clubs and restaurants, or with friends, so Littell suggested that a bachelor-flat building be run like a club, with membership fees and dues and a common dining room where the bachelor could find good food as well as privacy.

Bachelor flats and Stewart's Hotel for Working Women both suggested a modification to the assumed set of rooms for family needs, and with that modification some redefinitions of the boundary between collective and private spaces. Bachelors' apartments kept the private definition of a parlor, a bedroom, and a bathroom as other middle-class apartments of the 1870s had done. The women's hotel retained only private bedrooms, more like a college dormitory. Entertainment and dining activities were shifted to public spaces (dining rooms, clubs, restaurants, and roof terrace). Cooking was not considered a likely skill for bachelors to possess, so kitchens were omitted in proposals for bachelor-flat buildings. Young women (who were supposed to possess cooking skills) could not afford the space and equipment that private kitchens required on their meager salaries, so they were provided with collective dining facilities.

The lack of housing for these special groups had encouraged the production of designs especially developed for their needs, which were perceived to be different from those of families. However, not much was actually built during this period for tenants whose needs diverged from the family norm. The project to design for single people met with larger success at the turn of the century, when one finds many bachelor-apartment buildings for both men and women. By then one also finds the rigid notions of women's roles shifting so as to allow young single women to rent apartments like their male counterparts.[22]

Housework

Social uneasiness accompanied the first generation of apartments but so did appreciation of a new ease in the mechanics of running a household. If collective social interactions seemed at cross-purposes with images of home, the opportunities that communal settings and new household technologies opened up made housekeeping less of a problem than ever before.[23] New architectural designs of household space in apartment buildings allowed for improved efficiency in basic household work. The ways that apartment designers and clients understood the work of the household as it took shape in apartment buildings enabled a redefinition of the place of servants. Designers and clients reassessed the role of domestic work done outside the home and focused on the ways that architectural planning and newly available equipment could make housekeeping easier.

Modern readers in houses with running water and electrical equipment may find it difficult to realize the extent of the burdens of housekeeping, but nineteenth-century writers have recorded how hard housekeeping really was. "Our system of living in America makes life a tyranny to every woman," wrote Sarah Gilman Young in 1872, "so that, as John Stuart Mill justly remarks, 'there remain no legal slaves except the mistress of every house.'"[24] Young stated that American women lost "their bloom and youth" before their European counterparts did specifically because American houses were so badly designed and managed. Young based her recommendations for improved housekeeping on her experiences of living in European flats, where one-floor living, combined with citywide aids like bakeries and laundries, made all the difference. Intelligent layout of the household space could save women time, energy, and health.[25]

In the years before indoor plumbing and central heating, the housekeeper and her servants carried fuel up stairs to every room that needed heat; lighted and maintained the fires; carried water whenever it was needed, probably from an outdoor source; and heated the water when hot water was required. They used outhouses during the day and emptied chamber pots in the morning. They made various kinds of soaps and preparations to do all their own cleaning—not just of clothing but also of upholstery and drapes, and bedding. If urban life had its drawbacks, at least city dwellers had easier access to manufactured products such as soap and bread and clothing, as well as to indoor plumbing. Still, even urban household work encompassed both production and maintenance, so servants were essential.

"Housekeeping isn't fun," wrote Nora to the *New York Times* in 1874. "Already we young woman do in one day work indoors that would have killed our grandmothers. We want flats."[26] Nora's preference for a home on one floor echoed early reports from apartment dwellers and designers who agreed that one-floor living was always easier for the housekeeper. A private house of four stories required constant climbing up and down stairs to cook, clean, oversee children and servants, and entertain. An apartment on one floor eliminated much of the effort involved in carrying things and moving from room to room. Indeed, an architect, looking back from 1901, claimed that New Yorkers would never have taken to apartment life had they not "tasted the sweets" of easy housekeeping.[27]

Convenience as a theme of apartment life developed over the first generation of experience with these buildings, the 1860s and 1870s. By the time of the early middle-class apartment-house designs of about 1870, potential clients for apartments were already familiar with convenience and efficiency through elevators, gas lighting, and other urban-scale technologies. But, because of the large labor pool of servants available to perform household work, new technologies were not yet much in demand at home.[28]

Instead in this early period of apartment design, efficiency and convenience were understood to be present in the defining character of the apartment unit itself—its being on one floor. Having everything on one floor meant less running up and down and that the housekeeper had less trouble overseeing her servant's work. A flat was usually smaller than a whole house, and so required a smaller investment in furniture. Smaller and fewer rooms than a whole house and less furniture meant less cleaning and upkeep. Less cleaning meant fewer servants. In descriptions of apartments in the 1870s, convenience was one of the virtues claimed for apartment life, but this virtue was grounded in the new design idea of a one-floor unit, rather than in new technological conveniences.

The housekeeping chores of the new tenants at the Stuyvesant Apartments in 1870 were formidable by today's standards. The only services supplied to the building as a whole were gas for lighting and running water. Tenants had their own coal bins and had to light their own fires in individual fireplaces. There was no passenger or service elevator, although a rope-and-pulley dumbwaiter aided in bringing goods up, trash down, and laundry from basement washtubs to roof drying areas. Coal or wood had to be carried up to run the cooking stove in each kitchen, and ice had to be delivered to individual iceboxes. Families were expected to employ their own live-in servants. Compared with the technological conveniences introduced over the subsequent few years, the Stuyvesant's offerings were minimal. Each apartment unit in the Stuyvesant worked like a miniature private house of the period, conceiving of housekeeping as a labor-intensive problem and one internal to the household.[29]

Like the Stuyvesant, Bruce Price's French flat at 21 East Twenty-first Street provided individual kitchens in each family unit and no centralized cooking or dining. John Babcock at the Albany also conceived of its three- and four-bedroom apartments as designed for individual housekeeping. All of these buildings provided rooms for live-in servants but none of the additional services like meal service or cleaning that families living in hotels would have had. The apartment building of that era that did have centralized dining rooms and kitchens was the Stevens, and it was early converted to the Hotel Victoria, thereby stressing the public and collective nature of its facilities.

The Place of Servants

Middle-class households expected to have servants when the first apartment houses were built in New York.[30] This requirement, of course, had an effect on apartment planning. Family privacy demanded that servants be as invisible as possible, yet American families also mistrusted their servants enough to want to keep an eye on them. Servants' rooms were common in middle-class apartments and usually were labeled as such in plans. They were the smallest rooms, and when they had bathrooms of their own they had the smallest bathrooms. A servant's room was often placed so its window overlooked the light shaft and was usually linked to, or close to, the kitchen.

An alternative, based on European practice, was to provide a servants' dormitory in the attic of an apartment house, supplemented with dormitory rooms, usually for male servants, in the basement. Mistresses feared that their servants, when living in dormitories together with other families' servants, would both misbehave and gossip, spreading the family secrets to neighboring households. However, designers had to observe spatial constraints and were open to Continental ideas; servants' rooms were built in the attics and mansards of many New York buildings such as Price's 21 East Twenty-first Street French flat and the well-known Dakota, built in 1884. The attic seemed a likely place for servants to sleep because, in early apartment buildings, the roof was typically the servant's territory already. The roof itself had places for drying the laundry, and garret rooms or penthouses provided work space for servants. Whether bedrooms for servants belonged inside a family unit or in a special servants' zone remained an issue for apartment designers into the twentieth century, even as numbers of servants dwindled and technological aids to housekeeping increased.[31]

In New York during the era of apartment-building development, having and keeping servants was widely discussed as a problem. Some people explained that competent servants were hard to find, that too many were dishonest, and that they "took over" the household and ended up bossing around the mistress of the house. Furthermore, householders often expressed contempt for immigrants, who were "lower" than the native-born and who often came in for verbal (or worse) abuse from xenophobic employers. Florence Hartley's 1872 etiquette book reminded ladies that servants "come here from the lowest ranks of English and Irish peasantry, with as much idea of politeness as the pig domesticated in the cabin of the latter."[32]

These attitudes must be balanced by an understanding of the social context of the time. Most servants were recent arrivals to the city—either country girls who had few urban skills, or European immigrants whose cultures held different standards of both family privacy and housekeeping methods. New Yorkers, as we have seen, were especially conscious of privacy as a requirement for good family life and therefore resented having strangers in the household, even when their work was essential.[33]

Gwendolyn Wright suggests that after 1880 more and more servants who did work in American households lived in their own homes and that the preponderance of "servant's rooms" in architectural plans of the late nineteenth century were there mainly for display reasons.[34] She interprets it as a mark of middle-class status to possess a servant's room even if one did not have a servant. In a contrasting interpretation, the loss of a servant is used in *Sister Carrie* to mark the slide into poverty that Carrie and Hurstwood experience when he becomes unemployed. In their modest West Side flat they pay $35 a month and employ a "girl" to do the cleaning and some cooking. To save money they move to a $28-a-month flat and let the maid go.[35] The New York City 1880 and 1900 federal census data and letters to local newspapers written by apartment dwellers in New York indicate that even moderate-income families did employ a servant and had to house her—especially when there were children.

A special feature of apartment houses enhanced their ability to make housekeeping easier: the opportunities for collective, building-wide work, making use of new inventions. The era of apartment-house development coincides with the era of new mechanical conveniences and services for the house. Siegfried Giedion, in *Mechanization Takes Command* gave a summary of the appliances developed in the especially inventive decades of the 1850s and 1860s in the United States. Carpet sweepers had mechanical brushes patented in 1858 and 1859; in 1859 a patent was taken out on a vacuum cleaner. A dishwasher was invented in 1865; several washing-machine patents were taken out between 1850 and 1869; paring and coring machines made home food preserving easier; a gas-heated clothes iron was for sale in the 1850s; even a small artificial ice machine was patented in France in 1860.[36]

In their modern, powered form, these machines were developed and sold first for large-scale commercial use. Laundry machines that washed and ironed first appeared for commercial laundering establishments and did not receive their smaller household forms until decades later. In 1869 in their book *American Women's Home*, Catharine Beecher and Harriet Beecher Stowe recommended that every dozen families band together and establish a community laundry for themselves. In 1872 in *The Home*, Frank and Marian Stockton express surprise that more householders do not "club together" to establish their own laundries, buying the washing machines and hiring the labor to run them.[37]

Apartment buildings were in a position to take advantage of mechanical aids available at a commercial scale and to offer services representative of modern life to tenants several years, if not decades, earlier than they could hope to have them in individual private houses. For example, electrically powered vacuum cleaning equipment was first available as centralized machinery with a central suction source and outlets throughout the building. Refrigeration equipment developed in the same way, first for large-scale commercial applications. In the small size usable to individual families, such machines were not truly modern until the second decade of the twentieth century, when small electric motors became widely available. Apartments may thus have provided a kind of testing ground where residents first got used to, then came to expect, the kinds of household services and equipment that we take for granted as essential to modern life. The first apartment houses experimented with ways in which such mechanical aids and collective effort might affect housekeeping labor. Apartment buildings thus helped to solve the "servant problem." By the end of the 1870s, many apartment houses had central heating, plumbing, hot-water heaters, dumbwaiters, bells, and speaking tubes, which replaced the labor of lighting fires, carrying water, and running downstairs to answer the door.

A British observer in 1874 pointed to America as the inventor of a particular kind of modernity: that arising from collective effort. Contrasting American to British habits, the writer asserted that Americans banded together to get things done: a postal service replaced the individual messenger hired by the sender to carry a letter; central heating systems replaced the individual fire lit in each room and saved the individual servant's labor involved in that task. Deliveries could be made to the building's superintendent or door attendant and not to the individual household, once again saving the servant's efforts. "Modern life" was clearly heading toward collective effort to save costs and labor.[38] Apartment houses provided a perfect field for developing collective advantages.

Convenience to an individual family was often achieved by means of centralized labor: work done by apartment building staff rather than within the individual household. At the Bella Flats, almost every family had its own live-in servants to perform household work, but there was also a janitor in permanent residence. He, his family, and two additional servants in the employ of building management did all the general upkeep of halls and public spaces and the repair to individual units.

The Haight House, the fashionable apartment conversion at Fifteenth Street and Fifth Avenue, offered its 1870s tenants even more collectively organized services, more opportunities to have household work taken care of by servants employed by the house as a whole, not by individual families.[39] One single-family unit at the Haight House consisted of antechamber, parlor, dining room capable of seating eighteen, kitchen, pantry, three main bedrooms, two servants' rooms, bathrooms, and "water conveniences." There was a fireplace in each room; a steam heating system warmed the halls and was also available for private rooms if desired. Among the conveniences at the Haight House were hot and cold water day and night, a serviced steam laundry in the basement connected to apartments by dumbwaiters, and a general kitchen in the basement to prepare tenants' meals when requested. Here convenience was partly achieved by technological aids, partly by displaced labor: instead of the tenants and their personal servants producing family meals or doing family laundry, the house kitchen and laundry performed this work for all in common. While these arrangements at the Haight House raised some troublesome questions about the proper boundaries of the public and the private, at the same time they suggested a high level of convenience and comfort.[40]

Although many tenants and critics welcomed the centralized management of household work, it also led to centralized rules, as recognized by the architect P. B. Wight in 1870. He observed that the maintenance of good order in an apartment house is extremely important and is not just the result of controlling who is allowed to rent an apartment. It also depends on the efforts of a janitor or porter who enforces proper conduct and must perform "no inconsiderable amount of police duty." The journalist Christine Herrick noted that in her family's flat building the hall door was locked and the public corridor lights turned off at 9:45 each evening, a practice that she found in conflict with her social life.[41] The benefits of collectively supported work were counterbalanced by infringements on private choice, an ongoing issue in apartment life.

Collective Cooking

With the support of mechanical inventions, apartment buildings offered the potential of a housekeeping innovation: collective cooking. Many writers agreed that centralized food preparation was an ideal way to combine the efforts of many individual households for a savings of time, labor, and money. Considering the advantages of eliminating private kitchens in favor of collective efforts in cooking, E. T. Littell, writing in 1876, suggested: "to accommodate those who are willing to sacrifice a sentiment for substantial advantage, another form of apartment should be constructed; each suite to consist merely of hall, parlor, dining room, bedrooms and bathroom, with possibly a five by eight cooking closet furnished with a gas range. A restaurant should be provided . . . from which meals should be forwarded, in felt-lined boxes, to the private dining rooms of the tenants."[42] The family desiring its own meals privately cooked and eaten is in thrall to "a sentiment," as opposed to a real advantage. A cook hired by the house could buy in bulk, prepare food to order, and save individual families the expense of hiring their own cooks.

An apartment dweller writing to the *New York Times* in 1876 reported that she loved apartment living except for her private kitchen.[43] Kitchens attracted bugs, she said, and spread cooking odors through the apartment. Her recommendation was a central kitchen and cook who could send up prepared meals in the dumbwaiter. This system had the added advantage of keeping her own maid free from cooking chores and always presentable to answer the door. Both of these 1870s writers favored the idea of centralized cooking, but eating in private. The family members gathered together around their meals and did not want to share their dinners under public scrutiny, as the suspect families of Paris did. Writing in favor of collectivized housework in 1881, the *New York Times* pointed out the waste involved in building a "baking fire" for just a dozen muffins, when the same fire could cook for a dozen families. They doubted, however, that collective cooking could be made practical except in the case where the combined households are "colonized under one roof" in apartment buildings.[44]

The experience of dining in a fairly expensive apartment house of the later 1870s was described by a writer for *Appleton's Journal*. An apartment-dwelling family invites their visitor to stay for dinner, happy that they can spontaneously extend the hospitality that their collective dining arrangements allow. The hostess, a New York housekeeper exhausted from coping with her servant problems, says, "what a relief not to know what we are going to have for dinner!" They take the elevator down to the house dining room, encountering en route well-dressed tenants from other floors in the building. The ground-floor dining room is "handsomely furnished and frescoed," has separate, rather than group-sized, tables with fine napery, china, and silver. A menu and wine list are just like those in a good hotel, and meals are served by attentive waiters. While the food is well prepared, it retains a hint of the monotony associated with any food produced "in the mass." The writer praised the way such an apartment house could lessen so many of the housekeeping burdens of middle-class families. But, he cautioned, there is an unavoidably high level of socializing with one's neighbors because of collective dining, and the small size of individual apartment units makes large-scale entertaining impossible to accomplish privately.[45]

Many apartment houses provided such a restaurantlike dining room, either off the lobby or on a high floor, raising questions about the relation between collective and private values. Should family meals be private events? Then centrally located and staffed kitchens could cook meals for tenants to eat in private. At the thirty-five-unit Haight House, for tenants who wanted such privacy, a house steward received marketing orders for the family's favorite foods. House cooks prepared the meals centrally, which were then served in private. The Sherwood Houses on Fifth Avenue at Forty-fourth Street advertised its apartments in 1875: "Suites of 3 to 8 rooms . . . with every comfort and luxury, without the cares of housekeeping; meals supplied at table d'hôte or by private table." The Sherwood Houses are an example of the many apartment buildings where individual private kitchens were replaced by a single kitchen for the whole building. But buildings with elaborate food services were far too expensive to meet the needs of average families and were also defined by some as not *true* apartment houses, but rather some sort of "family-hotel," not quite a real home because of some loss of privacy.[46]

Between the lines of contemporary descriptions, one finds hints that women more than men preferred the collective dining potentials of apartment houses. The housekeeper who is relieved not to know what's for dinner has her burdens lifted; but the male breadwinner returning from his day at the bank wants the private atmosphere of a home-prepared meal. Although apartment buildings seem to have been ideally organized for an experiment in collective cooking, it was an idea that met with only sporadic approval. For one reason, dining in the apartment-house restaurant every night was expensive; then, some said, the menus became predictable and appetite was lost. Perhaps another reason was that collective cooking evoked "un-homelike" associations with dormitories, hotels, and other kinds of alternative, perhaps lower-middle-class, residential arrangements such as the 1850s Working Woman's Home. Apartment-house dining rooms also suggested restaurants, which the *New York Times* had condemned as destroying family values. None of these associations was necessarily repugnant, but all were antifamilial according to critics in the 1870s.

Neighboring

Inside the collective home simplified housekeeping and group dining provided advantages to those willing to try out the new apartment house. Another idea that helped apartment buildings become acceptable was the notion of seeing an apartment house as a neighborhood unto itself and partaking of the safety and comfort that the idea of neighborhood implied. "Neighborhood" has two meanings pertinent to this discussion: it means both "nearby location," and "community of interest." The first meaning of proximity and the second meaning of community preserve a historical change in the meaning of the word.[47]

In the New York of 1800, the word "neighborhood" indicated proximity alone; for example, people would advertise a house for sale "in the neighborhood of the docks."[48] The social homogeneity suggested by the second meaning of "neighborhood" developed in the early nineteenth century when real estate practice began to create districts of a purely residential nature. The new neighborhoods, such as St. John's Park, Washington Square, and Gramercy Park, created by developers between 1800 and 1840 could be counted on to contain only residential usages and the church that such usage required. Both proximity and social homogeneity were absorbed into the meaning of neighborhood in this new residential context. Such a neighborhood was of value because it could be relied upon as a safe and predictable place. Further control over the social homogeneity of Gramercy Park was provided by limiting access to its central green square, gated and locked, to which only residents of the neighborhood could have keys.[49] People of similar circumstances and incomes could feel assured of familiar neighbors; the turmoil of the city streets could be kept at a distance.

While the well-to-do could afford to indulge their desire for social homogeneity, less-established middle-class people were caught in the tumultuous real estate development of the post–Civil War years. The piecemeal, even chaotic, development of New York blocks, the portraits of which are preserved in the Buildings Department records, often resulted in the very opposite of neighborhood comfort and safety. The developer Benjamin Weber proposed plans for five contiguous lots on West Fifty-fifth Street, filed with the Buildings Department in 1869 (the same year as Hunt's Stuyvesant Apartments). He planned to erect five buildings containing a mix of stables, stores and warehouses, and family residential units. The intermingling of uses was the kind of thing that contemporary house hunters complained about as not encouraging to home life. The *Real Estate Record and Builders' Guide*, reporting on building activity on the Upper West Side in New York, lamented that such mixtures of uses in the 1880s drove away developers who wanted to erect high-quality, expensive buildings, because they feared that the value of their investments would be diminished by "poor" developments on nearby lots (fig. 41). Widespread unease about such mixed uses eventually led to the 1916 zoning law in New York, restricting particular uses to their own specific districts.[50]

FIGURE 41 Stables, workshops, and warehouses were interspersed with new apartment blocks in the mixed-use streets south of Central Park. View from Sixth Avenue and Fifty-seventh Street looking north toward the Central Park Apartments, taken c. 1889. Photo courtesy of the New-York Historical Society, New York City)

In the face of such mixed urban development, a large apartment building offered itself as constituting its own neighborhood. For those who could not afford the expensive social homogeneity of a Gramercy Park, apartments could be a refuge from the chaotic developments on normal mixed-use streets. Thus if tenants could be persuaded to view each other not as strangers but as neighbors, many desired qualities of social comfort would result from apartment living.

The potential of social homogeneity had been recognized by contemporary writers as a positive feature of apartments in the earliest years of apartment development. The Haight House was described in 1874 as an example of a New York trend toward "the clustering of particular social sets about particular centers." The writer felt that apartment houses had the capacity to encourage such groupings of like-minded people. In the case of Haight House, these were "artistic and literary people who are able to find home, society, recreation,—everything almost which goes to distinguish civilized life,—without passing from under their own roof."[51] While most New York apartment houses did not develop such extensive shared interests as are hinted at here, they often facilitated the social cohesiveness that at least a controlled income range of tenants could give. For any class with rising social expectations, an apartment building could have offered some welcome limits to the random pollution of a big city with a diverse population.

"An apartment house must be built to accommodate a class of tenants who are in a nearly uniform social scale," stated the architect P. B. Wight.[52] Nineteenth-century writers theorized that an apartment house, to be successful, must have more or less the same level of accommodations throughout, not cheap apartments on the top floor and more expensive at the first and second levels, so that the tenants would feel comfortable with each other. The authors of the pamphlet "The Central Park Apartments" asserted that Americans insisted on preserving the boundaries of social classes.[53] They intended their apartment house for people "socially suited to each other."

Still, the broader neighborhood character continued to be important throughout the end of the century in developers' calculations. "A careful study of the requirements of the class of tenants making their homes in the vicinity where the apartment is to be erected," cautioned Charles Israels in 1901, "is also absolutely essential to the successful plan." He advised that one could get such information through local realtors and carefully fit the social status of the building and its projected tenants to that of the existing neighborhood. Advertisers used the quality of a neighborhood as a selling point, sometimes suggesting that a neighborhood of private residences enhanced the social value of their buildings.[54] Even so, such conditions could never be guaranteed as permanent, and "degeneration from the better to the poorer type of house is always possible with the ever changing conditions in a large city."[55]

Builders showed a propensity to build similar-class apartment houses near each other, such as the development near the Central Park Apartments on Central Park South. By 1890 hundreds of middle-class tenants found homes on that street in the Hawthorne, the Alhambra, the Dalhousie, the Parkview, and several others. The same clustering went on along the west side of Central Park, which was seen in the late 1890s as a specifically middle-class apartment neighborhood (fig. 42). Later, other like-class neighborhoods of apartments would develop on West End Avenue and again on Riverside Drive. Apartment houses and neighborhoods, therefore, did not have to be viewed as risky; they could be seen through the lens of neighborliness as a means to combat exposure to strangers and live in social safety.[56]

"The tendency of the population to classify itself may be taken as irrevocable," reported an editorial in *American Architect and Building News*. The wealthy are sure to end up in one quarter, the poor in another, and the people of "moderate means" in their own part of town.[57] This theory about the economic geography of the city was a residue of private-house habits of thinking where a history of trickle-down housing accompanied changes in class. But a well-executed apartment house could apparently establish a high-quality neighborhood unto itself, even when not in a well-to-do quarter. Not only did builders choose their locations carefully to match class of building with class of district. They also found to their surprise that a good-quality apartment building could convert a neighborhood's class associations. In districts of the West Side where "single family houses of the better kind could not have been leased" at all, reported *Harper's New Monthly Magazine*, high rents were obtained from "comfortable and elegant flats." Flats constructed "in different parts of the city near stables, rum-shops, tenement-houses, rookeries, are occupied by refined, fastidious people," who find a district less objectionable if they share an apartment house in it.[58] Experience proved, against the common sense of private-house developers, that an apartment house could constitute a neighborhood within itself; one that had sufficient strength to defeat a socially questionable context.

Flats have introduced a new way of life, reported the *New York Times* in 1880, providing housing not just for those unable to rent a whole house, but for those in "easy, even affluent circumstances." The *Times* reported that women, once they got used to flat life, were unwilling to give it up because it made for much easier housekeeping. Flats were also ideal for families who traveled a lot, as many New Yorkers did, since the janitor kept an eye on the family abode, and leaving the country was as simple as locking the door. They housed increasing numbers of genteel New Yorkers, even while tenants, journalists, and the building profession expressed doubts about their ability to encourage properly private home-life. And amid doubts, these apartments also suggested a newly efficient and convenient housekeeping based on a combination of collectivized work and the beginnings of modern household technology. The small single- or double-lot French-flat type would continue to be erected for middle-class tenants on through the 1890s. The *Times* protested that, far from having too many apartment houses, Manhattan could hardly have enough; they foresaw that apartments would always be in demand.[59]

FIGURE 42 Central Park West looking south from West Ninetieth Street in 1906; the row of apartment houses visible from this vantage point included the Cayuga, the New Windsor, the Melbourne, the St. Urban, the Minnewaska, and the Mohawk. (Courtesy of United States History, Local History and Genealogy Division, New York Public Library, Astor, Lenox and Tilden Foundations)

5 THE FAMILY FLAT GROWS UP

MANHATTAN's population had reached 950,000 by 1870; within a decade it grew to 1,200,000, and by 1890 there were nearly 1,500,000 people living in New York—far more than in any of the other three largest cities in the United States: Chicago, Philadelphia, and Brooklyn. Broadway flourished as a theater district; such places as Madison Square Garden offered a range of entertainments in the 1880s from an orchestra and dancing, to a circus, horse shows, prize fights, balls, and fairs. For tragedy, comedy, and melodrama, in 1890 there were thirty-seven theaters. Additional entertainments could be had in New York's twenty-seven beer gardens and 7,579 saloons. More refined cultural experiences awaited visitors at the Metropolitan Museum of Art and the America Museum of Natural History uptown adjoining Central Park. Access to New York's districts was enhanced by an elevated railroad system that had been completed by 1878. City dwellers were also served by 135 miles of horse-car lines charging five or six cents a ride, and by the 1,500 cabs and hacks licensed in 1890. Newly constructed streets complemented the elevated rail lines, opening whole new territories to the west and north of Central Park for residential development.[1]

During the 1870s numerous French-flat buildings accompanied row houses in the development of new residential districts above Forty-second Street. Boston observers noted that the construction of flats in New York retained more vitality than other new construction during the financial recession of 1873. As the real estate and building industries recovered from the financial recession in the late 1870s, they were able to undertake increased numbers of new building projects. By 1880 almost all the land south of Forty-second Street had been built up, and major construction was underway all across town between Forty-second Street and Fifty-ninth, where Central Park began. Grim tenements below Thirty-fourth Street on the West Side gave way to fresh new flat buildings northward along Sixth Avenue. Most of the East Side up to Eighty-sixth Street from Central Park to the East River was also built up.[2]

New dwelling units under construction in 1883 numbered 10,174. Of those, 200 were single-family houses costing above $20,000, and 600 were single-family houses costing between $7,000 and $20,000. Apartment units for middle-class tenants numbered 5,700, and tenement units made up the remaining 3,674.[3] Some of the new housing was for working-class families just emerging from the slums of the old Lower East Side, able to find affordable housing uptown and to reach their workplaces by rail. At the northern edge of real estate development on New York's West Side, a set of early 1880s apartment houses suggested a new attitude in apartment design by their extra height, lavish architecture, and high rents. These were the 500 apartment houses designated "first class" in the *New York Times*'s 1883 list of buildings under construction. Their arrival on the scene was recorded in the New York Buildings Department's docket books under the category "French flat," a category they continued to use for grand apartment houses as they had for the small flat buildings of the 1870s. As the small walk-up French-flat type continued to be built, the new apartment houses impressed viewers by their large size, climbing eight, nine, ten stories into the air, their high floors made accessible by means of elevators.

Approaching the size that had earlier belonged to public or commercial buildings, these grand apartment houses radically changed the residential streetscape and raised many questions for architects, tenants, and critics. The buildings occupied sizable plots of land around Madison, Gramercy, and Union squares, on Broadway, on Madison Avenue, and south and west of Central Park. They constituted the new wave of residences for middle- and upper-middle-class tenants (renters, or sometimes shareholders in a cooperative) who could afford rents such as those advertised for the Central Park apartments in 1885: ten rooms for $1,800 a year, twelve rooms for $2,500 a year, or sixteen rooms for $3,000 a year. Bigger construction budgets attracted a wealthier clientele, and developers increasingly catered to these clients, creating the luxury end of the apartment market. Grand apartment buildings also carried a new range of meanings about home. If the small, single-lot French flat had presented ambiguous messages about its role as a proper home because it housed half a dozen families, the grand apartment house faced an even greater challenge: how to develop new strategies to make a convincing home for seventy or eighty households.

To enter into an experience of this generation of apartments, imagine a well-to-do family arriving in New York in 1883, after having lived in a private house. Two parents, their several children, and their servants need suitable living quarters and decide to look into the new Central Park Apartments, also called the Navarro, after the building's Spanish developer.[4] They take public transportation up to the neighborhood of Central Park—now over twenty years old—and stop, somewhat taken aback, at the corner of Seventh Avenue and Fifty-ninth Street (fig. 43). Rising before them is an apartment complex of eight ten-story towers linked by what appear to be flying bridges disposed around its own three-part courtyard. Eight hundred feet of entrance fronts on Central Park South

FIGURE 43 View of the Central Park Apartments that comprised eight linked ten-story towers around a triple courtyard. (*King's Photographic Views of New York* [1895], p. 665)

and Fifty-eighth Street and three stories of rustication at ground level give it a formidable appearance, but corner turrets and dormers break through above the cornice line and hint at domestic-scale spaces inside. Fearful of getting lost in such a mammoth block, the family is reassured when they find that each of the eight towers has its own separate entrance and name—Granada, Valencia, Tolosa, and so on—giving the building its nickname "Spanish Flats."

The apartment hunters enter through an imposing two-story-high front entrance to look at a one-floor apartment in the Tolosa, a corner tower. For privacy-loving people, the Navarro was perfect: only thirteen families lived in each tower—not like those "caravansaries where 50 or 60 families are crowded together without the least regard for social adaptability."[5] Our would-be tenants pass through the clean, tiled lobby, take the elevator up to the seventh floor, and find that theirs is the only apartment on the floor (fig. 44). They hope to feel nearly as independent as they did in their old private home. Coming out from the public hall into the private reception hall, they see the parlor in front of them, the library on their right, connected to the parlor by sliding doors, and a large billiard room. From the billiard room they walk through more sliding doors into the dining room, remarking at the convenience that this suite offers for entertaining—just like apartments in Paris—and at the wonderful views of Central Park through the bay windows. Walking back through the reception hall, they discover four large chambers, spacious and well lit, each with its own closet. They regret only that one of the chambers opens right into the library, a popular planning idea but a bit too Parisian for the parents' sense of propriety.

Passing along a narrower private hall, they see three more small chambers, separate enough for the servants' bedrooms, big enough for a baby and nurse, and all these rooms look over the interior court, where the family are delighted to see a landscaped fountain (fig. 45). From the servant's room it is a short walk to the kitchen with its own store room and pantry, which gives immediate access to the dining room. Furthermore, they have two bathrooms with bathtubs—one for the servants and one for themselves.

On reading the realtor's prospectus for the building, they find two unexpected things. First, this apartment, at 3,018 square feet, is bigger than their old eight-bedroom house, which had only 2,867 square feet. Second, they can feel just as stable and secure at the Central Park Apartments as they did when they were house owners, because tenants do not just rent their apartments—they actually buy shares in a joint stock company called the "Hubert Home Club." The family would own a perpetual lease to their apartment and, better yet, would be able to approve, along with the other lease owners, any new tenants wanting to join the club in their particular tower. Good neighbors were assured.[6]

The newcomers make up their minds on two other issues. They had always heard that apartments were terrible for children because they would be deprived of a front yard, but at the Central Park Apartments permanent open space was guaranteed in the expanses of Central Park itself unfolding under their windows. They also had heard things about New York neighborhoods—how you

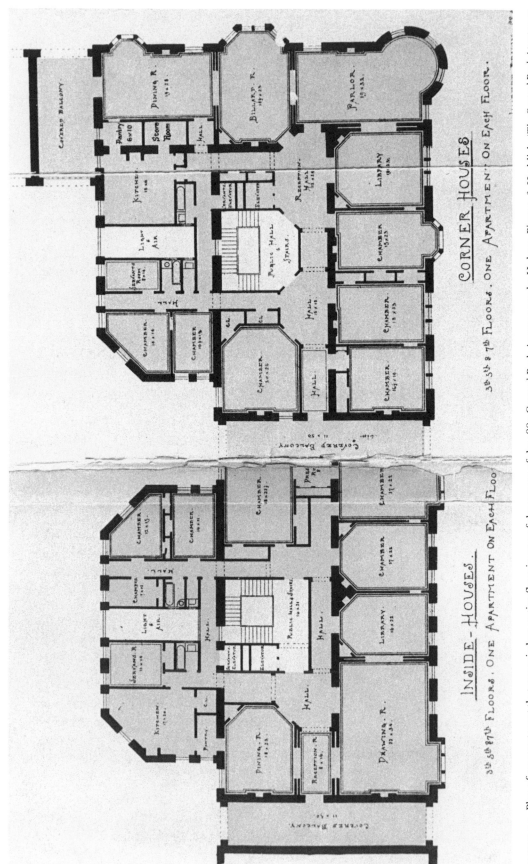

FIGURE 44 Plan of an apartment that occupied an entire floor in one of the towers of the 1883 Central Park Apartments by Hubert, Pirsson & Hoddick. (*The Central Park Apartments on 7th Avenue . . . Facing the Park* [1881])

FIGURE 45 Courtyard of the
Central Park Apartments with its
fountains. (Illustration by Harry
Fenn, in Everett N. Blanke, "The
Cliff Dwellers of New York," *Cosmopolitan* 15 [July 1893]: 357)

might find a stable or a coalyard under construction next door when you woke up in the morning, but Fifty-ninth Street was full of other fine apartment buildings under construction or already tenanted, assuring them of a respectable street as well as a socially homogeneous building. They decide to purchase shares in the Hubert Home Club and to try apartment life.[7]

Another (still standing) example of this new scale of French flat was completed the year after the Central Park Apartments. It is the well-known Dakota Apartments at Seventy-second Street and Central Park West, designed by the architect Henry Hardenbergh.[8] The original design was to house forty-two families in a quadrangular block with a private courtyard (figs. 46, 47). Initially budgeted for $1,000,000, its actual construction costs were nearly double that.

The Dakota filled the entire end of the block from Seventy-second to Seventy-third streets across from Central Park, about 200 feet square and nine stories high. It had such modern features as elevators, steam heat, and its own generator for electricity. Entering on Seventy-second Street, visitors would pass through a high arched entrance with pilasters at the sides enclosing a mezzanine window at the top, and into an interior courtyard, ninty-five feet across at its widest. At each corner were an elevator and public stairs to the several floors. The ground floor offered a spacious double room for a restaurant, a private dining room, and a reception room for guests. Upstairs, according to the description published by the professional magazine *Sanitary Engineer*, were about sixty-five suites ranging from four to twenty rooms on the main seven floors (rather than the forty-two originally planned) plus additional servants' rooms in the two extra stories of the mansard (converted in recent years to additional apartments).[9]

A third example of this new era was the Berkshire, a large apartment house at the corner of Madison Avenue and Fifty-second Street by the architect Carl Pfeiffer, under construction in 1883. At seven stories, with two more floors in the mansard plus a basement story half above ground, it was the same height as the Dakota. The exterior (figs. 48, 49) was busy with projecting bays and oriels, and the roof was alive with chimneys and dormers. The Berkshire had two apartments per floor—a four-bedroom unit whose servants' rooms were in the attic, and a three-bedroom unit that included one servant's room.[10]

Image from the Street

In the 1850s when the first articles recommending apartments had appeared, one view had promoted them as the hope for an impressive architecture of the type normally expected from public buildings. But in the 1890s Montgomery Schuyler speculated on the weakened potential of public buildings for creating a grand architectural presence. One effect of steel-frame and elevator buildings, Schuyler noted, was "to diminish the architectural importance of public buildings." He remarked that at the turn of the twentieth century when an institution

FIGURE 46 The Dakota, an elevator apartment house of 1884 by Henry Hardenbergh, still stands facing Central Park at West Seventy-second Street. (*Sanitary Engineer* 11 [February 1885]: preceding p. 271)

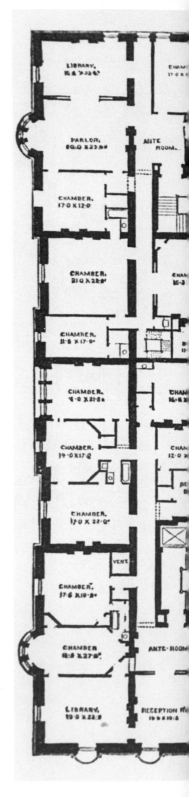

FIGURE 47 Plan of a typical upper floor at the Dakota.
(*Sanitary Engineer* 11 [February 1885]: 271)

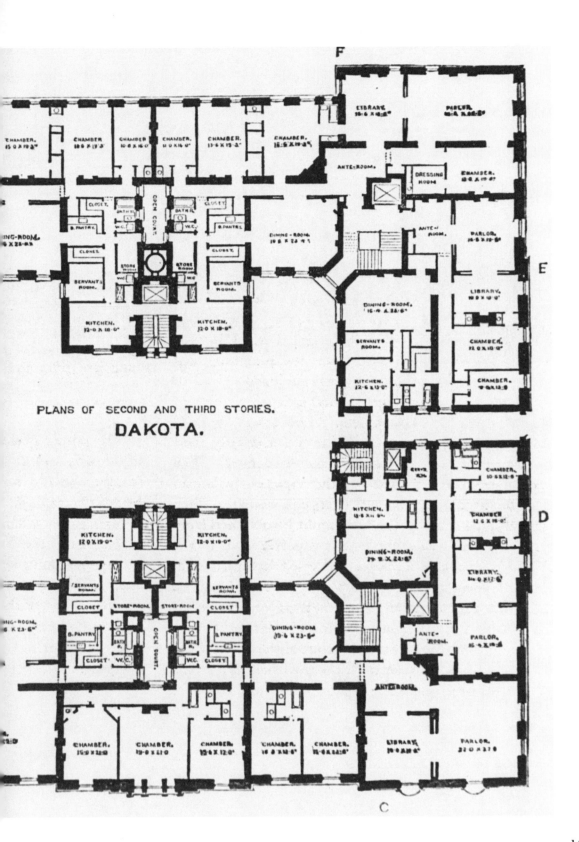

PLANS OF SECOND AND THIRD STORIES.
DAKOTA.

FIGURE 48 View of the Berkshire, corner of Madison Avenue and Fifty-second Street, by Carl Pfeiffer. (*American Architect and Building News* 14 [August 4, 1883]: pl. 397)

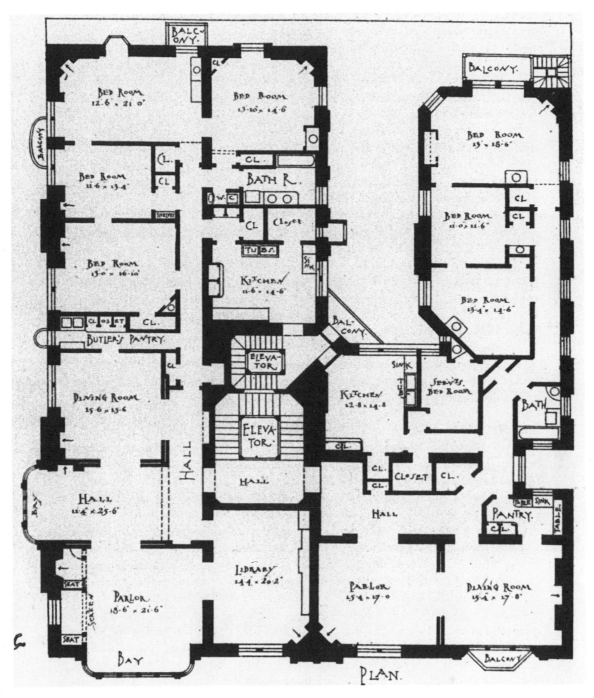

FIGURE 49   The Berkshire had two family units per floor. (*American Architect and Building News* 14 [August 4, 1883]: pl. 397)

wanted to house itself, it could erect a building of the proper size for its institutional needs and risk being dwarfed by the commercial giants around it, or erect a larger building but share interior space with others. Large apartment buildings, in contrast, could fill an imposingly scaled envelope with rental units, easily outstripping the size and assertiveness of churches and synagogues, schools, and institutional buildings nearby.[11]

Just twenty-five years after Olmsted designed Central Park as a refuge from all that smacked of "city" and urban pressures, the Dakota, the Central Park Apartments, and other such buildings of the early 1880s rose so tall as to be visible from all over the park. To Schuyler, looking back from the late 1890s, the Dakota seemed to enhance the park with its picturesque massing. But contemporary photographs suggest, rather, that the presence of large apartment houses recreated Central Park, changing it from a natural sanctuary as its designers Frederick Law Olmsted and Calvert Vaux intended, into a precinct walled on the south and increasingly confined on both east and west as urban development moved northward.[12] Apartment houses asserted their presence in ways that the mid-century had not foreseen, making a fully urban landscape of the neighborhoods around Central Park just as commercial buildings and flats had made of the streets around Union and Madison squares.

The problem of designing a suitable facade for large apartment blocks forced architects to deal with the tensions between privacy and publicity, commerce and images of home. Large apartment blocks could never capture the houselike scale available to designers of small French flats. Instead an individualism of style could mark out a large apartment block from nearby buildings. Fifth Avenue and Newport mansions of the post–Civil War years exhibited a fashionable eclectic, historicizing style. Architects of the 1880s apartment houses favored eclectic styles similar to those that mansion designers often used, and which in turn served as identifying markers for apartment buildings.

The window forms, tall roofs, and multitudes of dormers of the Dakota, for example (fig. 46), were loosely based on northern Renaissance sources. Contrasting colors for the walls and decorative details (now largely obscured by dirt) came from materials that included olive sandstone, terra cotta, a salmon-colored brick, and extensive wrought-iron ornament. Schuyler designated the style "French transitional" and praised the building's "picturesqueness of outline and effect."[13] For Schuyler a unified composition should be the aim of well-considered architecture, and such unity made the Dakota a building with a grand presence. Tenants in the Dakota and other large buildings could easily point out the imposing apartment house as their home, standing out through its assertive style from its city context.

But what of the individual family imagery that privacy-loving people might prefer? To passersby and to residents viewing the Dakota up close, the variety of color and ornament created an experience of difference from part to part rather than the experience of unity that Schuyler noted. The facade of the Central Park Apartments (fig. 50) shared this disjunctiveness, with its eight separate towers,

FIGURE 50 The entrance facade of the 1883 Central Park Apartments was filled with changes in surface texture and plane, with projecting balconies and porticoes. (Illustration by Harry Fenn, in Everett N. Blanke, "The Cliff Dwellers of New York," *Cosmopolitan* 15 [July 1893]: 354)

changes in color and texture, projecting bays, porches, and corner turrets. The Berkshire's exuberant ornament and variety of detail shifted from floor to floor as balconies picked up where projecting bays left off and the patterns of chimney ornament changed (fig. 48). These architectural details created variety and disrupted a single unified image.

The ornamented facades of this period led at least one critic to lament that both owners and renters preferred "palace-like" and "cheap and gorgeous" facades, but this ornament served a purpose in addition to being gorgeous. In a vast building, eclectic styles could also supply "clues" for single-family identification.[14] Because eclectic styles of the period stressed differences from part to part, residents could easily point out their own particular set of windows, towered corner, projecting bay, or bit of ornament on the exterior and say, "that's my part of this vast whole." No longer could families point to an individual house, or even (as at Price's French flat) their own full floor, but they could use stylistic details to break down a perhaps uncomfortably large whole building. Such identification would have been defeated by a more unified, smooth, or coherent architectural style such as the restful classicism favored for many luxury buildings in the next generation.

Another device for giving apartment houses a special and memorable identity was to give them exotic names. The Palermo on East Fifty-seventh, the Evelyn on West Seventy-eighth, and the Dundonald on West Eighty-third Street are just three examples of this trend in New York, all designed by the firm of Jardine, Kent, and Jardine in 1882. The Central Park Apartments was also called the Navarro, as mentioned earlier, and took the idea of special names to its extreme by having a name for each of the eight sections of the building—the Barcelona, the Cordova, and so on. When the owner, Edward Clark, named his apartment building the Dakota, a rash of western-named buildings broke out. In the nearby neighborhoods one could find the Wyoming, the Yosemite, the Nevada, and the Montana.

These names were sometimes ridiculed by contemporaries for being both pretentious and nonfunctional. Buildings that were clearly tenements, complained a writer of the 1890s, had names like Pembroke, Warwick, and Bayard bestowed by developers who wanted to upgrade the image of their buildings. And better-quality French-flat buildings sometimes were burdened with names like Amy or Lulu. Howells, in *A Hazard of New Fortunes*, made fun of apartment names when he sent the March family looking for the superintendent of an apartment called the Xenophon. The man could not be found, and the Marches were told that he must be in the Herodotus or the Thucydides next door.[15]

Where did the drive to give apartment houses names come from? Europeans were happy to identify their apartment houses by street address. The much longer tradition of middle-class apartment living in European cities made tenants comfortable with a large, undifferentiated building, and they did not feel the same need that Americans had to mark their homes out from the rest through a special name. Of course, American hotels also had traditionally used names rather than addresses to identify themselves, one more place where distinctions were blurred between hotels and apartment houses. The British may have provided the precedent for naming buildings, as in the name of the Albany, borrowed from a London building; it was also the trend in Victorian London to give apartment houses names like Grosvenor Gardens or Albert Mansions.

The original reason for giving a house a name can be found in English tradition, where the name identified a house in locations where there were no street numbers. In New York, since the streets did have numbers, every apartment house had a perfectly good address without its name. From a functional point of view, the name was beside the point. Furthermore, popular building names recurred; if someone gave his address as the Florence, one would have to ask which Florence. In the 1890s there were at least two Chelseas, three Nevadas, two Wyomings, three Manhattans, two Berwicks, and two Rockinghams among apartment houses in New York City.[16]

Given the situation of tenants learning to live in these new apartment buildings, the practice of naming eased the way. Advertisements for apartment rentals on the real estate pages of the *New York Times* always used the house name, giving would-be renters something extra to remember it by. Names might seem the product of inflated social ambitions, yet one can also imagine it was more comfortable to come home to the "Evelyn" than to a mere street number; the name gave the building a little more personality, a little more to identify as home. Apartment-building names were featured prominently in many editions of the *Phillips' Elite Directory*, adding a stylish touch to family addresses. And while grand apartment houses of the early twentieth century reverted to using addresses rather than names, again today names are being used as an identifying device for high-priced apartment towers.[17]

The Building Envelope

For the new, large apartment blocks of the 1880s, the overall building envelope was very different from smaller French-flat predecessors. The designers of the Dakota or the Central Park had large sites to work with, many city lots combined. Especially on the west side of Central Park, hundreds of vacant lots awaited development, some of which can be seen in a view from the Dakota roof (fig. 51). Small flat buildings of the first generation typically had to gather light and air for only five or six floors of flats, one or two flats per floor. Designers of huge blocks like the Dakota or the Central Park had many more apartment units within the building that needed proper light and air.

For an impressive and clear building envelope, the quadrangular courtyard block was admired, although infrequently used before the turn of the century. The Dakota (fig. 47), an example of the type, filled its plot of land out to the lot

FIGURE 51   A view of the developing West Side in about 1886 taken from the roof of the Dakota shows dozens of flat buildings along the avenues and dozens of empty lots awaiting development. (Courtesy of United States History, Local History and Genealogy Division, New York Public Library, Astor, Lenox, and Tilden Foundations)

line and reserved its center for its light and air supply. This kind of "square doughnut" scheme consolidated all the small indentations and light wells seen in other apartment plans like the Albany, into one broad, continuous space. The center courtyard provided potentially much better sunshine and air circulation than little light shafts did.[18]

American designers had learned from the French to use fireproof materials for all exterior walls including the indentations used for light wells, or *courettes*, the author of an article on courtyards for the *American Architect and Building News* commented. The architect-author believed that Americans soon became more original and "more successful from a hygienic point of view" than the French. Courtyards like the Dakota's, he reported, give "a safe, pleasant and sheltered place, under the eye of the Janitor, where tenants can enter, but thieves cannot, and where children can play, out of the street."[19] Because of the Dakota's success, he urged designers to learn yet more from Parisian apartments and to take up the theme of large internal courtyards.

The Central Park Apartments' architects developed a courtyard theme both for healthy air and for service functions. The firm of Hubert, Pirsson and Hoddick designed eight linked towers arranged to create three interior courtyards (fig. 52), giving light and air to all rear rooms in the apartments, as well as giving access to service lifts for deliveries. They installed a system of basement-level delivery tunnels, lit from the courtyard floor. Fountains in the center of each court enhanced the view from rear-facing apartment rooms.

Apartment-house courtyards might have provided a space for collective activity, but most architects did not interpret them in that way. The writer who suggested that Dakota-type courtyards provided a sheltered space for children's play was a solitary voice. Planned activities associated with courtyards were instead popular in the later nineteenth century for working-class tenement houses, such as White's 1890 Riverside Apartments in Brooklyn, where the large court served as a children's playground and had a bandstand for concerts. However, this level of collective activity out of doors seemed unappealing to middle class tenants, since it would expose them to unwanted observation and "publicity" and would suggest too close a kinship to tenements.

While contained, quadrangular courtyards seemed architecturally promising, most developers shied away from them until after 1900. Sometimes establishing a completely enclosed interior courtyard required too much land and was simply beyond the budget of a project. Other critics felt that an internal courtyard inhibited the free movement of air and was likely to produce stale or unhealthy air for tenants. Furthermore, although Parisian tenants found the lower-rent apartment units that faced only onto inner courtyards satisfactory and economical, because they belonged to a culture with a courtyard history, New Yorkers preferred outward-turning parlors with street views as they once had had in private houses. These combined arguments promoted a trend away from central-courtyard buildings in the 1880s.

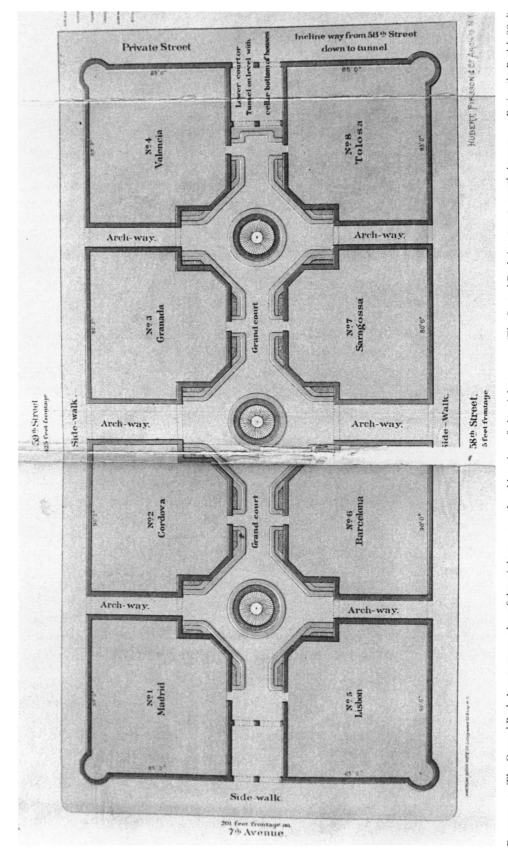

FIGURE 52 The Central Park Apartments, plan of the triple courtyard and location of the eight towers. (*The Central Park Apartments on 7th Avenue . . . Facing the Park* [1881])

The following labels appear within the plan:

Private Street

Lower court or Tunnel on level with cellar bottom of houses

Incline way from 58th Street down to tunnel

85' 0"   85' 0"

No. 4 Valencia   No. 8 Tolosa

97' 6"   93' 0"

Arch-way.   Arch-way.

No. 3 Granada   No. 7 Saragossa

Grand court

90' 0"   90' 0"

59th Street. 125 feet frontage   Side-walk.   Side-walk.   58th Street. 5 feet frontage

Arch-way.   Arch-way.

No. 2 Cordova   No. 6 Barcelona

Grand court

90' 0"   90' 0"

Arch-way.   Arch-way.

No. 1 Madrid   No. 5 Lisbon

85' 0"   85' 0"

Side-walk.

201 feet frontage on 7th Avenue.

HUBERT PIRSSON & Co ARCH'TS N.Y.

Another common type of plan that evolved for these larger buildings was an indented plan, a circulation core with wings filling the site and extending toward the street or the rear in the shape of a fat U, or wings extending in both directions like an H. Some plans were based on multiples of these shapes with many more wings of rooms separated by indented light courts. These plans maximized the exterior wall, thereby allowing the greatest number of windows for exterior light and air to every apartment. The Berkshire's plan is of the U type (fig. 53). Located on a street corner, it received light and air from its two street facades, from additional windows on its other side-wall, which overlooked a church, and from the windows in an indentation in the rear. Two more examples of the U-plan type are the Osborne and the Grenoble on Fifty-seventh Street (fig. 54).

Apartments with street-facing views always commanded higher prices. With more indentations and "peninsulas" of rooms facing the street, more apartments had street views, making the building more valuable to its owner, and probably more pleasant to its tenants. By the turn of the century there were many large apartment houses in the shape of an H, designed with indentations on the street sides to achieve these ends. This form can be seen as the opposite to Parisian courtyard types: the large apartment blocks of Europe were conceived of as suites of rooms wrapped around inner courtyard spaces, while American designers imagined a building as a solid body with extensions out into space.

Although these U- and H-plan designs probably gave better light and air than

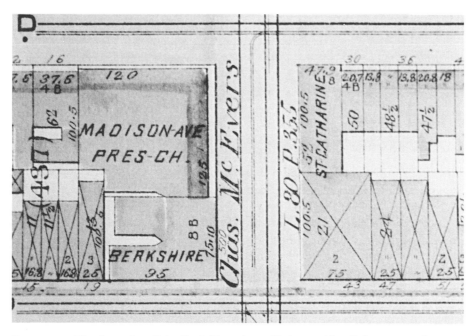

FIGURE 53 The footprint of the Berkshire takes a U shape with a light court at the rear. (*Atlas of the City of New York* [New York: Robinson and Pidgeon, 1890–93])

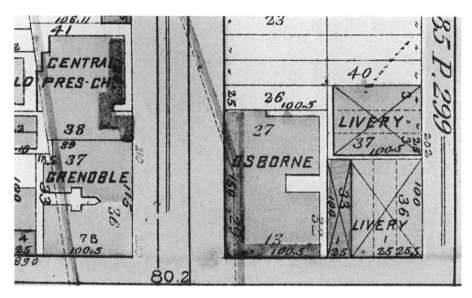

FIGURE 54   Both the Osborne and the Grenoble on Fifty-seventh Street show variants of the U-shaped plan with rear indentation for light and air. (*Atlas of the City of New York* [New York: Robinson and Pidgeon, 1890–93])

their narrow-lot contemporaries, they were not without faults. The U and H shapes did not allow very much distance between the wings of a building, and tenants could look across the court, as they could in tenements or the 1870s French-flat buildings with their narrow light courts, to see into their neighbors' rooms. However, since light and air were much better than in tenements, contemporary critics did not insist on this as a problem. One turn-of-the-century architectural critic found facade indentations to be aesthetically inferior. He wished that "the long straight facades . . . of Paris might be substituted for the restless and indented fronts of many American buildings;" although he recognized that in the real estate business the "implanted tastes of the public must be met, even if these tastes happen to be astray."[20]

Both the quadrangular block with an internal courtyard and the U or H plan maintained the continuity of the urban street wall. Unlike apartment towers of modern times that are set back from the street, these buildings rose from the edge of the sidewalk, set off at most by a railing and a "moat" that let light into basement windows. The indentations on facades, while they of course did interrupt the continuity of the street wall, were narrow, and architects tried to minimize the interruptions. Often such facades had a continuous ground floor or some bridging feature at the top linking one wing to the next, such as a continuous cornice across the break between wings. Designers of the large apartment house took their urbanistic job seriously, trying to sustain the early hope that apartment buildings' architecture would add grandeur to a plain city.

Public Spaces and the Line of Privacy

Relations between the apartment house and the street raised questions about what were the public, what the private elements of apartment buildings. Such negotiations extended into the interior of apartment houses as well. What were the proper boundaries between a private family unit and the public halls, landings, and stairs of each apartment floor? Further, what should be the balance between "public" and "private" within a family unit—public rooms being those for receiving visitors, and therefore on display as well as off limits to family activities; private rooms being set aside for family use only, yet constrained spatially by the desire to expand the "on display" parts of the household.

The entrance to an apartment building provides a focus for problematic definitions of what should be public, what private in such a collective building. Because of their increased scale, larger apartment houses of the 1880s often had doorways two stories high. Doorway enframements included columns, architraves, relief carving, and sometimes the name of the apartment house. The owners of the St. Honoré on Madison Avenue advertised seven- and eight-room apartments for rent in 1899, recommending the building for its marble staircase and "exquisite entrance." But critics objected to two-story porticoes, such as the one that served as the Somerset's entry, because they darkened the second-floor apartment whose windows looked out under it. They also objected to the tendency of landlords to lavish ornament on the front doors and lobbies of buildings whose other interior arrangements did not live up to that promise. As in the first small French flats, the separate stoop and entrance that a single-family house owner enjoyed was replaced by one main entrance for all tenants in most elevator apartment buildings. Although each of the eight towers at the Central Park apartments had a separate entrance with an arched canopy supported on columns, still, thirteen families shared one entrance (fig. 50).[21]

Prominently featured on the street, ornate two-story entrances shared the scale and stylistic ambitions of public-building entrances, yet of course tenants desired their buildings to preserve as much privacy as possible. Some recommended that entrances to apartments should always have a "porte cochère of some sort, by which people may enter and leave their carriages in comfort and under shelter, instead of being obliged to pick their way, often through a rough crowd, across a filthy sidewalk, to the waiting vehicle, as is now the rule here." Designers welcomed architectural devices that would clarify the nuances of publicity and privacy to the "rough crowd" of passersby and reassure tenants. This was the purpose served by the entrance to the Nevada shown in a drawing of 1893 (fig. 55). Depending upon the size and operating budget of an apartment house, the door would also be attended by a janitor, concierge, or doorman, whose duties included rejecting members of the public who did not belong inside.[22]

Guarding against the "rough crowd" may have assured a realistic level of

FIGURE 55 An awning claims some "private" space from the public sidewalk to shelter tenants of the Nevada. (Illustration by Harry Fenn, in Everett N. Blanke, "The Cliff Dwellers of New York," *Cosmopolitan* 15 [July 1893]: 358)

safety and comfort. Conceptually, however, tenants still had to deal with the paradox that home was private yet apartment houses had public spaces within. For those middle-class Americans who still felt the tenuousness of their social rank and feared strangers, architecture that was organized around collective spaces might be suspect. Because of tenants' nervousness about communal experience, designers had to control the public spaces in apartment houses to minimize the social unease of prospective renters. This could be done by curtailing shared spaces to the minimum circulation requirements, as in small French-flat buildings; by limiting the opportunities of meeting others in the public corridors by offering several vertical access routes, as at the Dakota, thereby cutting down on the numbers of tenants who would use any given public corridor or elevator; or by trying to improve the public experience by making such spaces either socially neutral, or glamorous and suggestive of exclusive drawing rooms, clubs, or hotels.

The public lobbies in large apartment buildings were often fairly sizable spaces. They had to allow for many tenants to reach the stairs and elevators and for door attendants to receive and direct guests and perhaps to accept and distribute deliveries and mail. Many larger buildings had reception rooms for guests and many also continued the 1870s innovation of restaurantlike dining rooms for tenants and for the public on the ground floor. Grandeur in public lobbies was a point of pride in some apartment buildings, where elaborate decorative schemes in the entrance, lobby, and main staircase could stun a first-time visitor or entice the not yet well-to-do with promises of luxury.

However, some critics condemned this gloss of luxury applied to apartment lobbies. The architects Hubert, Pirsson and Hoddick wrote in favor of simple, functional entrances, lobbies, and hallways. They felt that money was very badly spent on "useless luxury," and should go into solid construction instead of fancy draperies. Speculative builders were blamed for adding useless ornament to ordinary flat buildings. Their thoughtlessness was pointed out by the *New York Times*: "The money spent on the coarse and paltry ornamentation of these pretentious 'French flats' . . . would pay for making them healthful and habitable places."[23]

Decorated, showy lobbies and halls resembled the parlors in hotels. Sociable parlor associations thus claimed tenants' attention immediately upon entering the building, even though they were still in public space. In such a "parlor," tenants might feel obliged to interact with others, although they did not really know them. But hotel associations were to be avoided by genteel families seeking enhanced privacy. Simplicity in apartment-house lobbies aimed at a new and appropriate form for apartment buildings, distinct from hotels, and closer to a model that Philip Hubert called grouped houses along a public but neutral sidewalk. The more austere lobby and hall type may be interpreted as postponing an interior social experience until the tenants reached their own front doors and were clearly in their own space, just as they would avoid sociability when walking down the sidewalk.

The tension over interpretations of the public or private nature of apartment lobby space is illustrated in an 1885 story from the *New York Times*. Mrs. Lee, suspecting her husband of conducting an affair with Mrs. Ellis, visits Ellis's apartment house, the Madison Park Flats. Mrs. Lee, entering the lobby of the flat building from the street, enters public space. She intended to show the janitor a photograph of her husband and to find out for sure whether Mr. Lee had been living there illicitly. Mrs. Ellis meanwhile descends from her flat to breakfast with a female friend; she is at home, so the lobby to her is private space. Mrs. Lee confronts Mrs. Ellis and calls her "a hussy" in front of everyone—that is, in public. The janitor states that if he had knowledge that Mrs. Ellis was living with a man who was not her husband—that is, not observing the rules of the private home—he would put them out of his apartment building.[24]

While shared spaces continued to have ambivalent interpretations attached to them, they could present an occasion for architectural enhancement. Designers added dining rooms, gardens, and roof pergolas to the possibilities for collectively used spaces in more expensive apartment buildings. Occasionally, middle-class buildings also had meeting rooms, or party rooms that tenants could hire for a special evening. When these public rooms were carefully decorated, as in the oak-paneled reception rooms at the Dakota, or placed on a high floor to take in spectacular views as in Flagg's project for the 1883 Fifth Avenue Plaza apartments, they could make sharing palatable by making it elegant. Refined and well-decorated rooms for collective use suggested exclusive clubs or private drawing rooms, not unwelcome hotel lobbies.

The roof was a part of apartment-house space that was private to the tenants, yet publicly accessible, and had a mobile class identity. In many cases, roofs were collectively used, but by servants. They typically provided space for clothes drying in every scale of building from a tenement to a luxury house. Drying rooms of wood slats, stretched with clotheslines, were provided at the Stuyvesant and recommended for the garret of a proposed apartment building in 1878. In the flat building described by Christine Herrick, each household was assigned a day to use the clotheslines on the roof, so if it rained on the designated day, wet clothes had to be draped around the apartment. Here, strict ideas of privacy and individuality prescribed limits on the collective use of the public roof, sometimes causing problems for tenants.[25]

Yet roofs also had properties of the belvedere where a lovely view could be enjoyed by a select company. In the 1870s, the journalist O. B. Bunce recommended that apartment houses use plantings to develop their roofs as recreational spaces from which to take in stunning views of the city (fig. 56). In his article on bachelor flats, E. T. Littell suggested that part of the roof be fenced off, roofed with wood slats, and provided with benches for the tenants' recreation. In this case, since the tenants were all single men, Littell's roof garden would forestall their having raucous parties on their individual balconies, which would disturb other tenants and give the building a bad name.

In the 1880s, roof terraces of grand apartment houses could support a claim to exclusivity, since the grandest apartment blocks had the most splendid views,

FIGURE 56 The apartment-house roof could be treated like a belvedere with plantings, benches, and opportunities for tenants to take in the view. (O. B. Bunce, "The City of the Future," *Appleton's Journal* 7 [1872]: 156)

being substantially higher than neighboring buildings. During this period, roofs had a double identity as service spaces and as terraces and viewing platforms. The tiled roof of the Berkshire provided a promenade for tenants, reached by means of the passenger elevator. For the Dakota roof, Henry Hardenbergh designed gazebos, pergolas, and sunshades. Roof gardens associated with theaters took their places in New York nightlife beginning in 1882 with the roof garden on top of the Casino Theater, and another at Madison Square Garden. In these roof gardens theater patrons could enjoy informal entertainment such as vaudeville and cabaret after the more formal plays in the theater proper. Both in theaters with their fully public roof gardens and in apartment houses with their quasi-private ones, roof gardens provided spaces for people who arrived singly, in couples, or in small parties and who did not want to feel obliged to be sociable with all the others using the space.[26]

Roof gardens became almost a standard feature in high-quality apartment houses of the 1880s and 1890s. These spaces and the lobbies, reception rooms, and dining rooms of 1880s apartments gave tenants practice in accommodating themselves to more public pleasures. The shift from a roof for individual laundry chores to a roof for collective pleasure was facilitated by elevator rides to the roof and by new kinds of drying equipment introduced into apartment basements. Technological changes supported conceptual changes, and the notion of the roof as servants' territory was gradually reinterpreted after the turn of the century to the dream of a penthouse apartment for well-to-do tenants.

As lobbies and roof gardens brought tenants together, so did stairs, elevators, and hallways. Vertical circulation in the early five- or six-story French-flat buildings had been limited to stairs. In households where the tenants expected to have servants, service stairs and dumbwaiters gave additional and separate vertical circulation paths. But in the larger 1880s apartment houses, passenger elevators became the rule.

The Berkshire (fig. 49) had a single circulation core, with back-to-back passenger elevator and service elevator, each surrounded by its own staircase. Servants reached their stairs and elevator from the back of the building, tenants from the front.[27] In a courtyard building like the Dakota, a lavish budget made it possible to provide vertical circulation for guests and tenants at each corner of the court (fig. 47). Because there were so many passenger elevators, public hallways on each floor were unnecessary: where two apartments had to be reached from the elevator, a small foyer would give access to both, and in many cases at the Dakota, the elevator gave onto only one apartment on a floor. In that case, the elevator could open directly into a tenant's private foyer, with no public hall at all.

This solution of an elevator in each corner was ideal for a courtyard building, which, because of its shape, had no central point at which to cluster circulation. Multiple points of circulation cut down on the numbers of other tenants one met en route to one's own apartment. Big budgets enabled Hardenbergh to separate service stairs and elevators from those for tenants and their guests, placing the service circulation in the centers of the four sides of the Dakota's courtyard and accessible only from a service level one floor beneath the open-air courtyard. Thus servants were kept apart from tenant stairs and elevators, and tenants were kept relatively free of encounters with each other.

The Dakota and other grand buildings of the 1880s had had to supply their own steam or electricity to run the elevators, and that made for expensive construction, compensated by high rents. The typical elevator of the 1880s was a hydraulic machine with an ungainly and space-consuming apparatus installed in the basement to run it.[28] Generators had to be installed in each building wanting an elevator because city-supplied electric power was still not widespread.

In the 1890s a more streamlined electric elevator entered apartment houses. An electric elevator could save much of the basement space that the old hydraulic machinery had required, and designers could use that space instead for new conveniences and storage rooms. Its advantages, articulated by an engineer, George Harding, in the mid-1890s, were the more reliable control of speed, the smaller machinery needed to run the cars, and the independence of each car and shaft from the next. The electric system allowed much greater ease in planning building layouts, and the simplicity of installing electric elevators simplified scheduling during building construction. By 1898, with easily available electric power finally supplied by public utilities companies beneath the streets, the earlier small walk-up type of French flat like Bruce Price's 21 East Twenty-first Street was replaced in new construction by at least a double-lot-sized flat building, typically of seven stories, made profitable to developers through the appeal of elevators.[29]

The choice of vertical circulation in apartment houses had cultural implications. When walking up stairs was the rule, some rent differences could be expected. As in Paris, in New York's early French flats the highest floors might be reserved for servants, the next highest for poorer tenants who would be willing to pay less rent in exchange for walking up more steps, and the lowest floors for the most prosperous. A New York resident, George Andrews, had written in 1877 "two or three years [ago] the third story was as near the sky as it was possible to induce the better class of tenants to go, but the steam elevator makes the fifth and even the sixth accessible and habitable and the difference in rents where this vehicle is in use, is surprisingly small." Andrews hints that "better" tenants were committed to being near the ground, perhaps retaining the intimate link between parlor and street that had been an important feature of row-house life. When the elevator became widely available, suddenly landlords could raise the rents on the upper floors, more than compensating them for the expense of installing an elevator. When rents were equalized as an effect of the elevator, the result was a more homogeneous tenancy in apartment buildings. This trend made tenants feel more secure, as they recognized that all their fellow residents were of the same income bracket as themselves.[30] Perhaps the shift in character of the apartment roof from service to pleasure was linked to the social rise in rank of the upper floors of apartments.

Horizontal circulation required internal public corridors, and while designers tried to limit the length of such hallways, they were not always successful, given the demands of access to large numbers of units per floor when there was a single central elevator-stair access point. Lengthy public corridors were condemned strongly by contemporary critics but continued to be built on into the twentieth century. Many "long hall" plans of the H or U type had a central circulation core at the street or rear, requiring lengthy public corridors to get tenants from elevators to their own front doors. In courtyard buildings where budgets were not sufficient for a circulation core in each corner of the quadrangle like that at the Dakota, a single circulation core necessitated even more awkward long corridors around the central courtyard to units on the opposite side. It is easy to see how difficult horizontal circulation could become without a budget adequate for several stairs and elevators.[31]

John P. Putnam, discussing apartment-house circulation, assumed that issues of publicity versus privacy were easy to resolve: "Isolation may be made complete in the flat," he asserted. For Putnam "the private halls and front doors of each suite [are] in every respect the equivalent of those in the 'tower' [i.e., a freestanding private house]; the only difference being that with the 'flat' the outer world begins with the public hall and its elevator, while with the 'tower' it begins with the public street and its horsecar." However, in the experiences of the period, such boundaries were by no means so easy to discern.[32]

Public stairs and corridors might be the location for unexpected uses. An 1892 report described a family who were disappointed to find some tenants in their apartment building who were not as refined as themselves. They discovered a new family "on the stairs and landings which they used as a regular part of their holding, and where they appeared with a painful disregard as to their toilet."[33] In good weather the stoops were treated like parlors, this report continued, forcing the better class of tenants to move to the country so they would not be bothered by the population density on their own front stoop. In this building, the boundaries between public and private were not agreed upon by all. Some tenants might easily assume that halls, stairs, and front stoops were "part of their holding," since they were collectively used spaces. But this kind of communal use was horrifying to others, who treasured firm boundaries between public and private life.

Even with all the planning principles in place, the clear demarcation of private from public was not legible to everyone. A janitor in the apartment house at 208 West Eighty-fifth Street showed a well-dressed man one of his vacant apartments. When the man got to the bathroom, he locked himself in and proceeded to draw a bath. The janitor, unable to persuade him to come out, called the police. They removed him from the premises to a mental hospital, a response called for in part by the fact that he could not tell the difference between public and private.[34]

Collective Spaces, Cooperative Effort

Because apartment houses of the second generation gathered together greater numbers of families, each of whom had to have similar housekeeping done, it would have been reasonable to combine effort and have more of that work done centrally. This advantage of apartment life had been evident to tenants and designers of the first-generation of buildings, and it continued to be explored. The question was how much and what kind of centralized effort and equipment would make for the best living conditions while violating privacy the least. This careful balance was achievable when "different households touch only at such points . . . where cooperation is proper, convenient, and economical."[35]

Some of these decisions were easily made in the ordinary arrangements of an apartment building. It had been established in the French flats of the 1870s that apartment houses required at least a concierge or janitor, if not a full staff, to take care of some cleaning and repair work, both of the building as a whole and of the family unit. The flats of the 1880s also had more kinds of centralized equipment in more widespread use, such as central heating, elevators, water, gas, and other utilities, which all tenants shared. While these were not collective activities in the sense that tenants did them together, nonetheless they were possible only in a "co-operative" dwelling where the group's resources supported centralized labor and equipment.[36]

At the Central Park Apartments, collective dwelling enabled tenants to pool their resources to pay the wages of the janitor and "hall boys." Equipment paid for out of the group's combined rents included coal-powered central steam heat and hot water (water supplied by the building's own artesian well), gas for lighting, and a back-up installation of incandescent electric light, should anyone in the early 1880s prefer it to gas. Residents shared in the benefits of one service elevator and one passenger elevator for each of the eight towers of this large apartment house and paid the engineer (needed to run early elevators). These were items that did not impinge upon any family's privacy, or only required a small stretch of tolerance for strangers, as when people who did not know each other had to share a ride in the elevator.

Centralized preparation of meals, usually served in a group dining room like a restaurant, continued on from the 1870s as an offering of many larger apartment houses. Just inside its entrance the Dakota had both a restaurant and private dining room. Ernest Flagg's 1883 prospectus for a fifty-two-unit cooperative apartment, the Fifth Avenue Plaza (never built), included a dining room/restaurant. Not only did a house dining room and centralized kitchen save the tenants work and money, Flagg claimed, but the profits from this restaurant also could pay many of the general expenses of running the building. In addition, when wives and children went away for the summer months, the husbands who remained behind could still get a decent meal.[37]

Centralized cooking could also serve the desire for privacy. A nine-room "kitchenless" apartment in the Florence at Eighteenth Street and Fourth Avenue was for rent in 1890. In this apartment building, meals could be cooked in the building's kitchen by cooks employed by the management, then served in one's own dining room by a family-employed servant. Instead of a kitchen in these units, one of the Florence's features was a large pantry "with refrigerators, gas heaters, sinks, etc.," which complemented the full array of centralized kitchen equipment. This fully equipped pantry took up far less room than the standard kitchen, yet probably also allowed servants to create smaller meals, as well as serve larger ones. Like its predecessor the Haight House of the early 1870s, the Florence encouraged the privacy that was so crucial to family-centered life, yet lightened the burdens of housework through centralized equipment and labor.[38]

Parallel to these developments in ordinary apartment houses were more politically charged proposals for communal services, as seen in the writings of feminist reformers such as Helen Campbell and Charlotte Perkins Gilman. In a program to free women from "domestic slavery," they wanted to introduce professionalism into housework. Gilman claimed that the modern family was no longer a self-contained production unit as it had been earlier in the nineteenth century but an "outgoing," as contrasted with home-centered, group whose needs ought to be served by professionals. Middle-class women as housekeepers did not have to prepare their own foods or do their own laundry, since they could easily purchase these services in city neighborhoods. The home no longer needed to be a center for housekeeping but could become a center for peace, rest, and emotionally rewarding family life. Like many of the writers who dealt with apartment design in the 1870s and 1880s, these feminists believed that improved household design could lead to more freedom for women.

Campbell wanted to professionalize household work along the lines of efficient industrial production, introducing the concept of "domestic science," a rational and skilled pursuit. She put forward a proposal for suburban houses that would, like apartment houses, have a common kitchen and laundry, and she envisioned a domestic environment of "great clustering palaces; whe[re] the private houses ray out in wings and ells of lawn-ringed separateness, all its industries subservient and reduced to order, and the whole great building expressing the thought of human living at its best." Her suggestion fuses the idea of collective services with the suburban ideal of a house in its own lawn. However, Campbell herself discouraged families from living in traditional apartment houses, persuaded that urban congestion and strife could not enhance home-life.[39]

Interiors

Some general principles of spatial organization established in the first generation continued in the 1880s, pertaining to the whole range of income levels within middle-class apartment production. These features differentiated genteel aims in the organization of domestic space from working-class tenement space. There was always a "parlor," understood both as a room reserved for receiving guests and a room preserved from work. Many apartments had several such rooms; their names may have varied, but their defining features remained (and persist in the living rooms of the late twentieth century). Tenement units, in contrast, had too little space to set aside a room where people were required to be unproductive. In middle-class apartments there was always a bathtub, a toilet, and hot and cold water available inside the family's private space, rather than elsewhere in the building as was characteristic of tenements. Other than that, the middle-class apartment's features changed with budget, intended tenants, and conceptions of use.

When designers, tenants, and critics of the 1880s discussed the desirable qualities for a substantial family apartment, they seemed to express broad agreement about planning principles. They had learned certain lessons from Paris, on the one hand, and from the tentative and sometimes clumsy efforts of flat designers of the 1870s, on the other. Experiments with room groupings, spatial zoning, and various circulation patterns crystallized into an increasingly articulate series of requirements. From the statements of architects and from apartment plans, it is not hard to reconstruct a list of these principles of planning.[40]

Probably the most important rooms in an 1880s household were those for receiving guests. Here the family met the world, its best foot forward. According to the planning ideas of the 1880s, public, reception rooms should be located so as to have a view of the street whenever possible, should be grouped en suite, and should be near the main entrance to the apartment unit. The suite of public rooms at the Central Park Apartments are a good example. The rooms correctly included in this category could be several in a single apartment; their names are typically parlor, library, music room, billiard room, and sometimes drawing room. This reception category included any other spaces used specifically for receiving and entertaining visitors. Where possible, the dining room should also be included as a spatially contiguous part of the group.

Chambers, or sleeping rooms (excluding servants' bedrooms), were located according to two different guiding concepts. One concept understood the bedrooms as all one type of room, and located them all grouped together in a sleeping/sitting/private zone that maximized seclusion from the reception rooms. The sleeping zone would usually be reached by a corridor of its own and would be out of view of guests. This concept of grouping bedrooms together was anticipated in some first-generation buildings like the Albany. However, an equally common 1880s and 1890s method of locating bedrooms suggests that they could also be conceptualized as two types of rooms—a set of chambers in a private family cluster and a separate master/mistress chamber. Where the principal bedroom of the 1880s was not grouped with other sleeping rooms, but treated as the master/mistress room, it would be grouped with rooms in the "reception" category, following French precedents and the method used in many first-generation New York apartments. Locating the principal bedroom this way, as Hunt had at the Stuyvesant apartments, suggests that it would be used sociably, perhaps akin to a Frenchwoman's boudoir where close friends visited. Either way, each bedroom should have good, fresh air and should have independent access by corridor. And never should there be a bedroom whose only access was through another bedroom, as found in tenements.

Service rooms within an apartment unit included the servants' rooms, the kitchen, and the pantry as a proper grouping. Servants should have a separate entrance, their own stairs, and sometimes their own elevator. The kitchen should be next to the dining room and linked to it by a pantry, and well-ventilated by windows to the outdoors (or at least windows on an air shaft). Additional service spaces in the basement, penthouse, or roof of the apartment house as a whole were expected to supplement those within the individual apartment unit.

Some of these principles of spatial organization had been followed in the first generation, such as window ventilation for the kitchen and a street view from the parlor—a preference of Americans that Vaux had mentioned in 1857 in his argument for apartments. Other principles were not generally agreed upon: some planners preferred the dining room in the back, while others placed it in the front of the apartment. Experiment on the part of designers and experience on the part of tenants gradually led to a consensus that the principles listed above were in fact "correct" for middle-class apartments. Yet ironically by the turn of the century when these planning principles seemed fully worked out, the apartment unit that was spacious enough to incorporate all of them was already priced beyond the reach of most of the New York apartment market.

In grand buildings, the increased sophistication in planning showed the results of learning from experience, as well as the refinement made possible by extra-large budgets. Nonetheless, the planning of grand apartment units in the 1880s still seems tentative when compared with plans of the succeeding generation. The Dakota's plan, for example, was somewhat awkward (fig. 47). A typical apartment at the Dakota had an anteroom and sometimes a reception room leading to the parlor and library, always linked together. The dining room was sometimes adjoining, sometimes at some distance from the parlor. Dining rooms were always linked to pantries and kitchens for convenience and efficient service. Adjoining the kitchen were a servant's room, various storage rooms, and the principal (sometimes the only) bathroom. A service wing jutting out into the central courtyard in some units kept servants, kitchen, and pantries well apart from reception rooms and well ventilated. However, the reception rooms and the private family bedrooms were not cleanly separated from each other nor articulated as a grouping, nor did the individual rooms have any distinguishing shape or height characteristics.

In the smaller units at the Central Park Apartments (that is, where there were two units per floor instead of one), one chamber was grouped with the main public rooms, while the others were located at the back, either near to the servant's room and the bathroom or up one flight of steps in the duplex wing (fig. 57). The principal bedroom for master and mistress of the house was linked with reception rooms near the apartment's main entrance. Public rooms were generously laid out and well connected by sliding doors in wide openings, to afford opportunities to open these rooms en suite for entertaining. These rooms had fifteen-foot-high ceilings, preserving the traditionally higher ceilings found on the parlor floors of single-family urban row houses. Each reception room also had a distinctive floor-plan shape of its own, as bay windows, turrets, or chamfered corners gave variety to rectilinear room shapes.

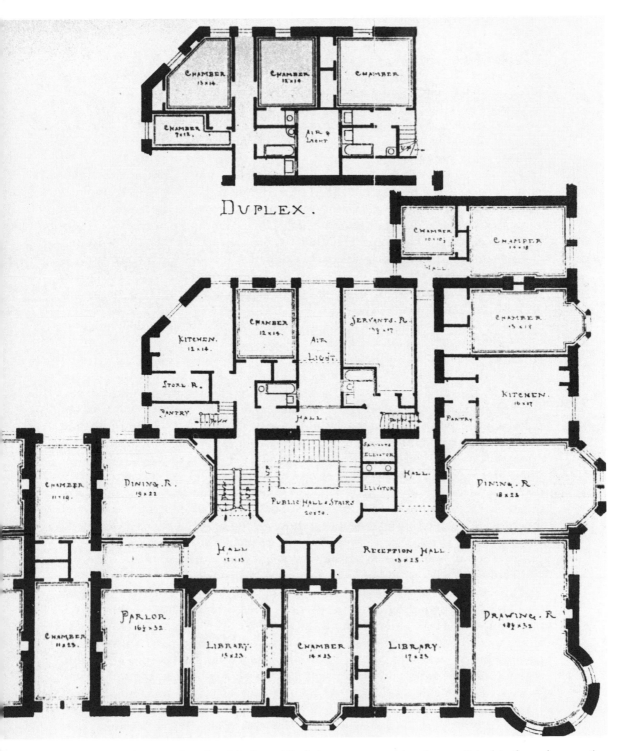

FIGURE 57 In the five-bedroom unit at the 1883 Central Park Apartments one chamber was linked to the main reception hall, while the others were pushed to the rear in a private zone or raised a level in the rear duplex wing. (*Central Park Apartments on 7th Avenue . . . Facing the Park* [1881])

A plan for an apartment house built about 1900 on Fifty-fifth Street by G. A. Schellenger (fig. 58) shows the difficulty of meeting all the requirements for ideally situated rooms and still producing a building that could rent for a reasonable amount. His H-plan apartment house had four units per floor. The front doors were located near the middle of the building next to the public stairs and elevator. Each unit had its dining room and parlor grouped together with good exposures to the outside air. But in order to get the best exposures for his reception rooms, Schellenger had to compromise. Some units got reception rooms overlooking the street in the preferred position, but some faced the rear court—a compromise in location necessitated by the conflicting requirement of fitting four independent units on each floor. Because of this placement of reception rooms, visitors had to progress down a private corridor past the bedrooms to get to the apartment's social space. The designer thus violated two principles—separation of guests from bedrooms, and the locating of public rooms next to the entrance—in order to satisfy the two other principles of grouping public rooms and giving them the best exposures.[41]

The decoration of interiors took many forms in 1880s buildings. Some developers put a lot of effort into creating rich-looking rooms, as at the St. Catherine Apartments on Madison Avenue and Fifty-third Street, where, advertisers claimed, the "cabinet work and decorations [were] not surpassed by any house in the city." This kind of interior was condemned by the architects of the Central Park Apartments, who called such buildings "ridiculous Lilliputian imitations of palaces, frescoed and gilded, and trimmed with all the woods of the Indies." In another approach to satisfying tenants' decorating tastes, apartment-house promoters often advertised that those who signed leases while the construction was still under way could have their choice of wall finishes and woodwork, choosing their own favorite colors or materials, and sometimes even choosing room placement. Advertisements in 1885 for the Dalkieth, near Mt. Morris Park, invited tenants to select their own decorations; those for the Berkeley Arms on Riverside Drive in 1899 stated that tenants could select their own decorations and wallpaper. Tenants also understood that they would often do decorating themselves, and could not rely on finding interiors to suit their tastes.[42]

While many apartment designers left private interior decor up to the tenants, Carl Pfeiffer designed a great many decorative features into his Berkshire apartment house. His plan had two family units per floor (fig. 49). At the front of the larger apartment near the main entrance was a group of social rooms—a hall, parlor, library, and dining room. The dining room was linked to the kitchen by a narrow butler's pantry and private hall. In an overlaying of functions, this same hall was also the only corridor to the family's bedrooms. The smaller apartment at the Berkshire had a more clearly organized plan, with the servant's room and kitchen acting as the hinge between a bedroom wing and the more social rooms at the front.

Individuality in configuration and elaborate woodwork distinguished the rooms at the Berkshire. For example, a built-in window seat, an inglenook, and a

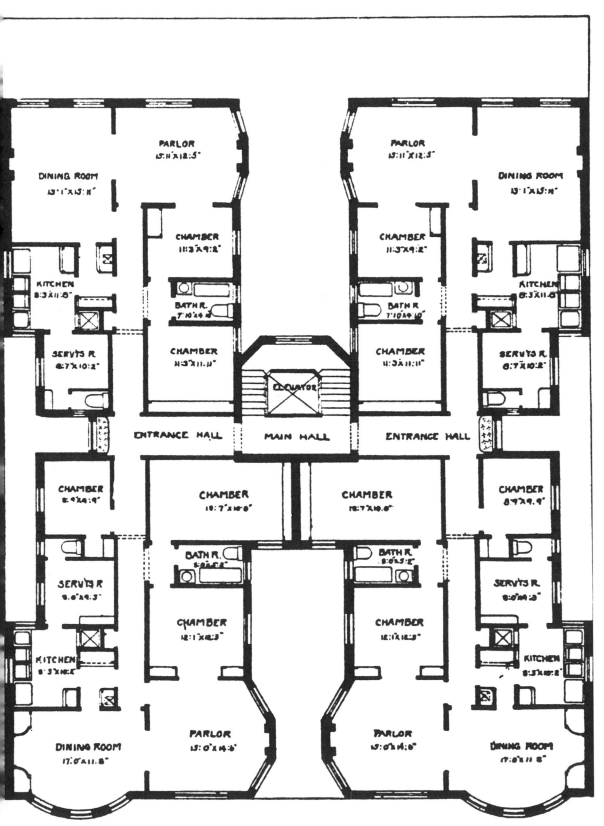

FIGURE 58 Chambers were embarrassingly near the main entrance and parlors inconveniently pushed down the hall in an apartment house by G. A. Schellenger. This was the result of competing needs to give social rooms the greatest exposure to light, air, and view, to give bedrooms privacy, and to centralize circulation. (*Architectural Record* 11 [July 1901]: 499)

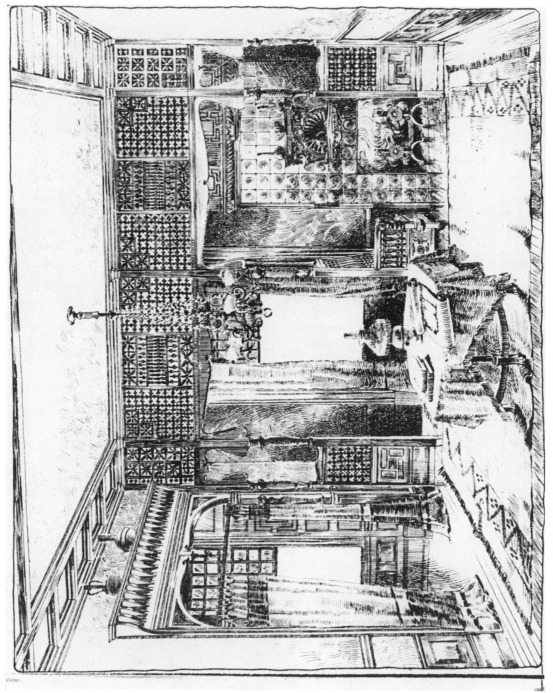

FIGURE 59 The interiors of the Berkshire apartments, by Carl Pfeiffer, were elaborated with wood carving, paneling, and turned work. Many other apartment houses left interior decoration up to the tenants. (*American Architect and Building News* 14 [August 4, 1883]: pl. 397)

broad bay window differentiated the parlor from the other rooms. Elaborate turned wood spindles created a screen demarcating the boundaries of the seating nooks. Wood moldings marked off a pattern of square panels around the edge of the parlor ceiling, from which a chandelier hung above a center table (figs. 59, 60, 61). The apartment's corner bedroom had a top-heavy wood overmantel on which to display favorite ceramic pieces. Even the bathtub was lidded and encased in paneled and carved wood. But the Berkshire was unusual in its development of interior decor. Professional journals focused more on elevations and plans, and advertisers cared more that renters knew about fresh air and light. The many publications describing apartment houses in the 1880s tended to reveal few details of interior unit decoration.

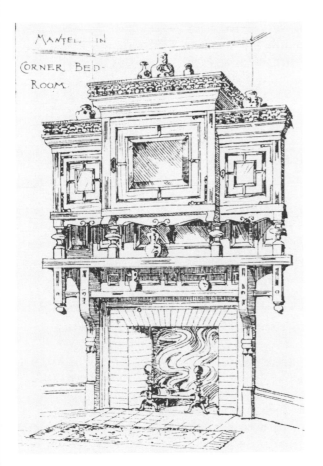

FIGURE 60 The mantel in a corner bedroom in the Berkshire. (*American Architect and Building News* 14 [August 4, 1883]: pl. 397)

FIGURE 61 A bathroom in the Berkshire. (*American Architect and Building News* 14 [August 4, 1883]: pl. 397)

Duplex Apartments

Apartments on two floors, called duplexes by writers of the period, and even on three floors, called triplexes, offered a direct, if expensive, solution to separating a home into zones of activity. Public and private could be separated by placing bedrooms on a different level from reception rooms. Two levels also allowed two ceiling heights, as in private houses, so designers could recapture the higher ceilings of the parlor floors and the lower ceilings of bedrooms.[43]

Duplex designs emerged very early in the development of American apartments. Calvert Vaux suggested in 1857 an apartment whose bedrooms were raised a few steps above the level of the reception rooms for privacy (see fig. 5).[44] Another duplex type where each apartment was "like a two-story house" was Charles W. Clinton's Knickerbocker, built in 1882 at Twenty-eighth Street and Fifth Avenue (fig. 62). Clinton emphasized the spatial image of a private-house interior by designing the whole building with alternating high-ceilinged and low-ceilinged floors—high for parlor, library, dining room, kitchen, and pantry; low for bedrooms. Staircases connected upper and lower levels, inserting a private vertical circulation system in the unit that duplicated the public circulation serving building-wide needs. Critics argued about wasted space, while designers and tenants focused on the staircase as a decorative feature, one which again reinforced similarities with private houses.[45]

A staggered duplex design gave some of the units of the Central Park Apartments front rooms with fifteen-foot ceilings and rear rooms with ten-foot ceilings. The street facade of the building thus had two floors for every three floors facing the rear court. A diagrammatic section for this type in Tuthill's *City Residence* (fig. 63) shows how the resulting low-ceilinged bedroom spaces would be either dropped below, or raised a few steps above, the reception rooms. Tuthill cautioned designers that such a scheme was wise only on an interior lot, since the staggered window patterns on the exterior that resulted from split floor levels could not be handled aesthetically. The architects solved that problem by having their lower-ceilinged floors face onto a private court.

Duplex schemes such as these were experiments to preserve both the room proportions and the functional zoning found in middle-class private houses. Architects tried varying designs, from the double-height parlor with two floors of single-height rooms, to whole buildings of alternating high and low floors, to staggered split-level plans. But these solutions obviously took up more space than a one-floor family apartment and were usually suitable only for upper-income tenants. Charles Israels stated in 1901 that duplexes were "an interesting experiment" but not a successful one, because they "neutralized one of the principal advantages claimed by the apartment dweller, namely economy in housekeeping arrangement and service due to dwelling entirely upon one level." The great majority of designers and tenants of nonluxury buildings apparently agreed, and relatively few moderate-rent duplexes were actually constructed.[46]

As New York's apartment designers became more sophisticated and capable of handling the planning problems of the one-floor home, they still compared

FIGURE 62 Charles W. Clinton designed the Knickerbocker apartments at Fifth Avenue and Twenty-eighth Street so every other floor had balconied social and living spaces, alternating with lower-ceilinged bedroom floors. (Courtesy of the Henry Francis du Pont Winterthur Museum Library, Collection of Printed Books)

themselves with their Parisian counterparts. The architect Paul Marcou explained the interior planning principles of late-nineteenth-century Paris apartments to American readers in an 1893 *Architectural Record* article. He broke the French plan down into three parts according to their importance. The most important zone of the household to French residents was that part reserved for the heads of household and their family, and within that zone, the wife's bedroom was of paramount interest. Then came rooms for the formal reception of visitors; last were the service areas. For Parisian families, intimate friends and their relations to the mistress of the household provided the primary motivation for planning decisions in regard to room location, use, and adjacency.[47]

In contrast, when American designers listed apartment rooms in order of importance, they always put reception rooms first. American families desired to present themselves to visitors in a formal space that would guarantee the "correct" assessment of family status and respectability. Comparisons with Parisian planning in the 1890s, much as in the 1860s, only served to convince American readers that Parisian plans could not just be borrowed: successful apartment architecture had to correspond to local culture.

In this generation of the 1880s a new, large version of the apartment house had been launched for an upper-middle-class clientele. The outward appearance of large apartment buildings was managed in a variety of eclectic styles, a diversity that would continue on into the twentieth century. Larger budgets allowed more rooms in an apartment, and the experience of architects and tenants prompted better room planning. Sustained concern for good light and healthy air influenced courtyard planning, placement of windows, and the location of kitchens. Larger lots allowed designers more latitude in achieving effective room adjacencies and more adequate light and air, but the sheer size of the grand apartment house caused a new problem.

The height of these new apartment houses was striking to contemporary viewers. A period drawing of the Osborne shows it "in perspective" soaring upward, the lines of its parallel side walls seeming to converge (fig. 64). But critics of urban development recognized that the taller the building the more it blocked off the sunlight from neighboring structures, and this perceived threat to health led them to press for height limits. In 1883, a committee produced a report that called for an immediate halt on high apartment houses. They recorded that the Buildings Department had granted permits for constructing 103 new apartment houses over 80 feet tall in the previous two years. Eleven of these were over 140 feet, and one had even been proposed with a cornice height of 182 feet and embellished further by a 40-foot-high cupola.[48]

Not only did these heights cut off light and air from neighboring residential structures, but their height also exceeded the firefighting capabilities of period equipment. A fire that demolished the St. George Apartments on Seventeenth Street in 1884 reinforced the city's resolve to limit the heights of apartment houses. The St. George was a "fireproof" seven-story (eight stories in the rear), fourteen-unit building whose apartments rented for up to $1,800 a year. But its stone front and marble-columned entrance concealed wood construction be-

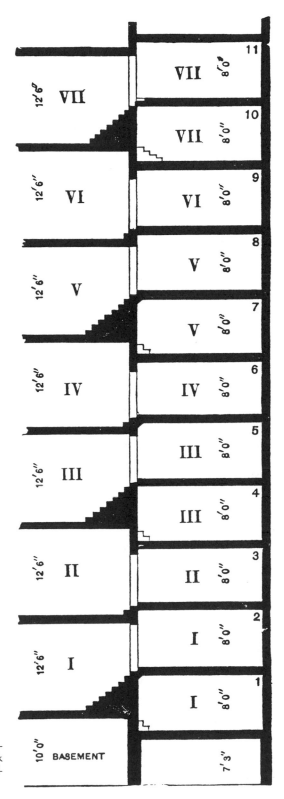

FIGURE 63 Section through a split-level duplex apartment, like those in the Central Park Apartments. (William B. Tuthill, *The City Residence: Its Design and Construction* [1890])

FIGURE 64 Ten- to twelve-story apartment buildings of the early 1880s like the Osborne at 205 West Fifty-seventh Street, by James Ware, caused legislators to push for height limitations, fearing that tall buildings would cut off the city's light and air. (Illustration by Harry Fenn, in Everett N. Blanke, "The Cliff Dwellers of New York," *Cosmopolitan* 15 [July 1893]: 361)

neath, which easily caught fire.[49] The vulnerable character of even expensive apartment houses brought home the dangers of unrestricted building to the middle class.

The grand heights for apartment houses were curtailed by a new law passed in 1885, limiting them in relation to the width of the street they faced onto. With the upward thrust of apartment houses momentarily halted, the next decades saw a consolidation of the apartment's strengths, as well as ever-increasing numbers of new apartment units. The Boston-based *American Architect and Building News* reported that as apartment houses were falling out of favor in other American cities, New Yorkers "clung to their flats" because private houses in suburban places were so hard to get to.[50] The rising middle class in Boston, Chicago, and Baltimore selected private houses in streetcar suburbs, but New Yorkers had built themselves too large a city and too few routes of escape.

6 THE MODERN APARTMENT HOUSE

New York grew not just in population but in area too at the turn of the century. Restructuring the city as Greater New York consolidated the surrounding towns in the boroughs of Brooklyn, Queens, and Staten Island, combined them with the territories of the Bronx and Manhattan, and produced, in 1898, the geographic size of the New York City we have today. By 1910 the population of Manhattan had reached 2,331,542, an increase of nearly a million since 1890. Both industrial wage earners and white-collar workers expanded in numbers from 1880 to 1910, so that by the end of the first decade there were 550,000 industrial workers and nearly 300,000 white-collar workers, a growing apartment-house tenancy.[1] Although this enlarged city afforded home seekers plenty of room for the expansion of residential neighborhoods, Manhattan itself remained the apartment-house capital. In 1910 census workers found that dwellings in the rest of the country contained an average of 5.2 people, but in Manhattan (where each apartment house counted as one dwelling) there were 30.9 people per dwelling. In 1876, at the beginning of French-flat development, one observer had estimated that there were 200 apartment houses in the city; by 1910 there were an estimated 10,000.[2]

In the greatly expanded New York City of the first decade of the twentieth century, the apartment as a building type fulfilled the hopes of its early apologists. The period of the 1890s and the first decade of the twentieth century drew the "archaic" period in apartment design to a close as it produced apartment houses that performed in ways that still make sense. Apartment houses now came in every size and very many architectural styles. The modern apartment as a building type diversified to accommodate the needs of varied family sizes, budgets, tastes, and styles of life. This variety and choice of accommodations occurred in part because of sheer numbers, the hundreds of new apartment houses built in a variety of neighborhoods. But variety was also a feature of individual buildings where apartments of many different sizes were offered in a single house.

Apartments of this era were the first modern apartment houses—not because they looked like modernist architecture, but because of the way they performed. They were spatially organized around notions of function still current in the late twentieth century, they depended on an assumption of technological aids replacing servants' labor, they celebrated convenience, and they both shifted and clarified the place of privacy as a centerpiece of homelife. Apartment houses had opened up a view of efficient, modern living that appealed to many, and the apartment itself was recognized as enabling this particular rationalized modernity to come into being.

The Interior Plan Matures

By about 1905, writers on middle-class-apartment design could say "it goes without saying" that the proper way to lay out a family apartment unit was with functionally differentiated social, sleeping, and service zones. Room groupings in the first and second generations of apartment design proceeded according to rules based in part on meanings assigned to family relations rather than on clearly utilitarian function. But the turn-of-the-century architect used rules of adjacency derived from function whenever an apartment had enough rooms to raise the problem of how to group them. These functional zones should be understood as ideals for designers. Only if budgets and sites were generous could most or all of their principles of room grouping be realized. But aiming at such ideals helped even lesser designers of lower-budget buildings achieve some clarity and convenience in planning.

The small flats of the 1870s continued as a type well on into the next two decades and have specific organizational problems of their own. While developers with ample resources might build very large apartment buildings, smaller developers continued to produce walk-up flat buildings for a less-moneyed clientele. Looking at the city's growth in 1892, the architect Phillip Hubert feared that developers were packing the streets with five-story, two-family-per-floor, twenty-five-foot-wide French flats. Such was their density that Hubert associated them with the close packing of tenements and suggested that these better-class buildings would themselves degenerate into tenements. He called for legislation to limit their proliferation.[3]

The interior arrangements of these small flat buildings are preserved in William Tuthill's *The City Residence* of 1890, in which he gave a variety of plans for small and large city dwellings. An idea for a one-unit-per-floor middle-class apartment plan (fig. 65) shows the dimensions of a modest flat and some of the conflict between grouping bedrooms, separating them from reception spaces, and getting adequate fresh air circulation.[4] Tuthill's flat was on a narrow 25-by-100-foot lot, and thus had to make use of air shafts. The bedrooms were 12 by 14, 10.5 by 12, and 8 by 12 feet. While they are grouped together, they are all ventilated on these air shafts, creating "sleeping rooms, the windows of which are in such close proximity that every act and every sound may be seen or heard by strangers." This was a problem that contemporaries identified as "subversive of common morals and decency." His plan also did not succeed in separating bedrooms from reception rooms, since the dining room at the rear could be reached only by an internal corridor that passed all the bedrooms.[5]

In an alternative plan for the same lot (fig. 66), Tuthill showed the social rooms grouped at the front. The parlor was 15 feet square; the dining room, 12 by 14 feet; and the library, 11.5 by 7.5 feet. All bedrooms were grouped at the rear, two of which looked out into the better light and air of the yard; in this variant only one of the bedrooms had to make do with an air shaft. This placement also guaranteed the complete separation of bedrooms from dining room, parlor, and library. To achieve this success, however, Tuthill sacrificed some of the kitchen requirements.

Tuthill's second apartment plan shows how hard it was to plan the service core in a narrow 25-by-100-foot building. When public rooms were grouped facing the street and bedrooms grouped facing the rear, the center, always the darkest and least well ventilated, had to take the rest. The requirements of the service zone were complicated for a small flat building, since they included a work-place—the kitchen and pantry—a place for the servant, contiguity to the dining room, and good ventilation. It is no surprise to find that architects were unable to fulfill all these needs all the time. Tuthill grouped the 8-by-12-foot kitchen with the dining room and a little service pantry. The 7.3-by-10-foot servant's room across the hall from the kitchen was not too far distant for convenience. Tuthill's main problem, as he admitted, was the poor ventilation of the kitchen, which looked out onto an air shaft. Kitchen odors traveled up and down those air shafts so that neighbors always knew the family menu.

A scheme for a two-apartment-per-floor, 50-foot-wide apartment building by Tuthill (fig. 67) had a very successful service room grouping at the rear of the apartment. Dining room, kitchen, and servant's room clustered at the back, giving both dining room and kitchen a free flow of air and perhaps a view. But this advantage could be achieved only by pulling the dining room away from its rightful companions, the parlor and library. Trade-offs like this were common in most of the moderate-cost buildings from the 1880s on, and sometimes their resolution lay in tenants' accepting the fact that they could not have all they wanted.

Given generous sites and budgets architects could come close to meeting all the requirements of a clarified, utilitarian spatial zoning. A good example of a rather complete resolution of room-planning problems is Israels and Harder's design for a seven-story corner building at 78 Irving Place (figs. 68, 69), completed by 1901 and still standing. With only one apartment per floor and a corner lot providing excellent light and air, Israels and Harder had fewer problems than many architects. Visitors entered the apartment from a stair and elevator landing, which gave a choice of vertical circulation paths, into the front hall, which widened toward the reception rooms into a little foyer. From this point guests could enter the parlor and adjoining music room. From the parlor a

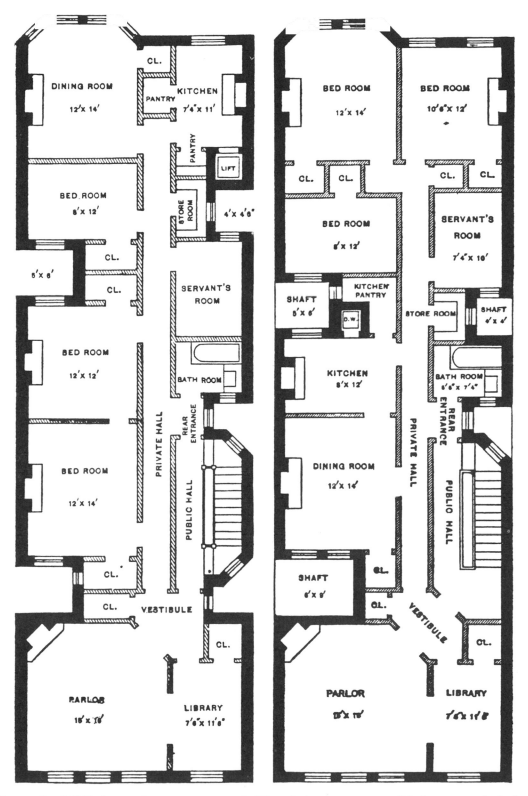

FIGURE 65 *(left)* Designers of narrow apartment buildings had to locate party-wall bedrooms on air shafts, which transmitted intimate sounds. In Tuthill's 25-foot-wide apartment-house plan, the kitchen and dining room are grouped at the rear, the bedrooms grouped in the center on light courts. (William B. Tuthill, *The City Residence: Its Design and Construction* [1890]: p. 39)

FIGURE 66 *(right)* The narrow flat could have party-wall dining room and kitchen, but at the sacrifice of good ventilation. (William B. Tuthill, *The City Residence: Its Design and Construction* [1890]: p. 39)

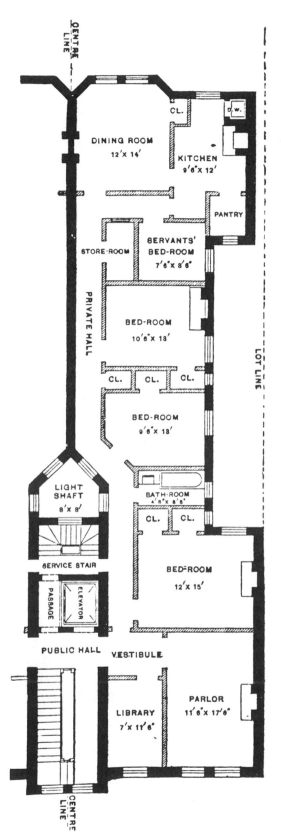

CENTRE LINE

DINING ROOM
12' x 14'

CL.

D. W.

KITCHEN
9'6" x 12'

PANTRY

STORE-ROOM

SERVANTS' BED-ROOM
7'6" x 8'6"

PRIVATE HALL

BED-ROOM
10'6" x 18'

CL. CL. CL.

LOT LINE

BED-ROOM
9'6" x 18'

LIGHT SHAFT
8' x 8'

BATH-ROOM
4'8" x 8'8"

CL. CL.

SERVICE STAIR

PASSAGE ELEVATOR

BED-ROOM
12' x 15'

PUBLIC HALL   VESTIBULE

LIBRARY
7' x 11'6"

PARLOR
11'6" x 17'6"

CENTRE LINE

FIGURE 67 A long hallway makes for a journey between parlor at the front and dining room at the rear in Tuthill's 50-foot-wide apartment house with two units on each floor. (William B. Tuthill, *The City Residence: Its Design and Construction* [1890]: p. 41)

FIGURE 68 An apartment house at 78 Irving Place by the architects Israels and Harder makes use of the newly popular classical architectural vocabulary with corner quoins and a prominent cornice. (*Architectural record* 11 [July 1901], p. 494)

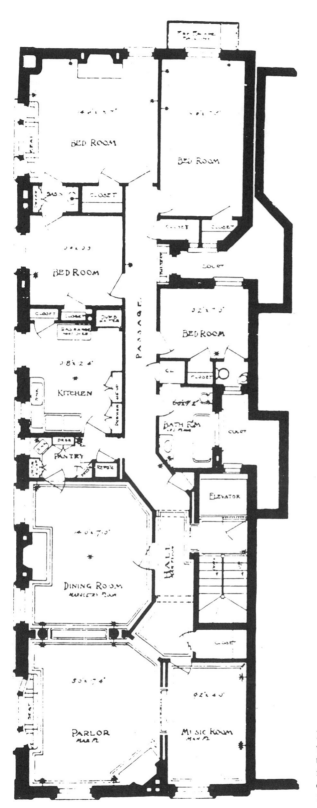

FIGURE 69 At 78 Irving Place visitors
would find all social rooms grouped near
the entrance and all private family bedrooms separated down a passage and buff-
ered by service spaces. (*Architectural Record*
11 [July 1901], p. 495)

wide opening led into a spacious dining room. These three front rooms, all with street views, gave tenants a suite of reception rooms clearly set apart, appropriate for entertaining, and akin to Parisian social spaces arranged en suite.

Critics noted that tenants wanted a handsome entrance hall, parlor, and dining room, even if bedrooms and service rooms were cramped as a result; "landlords and architects have learned to adapt their plans to this preference by making as much show as possible in the rooms in which their tenants receive visitors, even if they have to sacrifice for this purpose the humbler portions of the establishment." In order to help organize this "show" part of the house, a writer for *American Architect and Building News* in 1907 referred readers again to Paris. There a *galerie*, or new type of glamorous vestibule, was used to focus the social rooms, giving access to all of them from a circulation hub. By controlling the size of the social rooms (the author cites a clever plan by M. Sinell, in which the grand salon was only 13 by 16 feet), designers could avoid eating into the family and service parts of the unit.[6] Americans continued to refer to Paris in the layout of the social rooms of the house, as they had since the 1870s, to help them achieve the most successful reception zone.

Twentieth-century designers rationalized the bedrooms as a set of sleeping spaces, all for the same function. During the formative years of apartment planning, especially in the more expensive buildings, theory suggested that bedrooms for children should be located according to different rules from those used for the master/mistress chamber or for servants' rooms. After the turn of the century, it became unusual to see a principal bedroom separated from the other bedrooms of the apartment except for the servants' rooms. At Israels and Harder's Irving Place apartment building, family members could turn away from the reception rooms near the entrance and follow an angled hall to the family bedrooms, which were all grouped together, separated as much as possible at the opposite end of the apartment from the reception rooms. Each bedroom had its own door from a private hall, with good ventilation available to all from the street or end walls of the building. Such a functional grouping recalls Vaux's recommendation from decades earlier that all the bedrooms should be kept together to create a quiet zone.

Grouped in the center of the plan for 78 Irving Place was the service zone: the kitchen, pantry, bathroom, and servant's room (not so labeled on the plan, but properly located for a servant); the servant's is the only bedroom ventilated from a light court. The kitchen had windows onto the street and was linked to the dining room through a pantry, a favored arrangement that made serving meals more efficient. Of all the requirements of "good" family-unit planning that architects aimed to fulfill, only the principle of separate circulation for servants does not come into play at 78 Irving Place. Complete service-zone separation was expensive; perhaps only tenants who could afford more than one servant could afford the extra space required.

The way to design servants' rooms continued to be a point of discussion for

architects of expensive buildings. On this problem, they found the French precedent of little help. A critic in *American Architect and Building News* in 1907 remarked that in both France and America it was usual to herd servants together
in mansard rooms, as was done at the Dakota. This was inhuman, he asserted:
the maids and footmen were neither separated nor supervised, and since "there
is neither privacy nor protection for the innocent, the morals of all the members
of the little community are at the mercy of the worst among them." One solution,
this author suggested, to the worst evils of crowding servants together was to give
the men a separate floor from the women, both in the mansard. But in modern
American apartment houses where elevators were the rule, this writer noted, it
was foolish to squander top floor space for servants, since it was desirable for
tenants. Instead, the best American apartment houses of the first decade had at
least one servant's room within the apartment, although other rooms for additional servants might still be available in other parts of the building as they had
been in the large buildings of the 1880s.[7]

A "private" (which meant cooperative) apartment house designed in 1911 by
William Boring on Sixtieth Street and Park Avenue provided a plan (figs. 70, 71)
that integrated a complete service suite with all the other family zones seen at 78
Irving Place. In the plan the public, private, and service zones were worked out
skillfully to allow each zone to perform at its most effective level. The public,
entertainment zone included an entrance foyer, closets, and spacious drawing
room and library, contiguous to the dining room. Clearly separated from the
zone of publicity, the private realm of bedrooms and bathrooms had its own
separate corridor circulation. The service zone included three servants' rooms,
their own bath, the kitchen, pantry, and separate service elevator, with a discreet
route to the front door so that servants could admit guests without intruding on
the entertainments or the privacy of their employers. A service zone with its own
circulation was characteristic of first-decade designs for well-to-do tenants. Usually such spaces as the servants' sitting room or sometimes a pantry or the kitchen
itself functioned as part of the circulation path. The Boring building is a good
example of functional interpretations of room groups, which brought New
York's experimental era in apartment building to its culmination.[8] Such a functional interpretation is still used in residential design today.

While architects struggled to achieve comfortably ordered spaces in middle-
class units, they were of necessity working for anonymous clients and idealized
family forms. The arrangement of interior space for actual use depended upon
specific tenants' needs and economic ability. Tenants who respected the ideal
standards of refined housekeeping and entertaining still could live only in rental
spaces they could afford, and real life economies often compromised planning
abstractions.

The ways that rooms were used are almost impossible to discover from architectural plans, although, of course, architects always label their dwelling plans
with intended use names. The historian David Handlin has suggested that two

FIGURE 70 A cooperative or "private" apartment in the popular classical style by architect William Boring at 520 Park Avenue, corner of Sixtieth Street. (*American Architect* 100 [November 29, 1911], pl. 175)

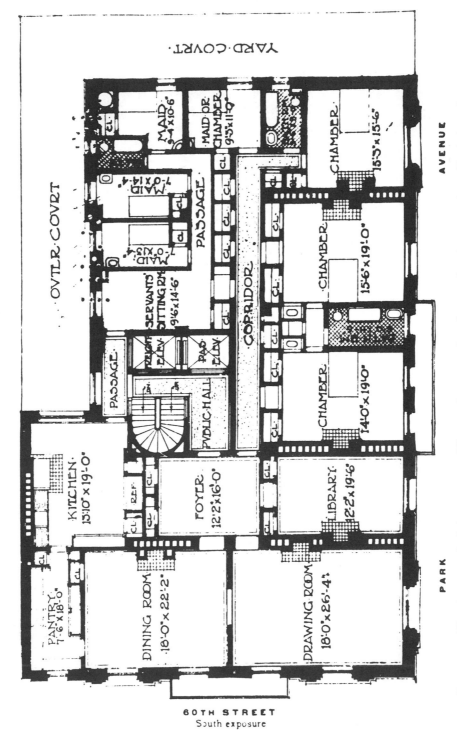

FIGURE 71 The plan at 520 Park Avenue exemplifies complete separation of servants' work space and provides independent circulation systems for family and servants. (*American Architect* 100 [November 29, 1911], pl. 175)

ideas were at work in planning the rooms of later-nineteenth-century houses. People wanted rooms with specific identities. "Just as the division of labor separated the contemporary economy from its predecessor, so the identification and parcelling out of specific household functions distinguished the modern from the primitive home." Later-nineteenth-century house plans with clear-cut room designations and different room shapes and equipment satisfied the desire for specificity. At the same time, Handlin believes that builders' guides of the period promoted room plans that were larger than their designated function and furniture required.[9] Such rooms were ready to accept additional unpredicted functions in their extra space.

Of course before apartments, people with cramped domestic quarters and large families had to make adaptations in room use. A well-known example is Catharine Beecher's 1841 design for a house whose parlor turns into a bedroom. Upon opening imitation "parlor doors" one finds not another parlor but a bed in a closet. In the same spirit of spatial economy, the *Appleton's Home Books* asserted that "in a small house, . . . bedrooms are more than places to sleep in; they are dressing-rooms, private sitting-rooms, sewing rooms, and nurseries." In a small house it was impossible to give each function in this list its own specific room. But one room could accommodate all these functions, if that room were designed with only one door. *Appleton's* stressed the importance of making each room in a house accessible from a passage.[10] Isolating a room from others guaranteed its privacy and uninterrupted quiet, which in turn allowed other potential uses.

While a modern nineteenth-century family would find specificity in room use a mark of cultural progress, in small dwelling spaces it was too expensive. Highly specific circulation spaces, for example, such as separate paths for servants and for family, cost too much; spatial luxury was a mark of conspicuous consumption reserved for wealthy house owners or the tenants of huge apartments. Smaller, middle-class apartments required the kinds of economy in spatial expenditure, overlapping in uses of space, that were more in keeping with Handlin's second notion of the room with extra uses.

Tenements, the least expensive multiple-dwelling units, had the greatest need for and a history of shared room uses. The "living room" was indeed an all-purpose family space in which cooking and eating, leisure and work activities, and even sleeping—by boarders or extra family members—took place. Designs for model tenements often show all the other rooms marked "bedroom" except for that living room. Of course, many of the activities that higher-income tenants would have incorporated into the dwelling unit, the poor carried on in public shared spaces. Public reading rooms, bathtub rooms, courtyard and rooftop laundry and recreation spaces compensated in a small way for the less-than-generous spatial allocations of tenement units.

In order to understand how an actual apartment worked for real clients, one would have to identify the uses that rooms served under the demands of daily life. Fortunately two published accounts of the period give us a glimpse of actual room use. Middle-class expectations for the use of space in small apartments sometimes clashed with the actual rooms provided, as we can see from an 1890 *Harper's Weekly* article.[11] When the journalist Christine Herrick, her husband, one baby, a nurse, and a cook came to live in New York, the apartment they rented was a typical single-lot-sized French-flat building. It had three reception rooms—a parlor, a sitting room or library, and a dining room. For services, it had a small kitchen and a maid's room. The private family area comprised two bedrooms. From Herrick's description, the plan of the unit was very close to the small flat plans published by Tuthill (fig. 66).

Then the Herricks moved in: the sitting room was given to the baby and its nurse for sleeping and nursery functions. The baby was put in a hammock because its crib was too big for the space. The maid's room, adjoining the kitchen, had to become a kitchen storage room since the kitchen was so small. The cook, who would have slept in the maid's room, had to use one of the bedrooms, which they had planned to use for guests. The parlor, meanwhile, had to serve as "best" room and at the same time a family room. It was impossible to keep a tidy parlor for entertaining, as Mrs. Herrick had expected to do, when that room was constantly in use.

These apartment dwellers seem to have come to their apartment expecting the rooms to perform as their designated names indicated. Finding that the room called "kitchen" was only big enough to service half the functions of a real kitchen came as a shock. Neither the tenants nor the management of the building had exploited the potential of apartment houses to accommodate displaced housework. The Herricks' habit of seeing all the work of the household as internal to their own private space led to conflicts over the use of that space.

The family stayed in their apartment for eighteen months but found it a struggle to maintain a respectable social image. Mrs. Herrick reported bearing in mind "that amusing account of a flat where every piece of furniture was something else than it pretended to be." She referred to the ingenious pieces of furniture marketed in the nineteenth century such as beds that folded up into desks or pianos during the day, or sewing machines that disappeared into tables. But they longed to go "upstairs to bed and downstairs to breakfast," so they finally moved back into a house where furniture did not have to do double duty and rooms were available to be used for the purposes originally intended.[12]

Another example of how tenants changed room uses to adapt their apartments to their own requirements was recorded in a 1902 *House Beautiful* article. Two young women shared a four-room apartment with rooms that they recognized as intended to be a kitchen, a dining room, a sitting room, and a bedroom. Their kitchen did double duty as a dining room; their dining room, because it had two large windows, became a painting studio for one of them; their sitting room was furnished with a cot so it could also become the guest bedroom; and the two women shared the remaining bedroom. The tenants reported this shifting of uses without surprise: they seemed to understand that apartments could be no more than generalized spaces, and to expect that they would have to adapt those spaces to their actual needs. That they could do this without much discomfort testifies to the flexibility of both the apartment and the tenants.[13]

An interesting progression can be traced in room uses from the houses of the early nineteenth century with their relatively undifferentiated rooms, to rooms differentiated for specific purposes with specialized plan shapes and equipment on the model of factory specialization of function, back to the rooms in smaller apartments whose function had again to be flexible to accommodate several uses in one space. Apartment designers did not report keeping this flexibility in mind, but tenants had to. Apartments designed for "average" tenants had to suit, in reality, tenants with very specific needs. The average tenants found themselves to be architects after the fact, designing their rooms to fit the uses they themselves determined. The family room, the all-purpose room, the eat-in kitchen, the living–dining room—these combined-function rooms were the results of tenants imposing their needs on generic spaces. Multipurpose living–dining rooms, later celebrated as "modern" in the one-floor suburban houses of the post–World War II era, reach back to the ad hoc sharing of functions in one-floor apartments.

Diversity of Rents

Throughout the 1870s, would-be tenants had complained that the new apartment houses were too expensive for members of the middle class with modest incomes and that apartments were too much the same in size, not accommodating the wide variations found in households. Some buildings in the 1870s had been erected with units for single people, and during the 1880s large-scale luxury apartment houses with larger family units had been added to the repertoire of middle-class multiple dwellings. In the 1890s spacious, if not tall, elevator houses and small French-flat walk-ups were going up at the same time. Increasingly apartments offered a greater range of sizes and costs, appealing to the more varied needs and incomes of city dwellers who chose them as home.

Stratification of incomes within the middle class was met by equally varied strata of apartment houses, with rents ranging in 1885 from about $30 a month in buildings just above tenement level, to $300 a month in lavish ones. Monthly rather than yearly rents were usually advertised for apartments at the low end of the rental spectrum and sometimes for those in more luxurious apartment houses too. Annual rents were the usual amounts listed for the best-quality apartment houses and for others whose owners wanted to discourage turnover in tenants. Near Stuyvesant Square on Seventeenth Street, one could rent a "23-foot front, second flat; seven rooms and a bath" for $55 a month. In the same street, eight and nine rooms were advertised for $30 to $50 a month. For a fancier apartment, one could try the "Sutherland, Madison Ave. corner 63d St.—suites from $90 to $150 per month; fashionable location; steam heat; elevator," while a furnished flat in the Van Corlear on Seventh Avenue between Fifty-fifth and Fifty-sixth streets was going for $200 a month. During that year, carpenters were striking for a pay raise, demanding to get $3.50 for a ten-hour day ($21 for a six-day week). Judged by the guideline of paying one-fourth of one's income in rent, the carpenter could have afforded none of these apartments, but he could have found others away from the more fashionable streets, perhaps of tenement quality, for even lower rents.[14]

A full four-story brownstone house near the Central Park Apartments cost $133 a month in 1885, while a ten-room unit, smaller than the house, in the Central Park Apartments rented for $150. In the same year a house in Harlem rented for $70 to $125 a month, twice as much as a similar-sized apartment in the same neighborhood. Such cost differences suggest major differences in the amount of space available to higher and lower incomes, as well as diverging organizations of space depending on expectations about use. But cost differences also reflect the real estate market's assessment of the value of various neighborhoods and the expectations of tenants about how much rent suited their budgets. By 1890 families might choose an apartment because they found one-floor living more convenient, because nothing else was affordable, because they liked the social homogeneity of an apartment house, because they were attracted by modern technological aids to housekeeping, or because this new form of dwelling seemed culturally progressive, novel, or glamorous.

In 1894 the *Times* summarized the rents available in different parts of Manhattan for dwellings in which one could make a "decent home in a safe neighborhood." The highest rents for this category of modest dwelling were found from Sixth Avenue to Park Avenue, and from Thirty-fourth Street to Fifty-ninth Street, where a three-story house rented for an average of $2,000 a year. West of Sixth and east of Park Avenues, the same size house could be rented for $1,500, and west of Eighth Avenue, for only $1,200. The rents for apartments varied more than those for houses, declining radically if the apartment had no steam heat. In the same midtown area, a flat of seven rooms and a bath with steam heat rented for $45 to $50 a month, while without heat it could be had for only $35.[15]

Rents and house prices at the end of the 1890s showed continuing diversity, an enhanced range of choices in size and location, for home seekers with few means and for those of wealth. The realtor Frank Fisher published a photographically illustrated catalog of houses for sale in 1899, either new or "unoccupied," on the relatively recently built-up streets of the Upper West Side. He listed more than six hundred expensive private houses, which ranged in price from about $25,000 to over $120,000. But for only $800 to $1,100 a year, one could rent older, three-story private houses along Sixty-eighth and Sixty-ninth streets east of Third Avenue. Around the corner on Sixty-eighth and the more commercial Third Avenue, six- and seven-room apartments rented for half as much—$420 a year. At Twenty-third Street and Avenue A, a working-class neighborhood, two- to four-room tenement apartments rented for $9 to $14 a month, or less than $100 a year for the small unit. At the same time a luxurious apartment on Madison Avenue and Eighty-third Street rented for $2,000 per year. Within a single building sometimes a diverse range of rents could be found, as at the Braender on Central Park West and 102d Street, where suites ranged from five to twelve rooms and from $1,000 to $3,500 per year.[16]

The diversity of people living in Manhattan at the turn of the century was analyzed as comprising six classes by E. Idell Zeisloft in *The New Metropolis* of 1899. The first class had inherited wealth, often from both husband's and wife's families and owned several houses (four or five in Newport, R.I., Lenox, Mass., and so on, plus one in New York). They traveled from house to house for the various social seasons with servants and children. The second class was very rich like the first but had only two or three houses.[17]

The third class was the merely prosperous, far below the upper two. It is they who "live in apartments of the highest class, commodious and elegant . . . sometimes of two floors." Professional men in law and medicine prevailed in this set, and the streets in the West Seventies and Eighties were filled with them. Their apartments had ten to twenty rooms and rented for $2,000 to $10,000 a year.[18]

The fourth class made between $5,000 and $10,000 a year and comprised the bulk of the people who lived in apartments that rented from $1,200 to $2,500 a year. Comfortably well off families with fewer servants than the first three classes, they lived within their means with just a cook, a housemaid, a laundress, and a children's nurse. Typical apartments for this class had ten to twelve rooms, which included a drawing room, a library, a den, a dining room, four bedrooms, a kitchen, two servants' rooms, and a bathroom.[19] The "comfortable" people just beneath them in incomes were a subset of this class—professional men, clergy, businessmen, and government officials hoping to rise into the more prosperous regions of the fourth class. The rents for their seven-to-eleven-room apartments ranged from $600 to $1,500 a year. Most of these apartments were in new flat buildings and suffered from one or more dark bedrooms, but some of the best were in old-fashioned converted houses.[20]

In Zeisloft's portrait the people in the fifth class lived in the cheapest French-flat buildings and were always scrimping; the sixth class was the tenement population. Some people, he asserted, made the social distinction among apartment types as follows: tenements were for working people, flats were for one-servant households, and apartments were for those more affluent.[21]

Variety of Tenants and Services

By the first decade of the twentieth century, apartment living incorporated a range of dwelling habits and physical frameworks that enabled many kinds of tenants to find affordable homes. Within this variety, one could find rentals or cooperatives, walkups or buildings with elevator, two rooms or twenty. Two specific types of multiple dwellings seemed notable to contemporaries: bachelor-flat buildings and apartment hotels. Both presupposed tenants with many middle-class values, but not the same values as the "stable" nuclear family, and these tenants, it was felt, deserved built-for-the-purpose apartment houses that had physical and planning characteristics different from those for nuclear families.

Bachelor-flat buildings had been proposed and built since the 1870s, part of the first flurry of interest in middle-class multiple dwellings. Executed bachelor buildings of the first decade are similar in room offerings to the bachelor flats proposed by E. T. Littell in the mid–1870s, but now such buildings were being erected all over town. By the turn of the century, advertisements for bachelor apartments appeared regularly in the newspapers. Some were available in apartment houses with mainly larger family units, and many occupied the upper floors of shops in the busy midtown area.

Bachelors who lived on $5,000 a year or more had splendid choices in the newer bachelor apartment houses built during the 1890s, wrote Zeisloft in *The New Metropolis*. For $600 to $2,500 (depending on size and address) a bachelor could have a three- to five-room flat in a fine building with heat and light included in the rent, and breakfast served in his room. Bachelor girls had less expensive, more "artistic" options. They might choose to live in the apartments at Carnegie Hall, or in other "buildings more or less devoted to artists' studios, for in them there is a greater freedom of life without cares than in any of the places given over generally to family life."[22] The female bachelor entertained friends from the literary, music, and art worlds, in contrast to her sisters, the underpaid working girls, in $1.50-a-week rooms.

Turn-of-the-century bachelor-flat design can be represented as a plan type by the Century, located at 119 West Forty-fifth Street, and in elevation by an executed bachelor-flat building at 22 East Thirty-first Street by Israels and Harder (figs. 72, 73). Seven stories high, markedly taller than its neighbor, a three-floor house, the Israels and Harder building has a stylish array of terra-cotta ornament on the facade and naked side walls. The exterior envelope at 22 East Thirty-first Street could easily contain layouts of the kind used in the Century. Each bachelor unit in the Century had two rooms, a parlor and a bedroom, measuring about 12 by 15 feet and 10 by 12 feet. Each unit also had a full bathroom and closets. Two front units overlooked the street; the two rear ones had a view of the yard.

Planning problems in designing a bachelor unit were reduced to the minimum. Since the flat was to accommodate only one person, privacy and separate circulation were not an issue. The bachelor walked directly into his parlor from the front door, and from there directly into his bedroom, and thence to his bathroom. No separate circulation meant a savings of space, and issues of room adjacency disappeared. The Century's plan bore remarkable similarities to the standard dumbbell tenement plan, because it occupied a 25-by-100-foot lot and included four units on each floor. Like the dumbbell tenement, stairs and plumbing were fitted into the center of each floor along with light wells. The individual unit plan is quite like that in a tenement in the size of rooms, although bachelors had their bathrooms within the unit rather than shared in the public hall. But of course, unlike the tenement plan, the units at the Century were intended for single people, not whole families.[23]

Another turn-of-the-century example of a bachelor-flat building is the Carlyle

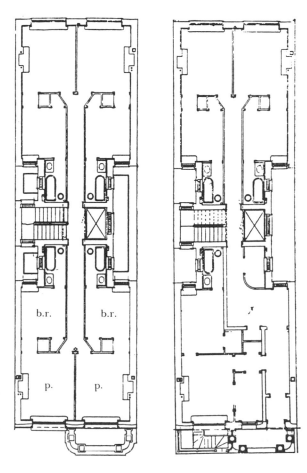

FIGURE 72 Bachelors, living alone, needed only a parlor (p.), a bedroom (b.r.) and a bathroom; all other services and entertaining went on outside the unit. Plan of the Century, a bachelor apartment house at 119 West Forty-fifth Street. (Charles Israels, "New York Apartment Houses," *Architectural Record* 11 [July 1901])

Chambers, by the architects Herts and Tallant at Fifth Avenue and Thirty-eighth Street, with small apartments over a jewelry store on the ground floor.[24] Most of the designers' attention went into making a pleasing shop with a dramatic curved corner window (figs. 74, 75); the apartments in the upper floors had only a parlor, a chamber, and a bath, like the Century. An advertisement for this kind of building from 1904 offered "service of the highest class obtainable. Unfurnished suites, two rooms and bath, open fireplaces, hot water heating, refrigerating plant."[25] The central refrigeration equipment that piped in cooled air to individual refrigerated boxes was a boon to bachelors, who otherwise had no kitchen equipment.

The "apartment hotel," suited to collective living, was especially important to a range of tenants at the turn of the century whom writers identified as less settled than the norm. This group of tenants included travelers, "bohemians" (usually business people without a more permanent home), those who were eager for the bright lights and entertainment of midtown, but also poorer middle-class families who could not afford all the rent and services for full-scale housekeeping.

FIGURE 73 Bachelor apartment house at 22 East Thirty-first Street by Israels and Harder made use of terra-cotta ornament on the facade but had plain side walls. (Charles Israels, "New York Apartment Houses," *Architectural Record* 11 [July 1901])

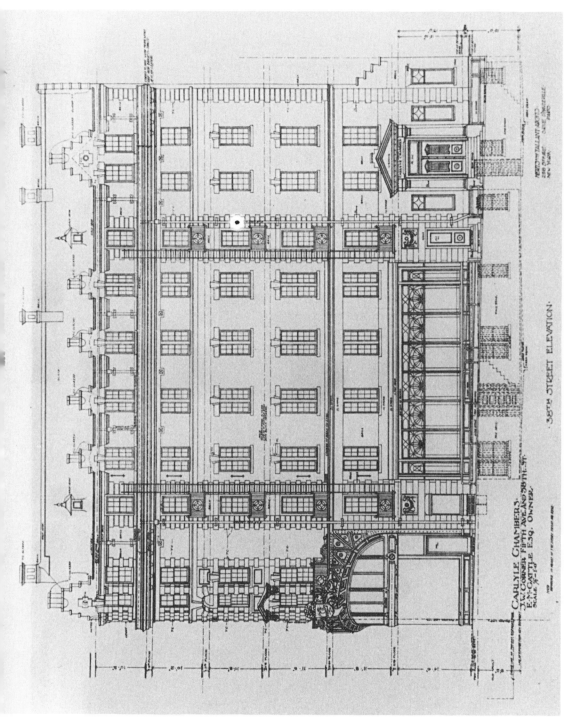

FIGURE 74 The Carlyle Chambers, a bachelor apartment house at Fifth Avenue and Thirty-eighth Street by Herts and Tallant, had a jewelry store on the ground floor. (*American Architect and Building News* 73 [September 21, 1901]: pl. 1343)

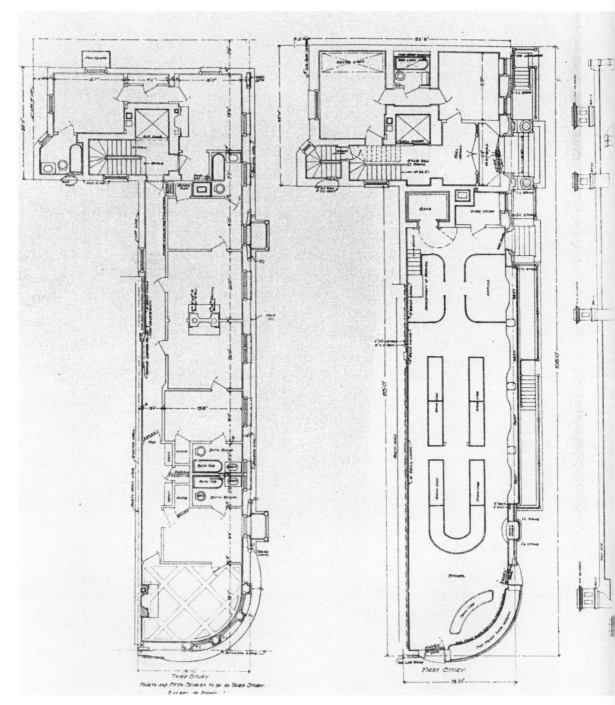

FIGURE 75 Some of the two-room-plus-bath bachelor flat units at the Carlyle Chambers had communicating doors so frien
could share. (*American Architect and Building News* 73 [September 21, 1901]: pl. 1343)

"They take to this life partly because . . . it can be made cheap, and partly because it reduces the trouble of living to a minimum." For tenants like these who depended on a high level of collective services, the apartment hotel became an acceptable and distinct variant of the middle-class apartment house.[26]

In the 1890s when the law limiting apartment-building heights had kept developers from investing in tall multiple dwellings, an unexpected boom occurred in hotel building. The *Real Estate Record and Builders' Guide* offered some reasons: people who lived in the suburbs liked to stay in a hotel after an evening at the theater; the journey uptown by elevated railroad was so lengthy that people with center-city jobs preferred to live in a midtown location; and many who had country homes where they entertained a lot in the summer liked to live in a hotel for the winter, where services were taken care of by management. But the author admitted that the underlying reason why so many developers were erecting buildings called "hotels" was that "apartments" were not a high-yield investment because of the height limit.

Of course there had been many apartment houses before this moment that did have hotel-like services to some degree, and which had been informally called by names like "family hotels." In the formative years of the new building type, apartment-house developers had tried a wide variety of arrangements, from completely self-contained private housekeeping in the Stuyvesant, to laundry services and central cooking at the Haight House. Almost since the beginning of apartment houses in New York there had been a tendency to convert them to hotels (as had happened with the Stevens in the 1870s). In those years the absolute difference between a hotel and an apartment house had never been made clear, and the buildings department itself had allowed hotels to slip back and forth between the categories of public buildings and multiple dwellings.[27]

"Why has the apartment hotel suddenly jumped into such popularity?" a writer in the *Architectural Record* wondered in 1903.[28] The answer lay in the new building law enacted in 1901 that allowed apartment buildings greater height: developers no longer had to falsify the character of a multiple dwelling with a disingenuous name. Now the name "apartment hotel" helped clarify genuine differences between apartment houses and the newer variant. The *Architectural Record* defined this new type to distinguish it from the family apartment building: the apartment hotel was a building that offered more privacy than hotels did in the way of meals and entertainment of personal guests but provided all the services of hotels in cleaning and upkeep so tenants did not need their own servants.

Many apartment hotels going up in New York were located near the center of the city and its amusements, appealing to people who liked to be out on the town night after night. The Gerlach was such a house, in the heart of the mid-town entertainment district (fig. 76). The advertisement accompanying the illustration in *King's Photographic Views of New York* in 1895 stressed this apartment hotel's location with a map and bird's-eye views of surrounding neighborhoods and a list of their attractions.[29]

FIGURE 76 The Gerlach Apartment Hotel in midtown Manhattan, close to the bright lights of the entertainment district. (*King's Photographic Views of New York* [1895]: p. 671)

Opened in 1902, Graves and Duboy's Ansonia (fig. 77), an apartment hotel still standing on Broadway and Seventy-fourth Street, is a good example of the apartment hotel's stylishness. In 1903 the British magazine *Cassier's* described it as an innovative new type and technologically ahead of all the hotels they were familiar with. Its ebullient exterior features corner towerlike shapes with bulbous French roofs, wrought-iron balconies, and a rusticated three-story base. More important, this building put flexibility in the foreground, providing large and small units for full family life or for single people, both with and without house-keeping equipment, serviced either by management or by tenants' own servants.[30]

The plan of the Ansonia is that of a large H; on each floor the public corridor traces the H, and separate apartments open off each side of each arm (fig. 78). Many indentations in the perimeter walls give additional space for windows to the outside. The use of indentations in exterior walls was very common in hotels and office buildings as well as apartment houses of the first decade. *American Architect and Building News* praised the Ansonia for its "substitution of deep recesses in the fronts for a central courtyard. [It] presents the obvious advantage that the rooms in the middle of the building look out on the street, instead of into an enclosed courtyard, and are much pleasanter and better aired in consequence."[31] At the Ansonia, additional air shafts are scattered throughout the body of the building, necessary because the apartment house is so large that, for all its indentations, many rooms still lack exposure to the outdoors.

Planned for 1,200 to 1,400 tenants, the building had 340 suites of rooms, but only 120 of them had kitchens. The full housekeeping apartments included a parlor and adjunct reception rooms, family chambers, rooms for the family's own servants, and the appropriate set of kitchen, pantries, and service entrances and lifts. These apartments were fully equipped with a gas or electric kitchen range, porcelain washtubs, and pantries with refrigerating compartments "with appliances for freezing artificial ice upon the spot." Miles of pipes, ducts, and lines wove through the Ansonia to keep these units supplied with heat, light, and power.

The other nonhousekeeping suites at the Ansonia were of varying sizes from "bachelor" size with only a parlor, chamber, and bathroom, to units with four or five rooms but still lacking kitchens, dining rooms, or servants' rooms. A 1907 observer reported in *American Architect and Building News* that in France people did not rent nonhousekeeping apartments or engage in the permanent living in hotels that American well-to-do families sometimes preferred. To the astonishment of the French, these Americans did no cooking at all but ate in restaurants all the time, "employing their servants only as housemaids or footmen in non-housekeeping apartments, or as lady's-maids or valets in hotels."[32] From the plans of the Ansonia's nonhousekeeping apartments one surmises that the lack of servants' rooms meant that renters of these units preferred to use building-hired staff to do the work that privately hired servants performed elsewhere.

Some suites at the Ansonia even had an optional extra room that could be

FIGURE 77 The Ansonia, an apartment hotel at Broadway and Seventy-fourth Street by Graves and Duboy, had suites for housekeeping and kitchenless apartments for those who would use the service staff of the building instead of their own servants. (*American Architect and Building News* 91 [January 5, 1907]: 7)

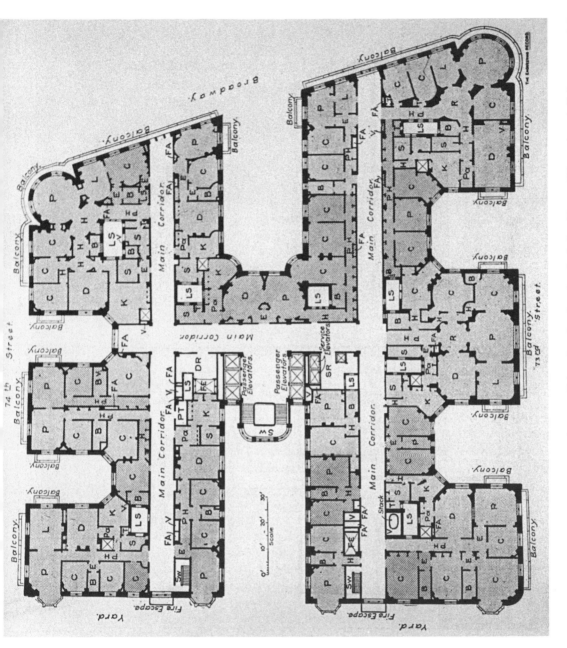

FIGURE 78 Plan of the Ansonia: P = parlor, D = dining, C = chamber, B = bath, L = library, PH = private hall, S = servant, LS = light shaft, K = kitchen, Pa = pantry. Apartments were offered at all sizes. (*American Architect and Building News* 91 [January 5, 1907]: 7)

197

rented to expand a small unit's space. Such a room had two means of access: one from an adjoining suite; the other from the public hall. The flexibility to allow tenants the option of changing sizes of apartments at the Ansonia was commended by *American Architect and Building News*, which reported that it had long been seen as essential in hotels to allow this choice, and now it was being offered in apartment houses.[33]

This apartment hotel also provided great numbers of public conveniences for its tenants: the basement had a fully staffed laundry with steam clothes dryers, an automobile garage, and a Turkish bath; the lobby had a bank, bookstall, cigar shop, telegraph office, doctor, and dentist. The building had a staff of cooks who prepared meals to be served in a seventeenth-floor conservatory dining room or in the private suites. Apartment hotels like the Ansonia attracted hundreds of families who found the hotel-provided services more economical than keeping their own servants and a full household's worth of rooms. After four decades of experience with multiple dwellings, living with many shops, services, and hotel facilities no longer seemed a threat but a boon to the middle class.

Apartment hotels represented a variant from the standard middle-class family planning theme. Here, unit planning was based on the same principles of room distribution and privacy seen in a typical middle-class apartment house, but the service, cooking, and dining rooms could be omitted from private space. Service and entertainment functions could be taken care of by the building management and the building-wide plan, rather than in individual units. As tenements had drawn the line between public and private space to exclude bath and toilet facilities from the private, now bachelor flats and apartment hotels redrew that line to exclude kitchen, dining, and socializing spaces from the private, when desired.[34]

For all its flexibility and convenience an apartment hotel could never be a home, lamented a wary writer for the *Architectural Record*, because it disrupted the traditional patterns of married family life. "It [the apartment hotel] could not have become as popular as it is now without the acquiescence of large numbers of women; and it is devoutly to be hoped that many more women will not be foolish enough to follow this example, thereby sacrificing the dignity of their own lives and their effective influence over their husbands and children."[35]

The observers of housing in the New York of the 1860s had found fault with hotel and boardinghouse life, especially for women. The publicity of shared housing was supposed to expose women to temptation and flirtation on the one hand and deprive them of housekeeping work, leaving them with nothing to do, on the other. Now, at the beginning of the twentieth century, another variant of the same problem for women was identified. "Foreign critics have frequently noticed and deplored the tendency which American women have shown to consider the care of the household a burden, and to believe that outside occupations, whatever they be—industrial, charitable, social or intellectual—are more interesting and praiseworthy than the domestic ones."[36] In the 1860s women would have had nothing to do if deprived of housework; in 1900 they had too much to do and should return to housework. Both these assessments of women's activities arose from concerns over the effects of multiple dwellings on traditional notions of "home" and women's role in it.

As the idealization of a secluded private house gave way to the realities of urban life, it was inescapable that women would want more latitude in their lives than that allowed by the domestic sphere alone. The collective home may have acted to facilitate women's enjoyment of the city, since apartment houses tended to be located on streets convenient to public transportation. Streetcars, elevated trains in the 1870s, and subways by the early twentieth century accompanied apartment houses as essential features of New York's real estate development. Thus women tenants without private carriages easily traveled to shop at McCreery's or Lord and Taylor's, to attend operas or lectures, and to eat in restaurants. Apartment hotels and all grades of other apartment houses brought women together in the daily flux of housekeeping, food shopping, child care, excursions, and visiting. Men complained that the New York women of 1900 wanted to be anywhere but waiting for their husbands patiently by the fireside.[37] Insofar as apartment houses and apartment hotels allowed women to meet each other and to have access to the city, they helped break down the notion of a private home as women's only proper sphere.

The Triumph of Convenience

Apartments, always understood as affording ease of housekeeping, remained within a developing culture of convenience. Sarah Gilman Young had stressed the desirability of single-floor apartments for ease of housekeeping when she reported on Parisian flats in the 1870s and 1880s. In her view women's health would be saved by simplifying housework. The "chief cause of the rapid growth of the apartment among us," wrote a skeptical *Scribner's* author in 1895, was the difficulty of obtaining servants and of doing housework; women willingly sacrificed identity and privacy, attributed to individual houses, in order to "escape from their trammels" in the ease of apartment life.[38]

Expanding on the thrust of this argument in 1890, the Nationalist theoretician John Pickering Putnam asserted that women's work outside the home was badly needed, both in public and for the health of the state. He urged that women's talent not be thrown away on "household drudgery" but be recaptured and used in professions such as architecture. To aid in this process by freeing women's time, he recommended apartment houses with their ease of housekeeping.[39]

Putnam developed his argument in favor of apartments by analyzing the waste engendered by large numbers of private houses and contrasting that to the economies of apartment living. He assessed the annual running expenses of an apartment building as compared with the same number of family units built as private houses: "Eighty independent Irish cooks give way to a professional chef and half-a-dozen attachés. The wages and maintenance of the 80 cooks would amount to an annual sum of not less than $40,000," but one cook and assistants could be had for $10,000.[40] His concept of professionalizing cooking by centralizing it could work only in a collective dwelling such as an apartment-house setting.

If women's labor was to be spared, then the labor women usually expended on child care must be considered as well as the normal chores of housekeeping; it was another feature of the housewife's work that apartment buildings could have taken on. A writer in *Harper's New Monthly Magazine*, concerned about housing problems in New York in 1882, asserted that apartments were not intended for children. Landlords sometimes refused to allow children in their buildings or charged extra rent to families with progeny. However, another observer had noted that the doorman or concierge kept an eye on children, who then could play safely in an apartment-house courtyard. By 1907 a writer for *American Architect and Building News* suggested that apartment-house developers would increase potential markets for their rental units by offering a central child-care service, akin to central laundry and food preparation, which had long been acceptable options in the large apartment house.[41]

Apartment houses should be differentiated from tenements in their ability to care for children. In surveying the apartments of the turn of the century, this 1907 architectural journalist found no "indication that their designers had ever heard of the word 'nursery.'" Tenement children must play in the streets, "but the child of the well-bred dweller in an apartment house must, if he too is to be well-bred, be kept out of the streets, and, if he is to be healthy and well nourished, must have a proper play-room for the daytime and an equally satisfactory nursery for the night." For economy's sake he recommended a common play-room at the top of the house or on the roof, along with a "hospital ward" and trained nurse to check the spread of disease among groups of children. Soon, this writer predicted, a landlord would consider a nurse as important a service as an elevator in selling his apartments.[42] However, centralized child care did not find a ready market in the early twentieth century. Contemporary commitments to private child rearing, the tradition of hired nurses for middle-class children, and fixed ideas of women's responsibilities and mothering roles prevented this service from being implemented.

Early apartment designers of the 1870s and 1880s had located themselves within a culture of convenience by producing a home all on one floor, but because of the competing tradition of labor-intensive housekeeping, they had not based the appeal of their designs on the array of technological innovations then available. Servants, however, had been declining in number as the nineteenth century advanced. In her study of domestic service, Faye Dudden records that there were an average of 250 servants per 1,000 families in the 1855 census in New York City. David Katzman shows that while New York families used 188 servants per 1,000 families in 1880 and 141 servants per 1,000 families in 1900, the number dropped drastically in the twentieth century; by 1920 there were only 66 servants per 1,000 families. This decrease in servants parallels an increase in available technological aids to housekeeping.[43]

The enhanced role of technologies and the decreasing place of servants implied some design changes, both in the individual units and in the layout of whole buildings. Architects speculated in the professional press about the most efficient arrangement of modern kitchen equipment or the best placement of electric outlets within the rooms of private apartment units, and individual rooms were rethought in terms of household technology. At the same time, apartment-house basements and top floors, once the habitat of servants, were reconceived as the sites for building-wide machines that could heat, refrigerate, wash, dry, or vacuum.[44] From a programming perspective, such conveniences raised a sociological question: who were these technologies for? should they be understood as individual conveniences for single households, or seen collectively, lifting the housework burdens for entire apartment houses and scaled and located accordingly?[45]

By the late 1890s electricity was finally supplied beneath the streets throughout all the developed areas of Manhattan, and electric lights and elevators became a feature of new moderate-rent apartments. In the first decade of the twentieth century, technologically aided convenience was expected in average buildings such as those filling the avenues and side streets of the Upper West Side. The Berkeley Arms at Riverside Drive and Ninety-fifth Street advertised in 1904 that the building not only had all-night elevators and electric lights but also a telephone in each apartment. The Wilmore Court at St. Nicholas Avenue and 126th Street offered refrigerators and shower baths; in the Strathmore on Broadway and Fifty-second Street, apartment tenants enjoyed the advantages of Otis elevators, steam heat, and telephones. Even low-rent houses offered both electric and gas light and gas ranges.[46] In 1907 an observer reported that large kitchens with their multiple servants were giving way to "a 'kitchenette,' consisting of a ventilated cupboard, opening usually out of the dining-room, and provided with a gas-stove and shelves, hooks, bins for flour and sugar, and other fittings."[47]

"The modern and up-to-date apartment," explained Israels in 1901, "offers to its tenants a measure of luxury and convenience totally beyond the reach of a man of average income living under his own 'vine and fig tree.'" Private houses once were very nice but now should be weighed against the modern conveniences available when living quarters were combined for the added benefit of all. A 1901 apartment could offer telephone service, central heating, filtered water, hot-water heaters, refrigeration, storage rooms, laundry machines, and clothes-drying equipment. Tenants need never be bothered by the coal or ice bill. This cooperative mode of living offered "the most economical and convenient living at the lowest cost."[48] Thus the apartment house presented itself as a fully serviced home, with the expenses of individual housekeeping shared among the many, and the work itself supported by advanced equipment and building staff. Such a full array of modern equipment was rarely available to private-house owners except for the wealthiest, whereas apartments made modern life accessible to the middle class.

Apartment buildings were the ideal way to collect and centralize both labor and costs, making life better for all. In this modern view, apartments were no longer seen as dangerously communal places where shared public spaces threatened the sanctity of family life; instead, communality could be viewed through the lens of modernity. The cooperative character of apartment living "follows a distinct tendency of this age of concentrated effort," wrote Charles Israels in 1901. "It eliminates the individual for the common good." Cooperation was "part of every great business," agreed the domestic reformer Helen Campbell, and was the secret of the success of business trusts; it was inevitable that housekeeping would join in the benefits of cooperative structure. As tenants learned to see collective dwellings not as hazards to privacy but as enhancements to modernity, they enjoyed the shared aspects of apartment life.[49]

Diversity of Styles

In the first decade of the twentieth century, as in earlier years, apartment builders had many style favorites. The eclecticism of the 1870s and 1880s continued on in apartment houses of the 1890s and through several decades of the twentieth century. Henry Hardenbergh pursued an architecture inspired by the French baroque in his design for a small apartment house at Sixtieth Street and Fifth Avenue, published in 1907. The Langham on Central Park West, by Clinton and Russell, retained some of the irregular profile of 1880s rooflines broken by multiple dormers, while developing a restrained classical elevation below the cornice. The exotically named Casa Alameda (fig. 79) was given a central baroque dome above the roofline, while at the porte cochere, delicate Renaissance carving framed the building's name.[50]

Developers tried to appeal to tenants by sometimes overblown and exotic exteriors. Architects occasionally tried advanced styles but more typically aimed at average taste. Many of the styling efforts of developers and architects met with disfavor, and a writer in *The Brickbuilder*, Elisha H. Janes, asserted, "It is well known that the majority of apartments were and are designed by a class of architects who . . . lack . . . training." Critics cringed at stylistic "aberrations" like the Dorilton, a large block at Broadway and Seventy-third Street that was ornamented with pretentious sculpture and built of "dishonest" materials like sheet metal. Imitating the forms of masonry, such materials did not express their own constructive properties, as critics felt good architecture should. The Hotel Somerset on the south side of Forty-seventh Street east of Longacre Square was cited by the *Architectural Record* as an example of the bad influence of steel framing, which had given rise to a tendency to ignore the sides of tall buildings while styling up the fronts. This writer also registered the common complaint, made about commercial buildings as well as apartment houses, that it was inappropriate to handle the exterior design of the several floors differently from each other "when everybody knows that the floors are internally alike . . . as arbitrary and absurd as it would be for bees to decorate one row of cells in a honeycomb. The

FIGURE 79 The Casa Alameda at Broadway and Sixty-third Street by the architectural firm of Glover and Carrell exhibited historical borrowing from diverse sources in its grand dome, corner turrets, and Renaissance portico. (*American Architect and Building News* 40 [May 27, 1893]: pl. 909)

bees are not so foolish." Thorstein Veblen, in his merciless *Theory of the Leisure Class* of 1899 criticized apartment houses because their facades were all tricked up with useless ornament just to make a show. He felt that the only good parts to apartment design were the naked sides and backs where architects had left them alone (cf. fig. 73).[51] But all this stylistic variety may have attracted tenants to rent apartments at times when there was a buyer's market; and when there was a lack of housing, tenants would not turn away from a suitable apartment just because they found a cornice or piece of sculpture imperfectly realized.

The height of large apartment houses responded to the elevator, but the ten-story and higher blocks planned from 1885 to 1901 were not approved under the Buildings Department's height-restricting laws. Quite grand buildings like the Yosemite (fig. 80), therefore, stopped at seven stories, while developers who wanted to go up higher had to call their projects "hotels" to escape the law. The problem was eliminated with the removal of height restrictions in 1901, when the construction of tall apartment houses resumed.

At the turn of the century the classical style, derived from either ancient or Renaissance architecture, became one of the characteristic architectural styles of large apartment houses. Historians have usually credited the 1893 Chicago World's Fair for this change in taste. The architectural firm of McKim, Mead and White anticipated the change in 1892 in the Yosemite apartments on Park Avenue (fig. 80). The classical vocabulary was used to produce such buildings as the elegant East Side apartment house still standing at 998 Fifth Avenue, built in 1910 by McKim, Mead and White (fig. 81), and the Apthorp, built in 1908 on the West Side by Clinton and Russell (fig. 82). Charles Israels praised this shift and argued the virtues of classicism to give apartment houses more dignity. The classical continued to be one of the favorite styles for New York's apartment houses on through the 1930s.[52] Quadrangular courtyard apartment blocks became more popular in New York after 1900; Graham Court, built by Clinton and Russell in 1901 (fig. 83), the Belnord Apartments, by H. Hobart Weeks in 1908, and the Apthorp Apartments, by Clinton and Russell in the same year, are good examples. These large courtyard buildings, paralleling and often exceeding in size the courtyard forms praised by observers of the Paris apartment, had their sources in the form of the Renaissance city palace.

This new classical architectural style presented the apartment house as a unified whole rather than as a set of fragments. In a reversal of the 1880s experience, passersby would register its unity first, then recall that apartment houses contained many separate families. By that time the once-popular disjunctive color and ornament of apartment facades, as seen at the Central Park Apartments or the Dakota, were judged to be out of place. This trend toward a more unified classicizing style coincided with a tenant clientele already used to apartment living. When tenants had come to accept the idea of living in large apartment buildings with many other families, their need for individualizing details to mark out their own part of a big building gradually faded into the background. The new conveniences that technologies provided to the tenants collectively

FIGURE 80 The Yosemite apartments on Park Avenue and Sixty-second Street, by McKim, Mead and White, was a grand building but only seven stories high to conform with building height restrictions imposed in 1885. (*American Architect and Building News* 31 [February 28, 1891]: pl. 792)

FIGURE 81 The classical taste influenced the design for a duplex apartment building at 998 Fifth Avenue by McKim, Mead and White. (*American Architect* 100 [November 29, 1911]: pl. 1875)

FIGURE 82   An enormous courtyard building, the Apthorp on Broadway between Seventy-eighth and Seventy-ninth streets, by Clinton and Russell, was given unity by the use of Renaissance-derived classicism. (*American Architect and Building News* 91 [January 5, 1907]: following p. 24)

FIGURE 83 Interior courtyards after the turn of the century could be generously dimensioned and ornamental. Courtyard at Graham Court at Seventh Avenue between 116th and 117th streets, by Clinton and Russell. (*Brickbuilder* 12 [1903]: 5)

were reflected in this unity of stylistic expression. Charles Israels's statement that modern convenience "eliminates the individual for the common good" finds its architectural form in the classical envelope. A building like the Apthorp, with its smoother detailing and single color, could satisfy tenants who had come to accept group living and admire it as the modern mode.[53]

Conclusion

By the end of the first decade of the twentieth century, apartment houses were fully established as a successful building type in New York. Whereas in 1890, 835 plans for single-family dwellings had been filed with the Buildings Department, in 1901 barely 100 were filed. Meanwhile the prices had skyrocketed from an average cost per dwelling of $16,700 in 1889 to $64,000 in 1902.[54] Single-family houses had become so expensive in Manhattan that they had nearly ceased being built, while apartments became the kind of dwelling every middle-class Manhattanite would expect to live in.

In the course of their forty-year development, apartment houses had made it possible for tenants to come to terms with the original oppositions at the heart of collective living. The physical fabric of the city changed radically during these decades; imposingly tall structures became commonplace in both commercial and civic architecture, made possible by the elevator and steel-frame construction. Apartment houses grew more varied in size, from a single lot to the entire span of a city block; and taller too, from the typical four or five floors in the early years to a typical seven to fifteen by 1910. Thus they took on something of the urban presence that early writers had hoped for, enlivening the streets with numerous architectural "statements" both elegant and gaudy.

Tenants learned to interpret the large block of an apartment building as home, both through architects' accommodations of style to tenants' tastes and through tenants simply becoming accustomed to the enlarged size of a group home. Tenants' own experience in living with others taught them the value of taking a positive stance toward close neighbors, thinking of them as potential community rather than strangers. A professional journal reminded apartment-house architects in 1907 "that their problem is fundamentally and primarily a sociological one, and that while they cannot contend successfully against all the evils of gregarious living, they can do much good by segregating each independent home with the most sedulous care to protect its privacy at every point."[55] People discovered that they could live privately in a group dwelling, because architects developed adequate ways to protect the privacy of tenants while making shared spaces useful and comfortable.

Years of experiment in interior unit layouts led to rationalized plans that secured tenants some privacy from each other, and separated residents from guests, servants from residents, work from pleasure and from rest. These planning moves were accompanied by advances in technological supports for household work, both within the family unit and external to it in the form of building-wide services and equipment. So much did one-floor living in a well-staffed building enhance the ease of housekeeping that the use of servants by moderate-income families declined rapidly after the turn of the century.

While apartments represented a new vision of cooperation for the common good, advancing technology also had the paradoxical effect of reemphasizing the individual nature of housekeeping. As the historian Ruth Cowan has shown, the array of household machinery took on more compact forms in the first and second decades of the twentieth century; it moved into individual households, making each more self-sufficient. Appliance advertisements of the first decade of the twentieth century illustrate the choice made by manufacturers to shrink appliances to fit individual apartment units as well as to produce centralized machinery intended for the apartment house's tenants collectively. For example, centralized refrigeration units did exist and were installed in various buildings, but the trend toward autonomy of the household unit favored small refrigerators instead.[56] These devices grew in numbers and availability as the supply of servants diminished, leading to smaller, more tightly organized, servantless households in both private houses and apartments.

The multiple dwelling had provided a potentially innovative ground on which to reconceive of an individual household's work in a large building with a ready pool of cooperative members, but the ideology of family privacy was too strong to allow such alternatives to be taken very far. The early ideas about collective cooking with a choice of public dining rooms or privately served meals faded away. The extensive staff of laundresses who not only cleaned but also repaired clothing and linens is no longer included in the rent, yet collectively used washing and drying machines are often still part of the building-wide equipment in an apartment house. The point at which publicly managed services and equipment are in perfect balance with private needs remains in question.

Collective spaces and occasions for meeting were built into apartment houses and homogeneity of income was likely to reinforce a sense of neighborliness among a building's tenants; however, other social barriers could be, and were, erected. In a 1911 article in the *Architectural Record*, the author cautions against allowing a "peroxide Juno" or a "hook-nosed tenant" to move in, destroying privacy and impairing the value of investments. Each generation finds its "others" and creates devices (like modern co-op boards) to filter us from them.[57]

Sounding another familiar note, a 1907 critic asserted that the true evil that lurks in multiple-dwelling life is rivalry among families to impress each other. If one family with a better income moves in, twenty others, previously happy, will become envious and the poorer tenants will go into debt to keep up. The same evil lurks in "the higher grade of tenement house colloquially known as the apartment-house," where people are led on by rivalry to indulge in fur coats, theater parties, and automobiles, paid for by gambling at the stock exchange.[58]

Apartment houses from their inception in the 1860s were discussed in terms of the danger they posed to private family life. But there had already been decades of living in shared dwellings before the Stuyvesant Apartments opened its doors in 1870. What was really new in the apartment house was public space, designed as such. Architects introduced lobbies, reception rooms, roof terraces, and dining rooms to tenants for whom sharing a dwelling was a disconcerting novelty. While the discourse in print remained preoccupied with the issue of creating and preserving privacy, the building designers were occupied with creating comfortable and genteel public spaces for controlled social interaction.

Even with all the apartment's successes, some early-twentieth-century commentators still interpreted sharing a roof with others as destructive of precious homelife. To others, like Sister Carrie and her sisters, confined by housekeeping or child-care duties to the home, gregarious living was the special benefit and saving grace of apartment life. These oppositions between publicity and privacy, between group and individual, were mediated by and in apartments, but they were not solved and never seem to be. Balancing group against individual needs remains an open issue in the design of current and future apartment houses.

NOTES

Introduction

1. Gwendolyn Wright, *Moralism and the Model Home . . . in Chicago, 1873–1913* (1980), traces attitudes toward home owning in turn-of-the-century Chicago; Constance Perrin, *Everything in Its Place: Social Order and Land Use in America* (1977), provides a sociological study of contemporary attitudes toward renting (irresponsible, immature) and owning (correct, adult) a home. John Hancock, "The Apartment House in Urban America," in *Buildings and Society*, ed. Anthony King (1980), pp. 151–89, stresses the role of apartments in the segmentation of American housing to express social differences.

2. For the early-nineteenth-century creation and conduct of real estate markets in New York, especially as regards housing, see Elizabeth S. Blackmar, *Manhattan for Rent, 1785–1850* (1989).

3. Theodore Dreiser, *Sister Carrie* (1981), p. 81. Compare Julia McNair Wright, *The Complete Home: An Encyclopedia of Domestic Life and Affairs* (1885), who stated that our homes have a sacred dimension as they stand between the "Home set up in Eden, and the Home before us in Eternity" (pp. 3–4).

4. For antimodern attitudes, see, for example, T. J. Jackson Lears, *No Place of Grace* (1981). His "Biographical Appendix," giving the major figures who expressed antimodern ideas in the period 1880–1920, interestingly includes males almost exclusively.

5. The concept of "building type" incorporates notions of use plus form and is one of the basic concepts used in building laws, zoning, fire-insurance ratings, and other regulatory codes. See Robert Shibley, Lynda Schneekloth, Ellen Bruce, and Elizabeth Cromley, "'Building Type': An Examination of the Construct," National Endowment for the Arts, #5242520071 (1988, typescript).

6. This case is recorded in *American Architect and Building News* (hereafter cited as *AABN*) 3 (February 9, 1878): 45. The court decided that a significant difference between apartments and tenements was that apartment houses had dining in common, while tenement houses did not, but *AABN* writers said this "plainly leaves the real issue untouched . . . the number and kind of neighbors it [the tenement] brings." Another similar court case was reported in "Notes and Clippings— Apartment Houses Not Tenements," *AABN* 76 (April 5, 1902): 8, where Judge Truax decided to uphold the popular usage of "tenement"—housing for working-class tenants—rather than the legal meaning of any multiple dwelling with three or more units. Jno. Gilmer Speed, "Naming Apartment Houses," *Harper's Weekly* 38 (March 24, 1894): 283, explains the subtleties of the words "tenement," "apartment," and "flat" as cultural-level identifiers. The art historian T. J. Clark says, "Society is a battlefield of representations, [which] are continually subject to the test . . . of social practice. Social practice *is* that . . . overlap and interference of representations; it is their rearrangement in use; it is the test which consolidates or disintegrates our categories, which makes or unmakes a concept" (*The Painting of Modern Life* [1985], p. 6). This making and unmaking seems pertinent to the fluctuating names for kinds of multiple dwellings that represent social distinctions.

7. *New York Times*, October 19, 1866, p. 4.

8. *Phillips' Elite Directory* (1874–1903) is preserved on microfilm in the New York Public Library. In *The Painting of Modern Life*, Clark allows the possibility of talking about certain forms as being "bourgeois," but cautions against saying that anything is "inherently bourgeois," for "what we are pointing to is relation, not inherence" (p. 7).

9. Discussions of class that I found useful were Peter Gay, *The Bourgeois Experience*, vol. 1, *Education of the Senses* (1984), pp. 17–44; several of the essays collected in Anthony Giddens and David Held, eds., *Classes, Power, and Conflict* (1982); and Stuart M. Blumin, "The Hypothesis of Middle-Class Formation in Nineteenth-Century America: A Critique and Some Proposals," *American Historical Review* 90 (April 1985). Gay problematizes the very defining of *bourgeois*, showing its multiplicity of meanings. Giddens and Held describe various historical definitions of "class" such as Weber's: "Classes consist of aggregates of individuals who share similar sets of 'life chances' in labour and commodity markets." In contrast, "status groups are founded upon relationships of consumption rather than production and take the form of 'styles of life' that separate one group from another" (p. 10). Blumin summarizes the positions of many other historians as regards the formation, indeed the existence, of a "middle class" in the nineteenth-century United States. As evidence that a middle class does exist, Blumin cites recent studies of distinctive working-class and patrician cultures in the United States that demonstrate that forms of economic inequality increase in the antebellum era and are maintained throughout the nineteenth century. "It is becoming increasingly clear, in short, that Americans diverged widely in their economic circumstances and that they translated their economic differences into significant differences in life style, outlook and aspiration" (p. 304). Blumin points to the paradox in the formation of a middle class that it "binds itself together as a social group through the common embrace of an ideology of social atomism" or individualism (p. 305). Also useful is the definition provided by Adam Przeworski: "'Class' then is a name of a relation, not of a collection of individuals. . . . Individuals occupy places within the system of production; collective actors appear in struggles at concrete moments of history. . . . Class is the relation between them" (*Capitalism and Social Democracy* [1985], p. 81).

10. Michael Katz, "Social Class in North American Social History," *Journal of Interdisciplinary History* 11 (Spring 1981): 579–605. Stratification denotes no particular terrain being contested (pp. 580–81); no struggle for the definition of space exists between the apartment with several maids' rooms and that with only one—the difference is only one of rent. Thus I do not use the term "upper class" for apartments where there are multiple servants' rooms or very high rents implying wealthy tenants.

11. See Christine Stansell, *City of Women: Sex and Class in New York, 1789–1860* (1986), for an analysis of women's ability to support themselves and their dependents through street-oriented activities, and her analysis of the metaphoric and conceptual uses of "the street" by reformers who identify children playing in the streets as a sign of the failure of the poor to provide homes and as evidence of their pathology (pp. 209–11).

12. Mary Ryan, *Cradle of the Middle Class: The Family in Oneida County, New York, 1790–1865* (1981), pp. 14, 15.

13. "Apartment-Houses," *Appleton's Journal*, n.s. 5 (1878): 535.

14. Andrew Alpern, *Apartments for the Affluent: A Historical Survey of Buildings in New York* (1975); Thomas E. Norton and Jerry E. Patterson, *Living It Up: A Guide to the Named Apartment Houses of New York* (1984). For other recent works on the apartment, see Amy Epstein, "Multi-family Dwellings and the Search for Respectability: Origins of the New York Apartment House," *Urbanism Past and Present* 5 (Summer 1980): 29–39; Robert A. M. Stern, "With Rhetoric: The New York Apartment House," *Via* 4 (1980): 78–111. My subject is limited to New York apartments, and so while many of the nineteenth-century ideas discussed here had national scope, the building forms themselves responded to the peculiar real estate constraints of Manhattan; Chicago's or Washington's apartment history would take a form somewhat different from this one. James Goode has completed a history of Washington, D.C., apartment houses, *Best Addresses: A Century of Washington's Distinguished Apartment Houses* (1988); Carroll William Westfall has written a catalog essay on the history of Chicago apartments in John Zukowsky, ed., *Chicago Architecture, 1872–1922: Birth of a Metropolis* (1987); on the first apartment house in Boston, see Jean Follett, "The Hotel Pelham: A New Building Type for America," *American Art Journal* 15 (Autumn 1983): 58–73; Rebecca Zurier wrote a master's thesis at Yale University in 1982 on apartments in Boston by John Pickering Putnam.

15. The period of this study is also the period when the architecture profession in the United

States was organizing itself. In the 1850s the American Institute of Architects was founded; in the years just after the Civil War, America's first architecture schools were founded; and not until the late 1890s were the first state licensing procedures initiated. Thus it is not entirely clear, as it is clear today because of state licensing laws, what we can rely on when calling someone an "architect" before the turn of the century.

16. For the history of New York City's tenements see James Ford, Katherine Morrow, and George N. Thompson, *Slums and Housing* (1936); Catherine Bauer, *Modern Housing* (1934); Edith Elmer Wood, *The Homes the Public Builds* (1940); Roy Lubove, *The Progressives and the Slums: Tenement House Reform in New York City, 1890–1917* (1962); Edward Lubitz, "The Tenement Problem in New York City and the Movement for Its Reform, 1856–1867" (1970); Anthony Jackson, *A Place Called Home: A History of Low-Cost Housing in Manhattan* (1976). For other useful perspectives on the social context of housing see Kenneth Jackson and Stanley Schultz, eds., *Cities in American History* (New York: Alfred A. Knopf, Borzoi Books, 1972).

17. David P. Handlin, *The American Home: Architecture and Society, 1815–1915* (1979); Gwendolyn Wright, *Building the Dream: A History of American Housing* (1981); Dolores Hayden, *A Grand Domestic Revolution: American Visions of Household Liberation* (1980); see also Richard Plunz, *A History of Housing in New York City* (1989).

18. Clark, *Painting of Modern Life*, states, "The sign of an ideology is a kind of inertness in discourse: a fixed pattern of imagery and belief, a syntax which seems obligatory, a set of permitted modes of seeing and saying. . . . Ideologies naturalize representation, one might say: they present constructed, disputable meanings as if they were hardly meanings at all, but, rather, forms inherent in the world-out-there which the observer is privileged to intuit directly" (p. 8). Thus whenever we think that meanings of "home" are natural, we are in the world of ideology.

1. Making Do

1. The population was analyzed in the 1850 census report as 93,608 families, living in 37,677 dwellings (Joseph Kennedy, *Preliminary Report on the Eighth Census, 1860* [1862], p. 243).

2. M. Christine Boyer, *Manhattan Manners* (1985), pp. 89–98; Kennedy, *Preliminary Report on the Eighth Census, 1860*, p. 232.

3. "Houseless," *Harper's New Monthly Magazine* 26 (May 1863): 789–90; "Apartment Houses," *Real Estate Record and Builders' Guide* 3 (July 17, 1869): 3.

4. "Houseless," 789–90.

5. *New York Times*, October 19, 1866, p. 4; September 25, 1869, p. 4, April 16, 1871, p. 3. In 1864 ("Houses and Rents," February 19, p. 4), the *Times* blamed high house rents on an influx of southerners and spendthrifts who drove up prices and caused housing shortages for decent local families.

6. Elizabeth Blackmar, "Housing and Property Relations in New York City, 1785–1850" (1980), gives extensive documentation of changes in this period. Her arguments are summarized in Blackmar, "Rewalking the 'Walking City': Housing and Property Relations in New York City, 1780–1840," *Radical History Review* 21 (Fall 1979): 131–48; see also Blackmar, *Manhattan for Rent*, for a detailed view of changing housing practices in the first half of the nineteenth century. On changes in the relations between servants and mistresses, see Carol Lasser, "The Domestic Balance of Power," *Labor History* 28 (Winter 1987): 5–22.

7. Faye Dudden, *Serving Women: Household Service in Nineteenth-Century America* (1983): 12–20, 45–55.

8. Bad fires in 1835 and 1845 wiped out hundreds of houses that would have filtered down to the working class (James Ford, Katherine Morrow, and George N. Thompson, *Slums and Housing* [1936], p. 868). Blackmar, "Housing and Property Relations," p. 435, shows that it was common to subdivide houses in the 1830s within one decade of construction.

9. *New York Times*, August 2, 1869, p. 1. See also Charles Lockwood, *Manhattan Moves Uptown: An Illustrated History* (1976); M. Christine Boyer and Jessica Scheer, "The Development and Boundaries of Luxury Neighborhoods in New York, 1625–1890" (1980); James Richardson, "The New Homes of New York," *Scribner's Monthly* 8 (1874): 70.

10. "Hotel Morals," "Man about Town" column, *Harper's Weekly* 1 (September 5, 1857): 563; H. C. Bunner, *Story of a New York House* (1887); Richard Grant White, "Old New York and Its Houses," *Century* 26, n.s. 4 (May–October 1883): 845–59.

11. *Women's Own Book* (1873), p. 99. The author recommended a parlor, a kitchen, a separate sitting room or one combined with the kitchen, and two bedrooms.

12. *New York Times*, May 1, 1854, p. 6.

13. Ibid.

14. *New York Times*, April 10 and 13, 1865, pp. 3, 8.

15. William Dean Howells, *A Hazard of New Fortunes* (1890; reprint, 1965), p. 42.

16. The percentage of income paid in rent varies according to the actual dollar amount of income, but between 16.5 percent and 25 percent of income was judged to be a suitable proportion to spend on rents in 1863 ("Houseless," p. 789); Robert Coit Chapin found that people he interviewed spent between 15 percent and 28 percent of their income on housing in 1907, with the larger wage earners spending a smaller percentage of the whole (*Standard of Living among Workingmen's Families in New York City* [1909], p. 72).

17. "Houseless," p. 790.

18. Lubitz, "Tenement Problem in New York City," p. 542, table 6.

19. *New York Times*, August 2, 1869, p. 1.

20. Even though the depression of 1873 affected wages and prices, the same figures of $1,500 to $3,000 for the rental of a nice house were given in "Apartment Houses," *Real Estate Record and Builders' Guide* 3 (July 17, 1869): 3, and nine years later in "A Revolution in Living," *New York Times*, June 3, 1878, p. 4. The *Record* said, "Many people of moderate means rent four-story brownstone built houses, and in point of fact keep boarding houses, when they don't acknowledge it" (p. 3). The wife, it said, spends all her husband's income in rent, then makes back enough for food, clothing, and so on by taking in boarders.

21. *New York Times*, November 21, 1865, p. 2; Junius Henri Browne, *The Great Metropolis: A Mirror of New York* (1869), chap. 21.

22. *New York Times*, May 1, 1854, pp. 5, 6; April 2, 1865, p. 6.

23. Federal census, 1880.

24. "New York Daguerreotyped—Hotels, Stores, and Banks," *Putnam's Magazine* 1 (April 1853): 367.

25. Jean Follett, "The Hotel Pelham: A New Building Type for America," *American Art Journal* 15 (Autumn 1983): 58–73; an editorial, *AABN* 76 (June 28, 1902): 97, states that the New York apartment "had been newly imported from Boston" twenty years ago, a lineage not given credence by New York reporters who wanted to preserve distinctions between the hotel and apartment-building types.

26. "How We Live," *New York Times*, November 22, 1873, p. 4.

27. In her real estate history of nineteenth-century New York, *Manhattan Manners*, M. Christine Boyer maps the growth of this fashionable hotel zone, pp. 55–62; Browne, *Great Metropolis*, p. 391.

28. Detailed description of Broadway (formerly Grand) Central Hotel in the *New York Times*, August 6, 1870, p. 5.

29. This building had been opened as the Stevens apartment house, designed by Richard Morris Hunt in 1871, but it was soon converted to a hotel. Advertisements for the Stevens offered "elegant apartments . . . at reasonable rates. First class board at a fixed price in the restaurant" (*New York Times*, April 13, 1874, p. 7). The Stevens was described in [Lewis Leeds], "Parisian 'Flats,'" *Appleton's Journal* 6 (November 18, 1871): 561–62. Tenants identified in the 1880 Federal Census of New York City.

30. Calvert Vaux, "American Institute of Architects Address" (hereafter cited as "A.I.A. Address"), *Crayon*, July 1857, p. 218; and Vaux, "Parisian Buildings for City Residents," *Harper's Weekly* 1 (December 19, 1857): 809–10.

31. Browne, *Great Metropolis*, p. 208. For a capsule view of the distasteful qualities of boarding, see "Apartment-Houses," *Appleton's Journal*, n.s. 5 (1878): 530.

32. "Letter," *New York Times*, September 25, 1869, p. 4; *New York Times*, October 31, 1875, p. 5.

33. "Hotel Morals," p. 563; *New York Times*, November 21, 1865, p. 2.

34. Among numerous studies of women's roles in nineteenth-century American culture are Kathryn Kish Sklar, *Catharine Beecher: A Study in American Domesticity* (1973); Ann Douglas, *The Feminization of American Culture* (1977).

35. Catharine Beecher, *A Treatise on Domestic Economy* (1841; reprint, 1977), p. 9.

36. "Boarding Out," *Harper's Weekly* 1 (March 7, 1857): 146.

37. "Prattle and Tattle" column, "Where Shall We Walk?" *Harper's Weekly* 1 (June 13, 1857): 382.

38. *New York Times*, June 22, 1879, p. 10.

39. *Women's Own Book*, p. 99.

40. "Hotel Morals," p. 563.

41. Browne, *Great Metropolis*, 398.

42. Ibid., 213.

43. *New York Times*, August 6, 1871, p. 5. Men who had formerly eaten mid-day dinner at home had to use restaurants as their workplaces grew ever more distant from home in the expanding city (Browne, *Great Metropolis*, 443; Boyer, *Manners*, 80–83). Browne devotes his chap. 28 to the restaurant question.

44. *New York Times*, August 2, 1869, p. 1.

45. Edith Wharton, *The Custom of the Country* (1913), p. 15.

46. Richardson, "New Homes of New York," p. 67. Richardson uses the strong term "degenerate."

47. Howells, *Hazard*, p. 103.

48. Louise E. Furniss, "New York Boarding Houses," *Appleton's Journal* 5 (March 1871): 259–61; she calls this life "young Paris" because of the people's reliance on city shops and services to sustain the household, as opposed to their doing all the cooking, cleaning, and other such chores internally as in the ideal American private home.

49. "Flathouse Thief Arrested," *New York Times*, April 8, 1898, p. 9; *New York Times*, April 3, 1898, p. 8.

50. "New York Daguerreotyped—Private Residences," *Putnam's Magazine* 3 (March 1854): 233.

51. Here $1,000 to $3,000 a year was considered low enough rent for nice apartments that young middle-class couples could afford (*New York Times*, August 2, 1869, p. 1); Richardson, "New Homes of New York," p. 65.

52. *New York Times*, October 19, 1868, p. 4.

53. Vaux, "A.I.A. Address," p. 218; and Vaux, "Parisian Buildings for City Residents," pp. 809–10.

54. Abundant transportation would preclude the need for "Paris flats," wrote a reporter in "Apartment Houses," *Real Estate Record and Builders' Guide*, p. 3. In contrast to Manhattan, the streetcar systems of Boston and Buffalo were established at a time that coincided with expanding housing needs and enabled most of the middle-class population to move away from downtown. But New York's population expansion always kept ahead of its public transportation system, reinforcing the trend toward multiple dwellings.

2. *Reference Points: Good and Bad Dwellings*

1. Attitudes toward home owning in Charles Israels, "New York Apartment Houses," *Architectural Record* 11 (July 1901): 477; Charlotte Perkins Gilman, "The Passing of the Home in Great American Cities," *Cosmopolitan* 38 (December 1904): 138.

2. Montgomery Schuyler, "The New New York House," *Architectural Record* 19 (February 1906): 83–84; Schuyler, "Henry Janeway Hardenbergh," *Architectural Record* 6 (July–September 1896): 352.

3. For a survey of single-family urban house design developments, see Charles Lockwood, *Bricks and Brownstone: The New York Row House* (1972); for end-of-the-century houses of the wealthy, see Herbert Croly, "The Contemporary New York Residence," *Architectural Record* 12 (December 1902): 716.

4. "Looking for a House," *New York Times*, April 9, 1871, p. 5.

5. "New York Daguerreotyped—Private Residences," p. 245.

6. C. Vaux, "A.I.A. Address," p. 218; Richardson, "New Homes of New York," p. 67; Beecher, *Treatise on Domestic Economy*, 337–38.

7. Robert Tomes, "The Houses We Live In," *Harper's New Monthly Magazine* 30 (May 1865): 739.

8. Ella Rodman Church, *How to Furnish a Home*, vol. 1 of *Appleton's Home Books* (1884): p. 10. Anticipating the bungalow craze by two decades, she borrowed her reasoning from advocates of apartments who praised plans that would eliminate stairs entirely and make housekeeping easier.

9. Well-to-do families after the Civil War increasingly built impressive city houses whose numerous rooms required increased servants. In 1880 a private house at 3 Madison Ave. was home to William Appleton, the publisher; his son, also in publishing; and his wife. She took care of two younger children and oversaw the work of eight: one cook, one waiter, one coachman, one groom, one maid, one kitchen maid, and two "servants," all of whom were in residence at this address. The Adams family resided at 8 East Twenty-fourth St. The husband, a clergyman, and his wife lived with a married daughter, son-in-law, and three grandchildren. Helping to run the household were ten Irish and Scottish servants: a coachman, two nurses, two laundresses, a waitress, a maid, a seamstress, a housekeeper, and an elevator boy (federal census, 1880).

10. Some examples of articles dealing with Paris apartments for American readers are "Sketches in a Paris Café," *Putnam's Magazine* 2 (October 1853): 439–44; James McCabe, *Paris by Sunlight and Gaslight* (1869); Olive Logan, "At Home in Paris," *Putnam's Magazine*, n.s. 3 (March 1869): 352–57; Sarah Gilman Young, "Foreign Modes of Living," *Galaxy* 14 (1872): 474–82; Sarah Gilman Young, *European Modes of Living, or the Question of Apartment Houses* (1881); Hubert, Pirsson, and Hoddick, "New York Flats and French Flats," *Architectural Record* 2 (July 1892): 55–64; Paul F. Marcou, "The Modern House in Paris," *Architectural Record* 2 (January–March 1893): 324–31; Fernand Mazade, "Living in Paris on an Income of $3000 a Year," pts. 1–3, *Architectural Record* 13 (April, May, June 1903): 349–57, 423–32, 548–54. See also Robert A. M. Stern, "With Rhetoric: The New York Apartment House," for an interpretation of the use of French-inspired courtyards in New York apartment houses mainly in the early twentieth century; and Helene Lipstadt, "Housing the Bourgeoisie," *Oppositions* 8 (Spring 1977), for a historical view of Daly and the housing situation in mid-century Paris.

11. "Sketches in a Paris Café," p. 441. Richard Sennett, *The Fall of Public Man* (1978), pp. 212–13, 217, offers an alternative interpretation: the life lived by Frenchmen can be seen as not very sociable. Sennett, a sociologist, has shown, through his analyses of the art and literature of the period, that individuals in the cafés and restaurants rarely engaged each other in conversation; they wrapped themselves in a cocoon of silence, observing but not mixing with all the others similarly out in public.

12. McCabe, *Paris by Sunlight*, p. 653.

13. P. B. Wight, "Apartment Houses Practically Considered," *Putnam's Magazine* 16 (September 1870): 308.

14. Edith Wharton, *The Age of Innocence* (1968), pp. 28–29; the setting in the novel is dated by Wharton in the early 1870s (p. 3). This passage has been cited by many writers on apartments, including Stephen Birmingham, *Life at the Dakota* (1979), p. 15; Alpern, *Apartments for the Affluent*, foreword, n.p. The scandalous behavior of expatriates following Parisian mores is recounted in Lucy Hooper, "French Society and Parisianized Americans," *Appleton's Journal* 12 (September 1874).

15. Sennett, *Fall of Public Man*, pp. 134–35; Norma Evenson, *Paris: A Century of Change* (1979): 201–3. Anthony Sutcliffe, ed., *Multi-Storey Living: The British Working Class Experience*, (1974), p. 6.

16. Siegfried Giedion, *Space, Time, and Architecture*, 3d ed. (1956), pp. 670–72; Evenson, *Paris*, p. 201; McCabe, *Paris by Sunlight*, p. 655. Paul Goodman and Percival Goodman, *Communitas: Means of Livelihood and Ways of Life* (1947; reprint, 1960), 244–45. The Goodmans suggest modeling modern communities on the mixed use and mixed-class buildings of Paris as an alternative to the over-specialized single uses and single-class districts of the modern city.

17. Sennett, *Fall of Public Man*, pp. 134–35, uses the concept of "turfs"; Evenson, *Paris*, p. 203, reports on the class homogenization resulting from Haussmann's reorganization of the city.

18. Daly's work is described and quoted in Richard Becherer, *Science Plus Sentiment: César Daly's Formula for Modern Architecture* (1984), pp. 218–27: "With the transformation of the client-architect relationship, the designer now created for an anonymous user. Schematized class structure took the place of the personality and idiosyncrasy of the individual patron. Plan, although still considered part of the private realm, was now standardized and stripped of personal imagination" (p. 225). As in New York, the new dwelling unit was designed for the "average man."

19. See Beecher, *Treatise on Domestic Economy*, for antebellum fears of social risk in encounters with strangers. Karen Halttunen, *Confidence Men and Painted Women* (1982), explores the continuing history of Americans' suspicions of strangers through the 1870s.

20. Sarah Gilman Young, "Foreign Modes," pp. 475–76.

21. See Dolores Hayden's discussion of Young's contemporaries in the United States and their concerns for easier housekeeping in *Grand Domestic Revolution*. However, many of the suggestions for convenient housekeeping that Hayden identifies as contributions of what she calls "material feminism" were ideas also suggested by other thinkers (see my Chapters 4 and 6) who were allied more generally to modern convenience in living and less specifically to feminist issues.

22. Lipstadt, "Housing the Bourgeoisie," pp. 35–47; she discusses César Daly's 1864 *Architecture privée sous Napoleon III*: Daly preferred the private house and even the suburban villa to apartment buildings for middle-class use. Wight, "Apartment Houses," p. 310, mentioned Daly's book as a demonstration of apartment plans that lacked the conveniences in circulation that Americans required.

23. *AABN* 26 (December 14, 1889): 284, responded to a reader's request for information on apartment design by recommending both Daly and the French architectural magazine *La Semaine des constructeurs* for "most ingenious" plans. Recent Parisian apartment-house plans were published in "Apartment Houses," pt. 2, *AABN* 30 (November 15, 1890): 97–100.

24. Ford, *Slums and Housing*, p. 867. Other major works on tenement problems are cited in my Introduction. Lubitz, "Tenement Problem in New York," p. 539, table 3, shows that in 1855 the population of New York City was 622,924 people, of whom over 52 percent were foreign-born. In 1820, the population had been 123,706. The *Plumber and Sanitary Engineer* mentions a tenement built in 1824 and still in use in 1879 (December 15, 1879), p. 26; Alpern, *Apartments for the Affluent*, p. 12, gives 1833 as the earliest tenement, located on Water Street; Alfred Treadway White names an 1838 building on Cherry Street as the first tenement (*Better Homes for Working Men* [1885], p. 1). Before mid-century, it was widely acknowledged that New York had a "tenement problem." The Board of Health inspector Gerrit Forbes published a report on overcrowded and unhealthy housing conditions among the New York poor in 1834, and the first proposals for model tenement plans were presented by the Association for the Improvement of the Conditions of the Poor in 1846. At the urging of that association, the state legislature began to investigate housing conditions and proposed a law in 1856 that would set standards for workers' housing. Sidetracked for several years by the Civil War, the legislature enacted the first tenement law in 1867. Lawrence Veiller discusses the first "model" tenements in de Forest and Veiller, *Tenement House Problem* (1903), 1:71–118. See also Jacob August Riis, *A Ten Years' War: An Account of the Battle with the Slum in New York* (1900), for views of turn-of-the-century slum life. It should be noted again that the term "tenement" was used in New York law to cover all multiple dwellings having three or more independent units, so tenement law applied to all multiple dwellings of all classes.

25. William F. Thoms, *Tenant Houses: Their Ground Area, Cubic Feet of Air Space and Ventilation* (1867), p. 3 (cf. Lubitz, "Tenement Problem in New York," p. 543, table 8, for the slightly lower figure of 15,309 tenement houses). Lubitz, "Tenement Problem in New York," p. 546, table 9. Marcus Reynolds, *The Housing of the Poor in American Cities* (1892), p. 69; some examples of tenement plans from the mid-nineteenth century published by Reynolds show common problems in this prelegislation era of tenement design. The tenement law enacted in 1867 required for the first time that tenement builders provide fire escapes, that there be at least one privy for every twenty residents, that inhabited cellars be no less than seven feet high, and that no animals be kept in dwelling units except dogs and cats.

26. The figures of 25 percent and 5 percent profits were given by Alfred Treadway White, *Improved Dwellings for the Laboring Classes* (1879), when he argued that more men of goodwill should become involved in "5% philanthropy" housing. See R. R. Bowker, "Working Men's Homes," *Harper's New Monthly Magazine* 68 (April 1884): 781–84; the investors in the Improved Dwellings Association's model tenements designed by Vaux and Radford and opened in 1882 were paid a 7 percent return. Bowker cites a case in Philadelphia where a wretched slum building worth only $500 was bringing in a yearly income of $960 from "beggars and thieves."

27. "Urban Housing in New York," pt. 3, *AABN* 3 (May 18, 1878): 173. The *Plumber and Sanitary Engineer* 2 published entries and winners in March 1879, pp. 103–6; April 1879, pp. 131–32; May 1879, pp. 158–59. Variants of the winning Ware plan were published, for example, in Reynolds, *Housing*, p. 71, figs. 6 and 7, and in Edgar Kaufman, ed., *Rise of an American Architecture* (New York: Praeger, 1970), p. 176. Scrapbooks compiled by Charles F. Chandler, Commissioner of the New York Board of Health, 1873–83, who was one of the judges of the competition, are at Avery Library, Columbia University. A landlord wrote to *Sanitary Engineer* 11 (1884–85): 191, to say that tenants dumped all manner of trash into his new indoor water closets, so he planned to remove them and replace the old outdoor privies in the yard.

28. Jackson, *A Place Called Home*, p. 77; J. McCabe, *New York by Sunlight and Gaslight*, p. 562; "How the Italians Live—Packed Like Sheep in Dirty Unventilated Rooms" is the headline for an article on houses at nos. 11, 13, 15 Jersey Street filled with 111 persons and only one "closet" for the three houses (*New York Times*, April 4, 1885, p. 8). The *Times* reported that "all these Italians find their food in the ash barrels. . . . In every room a bright fire is kept day and night, and no window is ever open during the cold weather," because these tenants did not understand the need for fresh air. Stories like this kept alive middle-class worries about immigrant life and unhealthy tenement conditions.

29. Alfred Treadway White published several books on his reform principles and the buildings he sponsored: *Improved Dwellings for the Laboring Classes* (1879), *Better Homes for Working Men* (1885), *Riverside Buildings of the Improved Dwellings Co.* (1890), and *Sunlighted Tenements: Thirty-five Years' Experience as an Owner* (1912). For White's sources in British tenement reform, see Sutcliffe, *Multi-Storey Living*; and John Nelson Tarn, *Five Per Cent Philanthropy: An Account of Housing in Urban Areas between 1840 and 1914* (1973).

30. Editorial, *AABN* 7 (April 1880): 138. White, *Sunlighted Tenements*, described the Riverside

Buildings: 201 feet on Joralemon, 307 feet on Columbia Place, 288 feet on Furman (fourth side not given). The four-room apartments included a living room (with scullery extension) of 10 by 18 feet; two bedrooms, 8 by 16 feet and 7 by 16 feet; and a parlor, 8 by 16 feet. The three-room apartments included a living room, 10 by 16 feet; a parlor, 8 by 15 feet; and a bedroom, 10 by 16 feet. Apartments on lower floors were more expensive than those on upper, with the rents for a three-room unit in 1912 ranging from $1.40 to $2.40 a week, the same rent as in 1890. Family size in the Riverside Buildings was mainly from two to four persons. In one-fifth of all households the bread-winner was female. The women breadwinners worked as house cleaners and house workers, office cleaners, laundresses, dressmakers, and nurses. The male breadwinners were laborers, longshore-men, waiters, carpenters, painters, metal workers, machinists, electricians, boatmen, clerks and book-keepers, porters, watchmen, janitors, elevator men; some were professional men, including one priest and one minister.

31. *The Astral Apartments* (pamphlet, 1895), pp. 7–9, quotes the *Brooklyn Eagle* of December 5, 1885, for its description of the Astral's "noble Norman archways" and "artistic cornice." Another important courtyard tenement was Vaux and Radford's design for the Improved Dwellings Association of 1879–81 on First Avenue between Seventy-first and Seventy-second streets in Manhattan; illustrated in Ford, Morrow, and Thompson, *Slums and Housing*, pl. 5H, and described in the "Appendix: Notes on Plans," p. 882; illustrated are an elevation, fig. 116D, and a view of the buildings, still in use in 1938, fig. 38. Vaux and Radford's reform tenement buildings for the Improved Dwellings Association were discussed in "Model Tenement Houses," *Carpentry and Building* 2 (October 1880): 191. Courtyard buildings were encouraged by the 1901 "New Law" that required bigger and lighter courts than could fit on a 25-foot-wide lot. New tenement types fitting these requirements are given in T. M. Clark, "Apartment Houses," *AABN* 91 (January 1907): 3–11, figs. 18 and 19. Thomas Short's winning design of the 1900 tenement-house competition was published in de Forest and Veiller, *Tenement House Problem* (1903), p. 116, and in Ford et al., *Slums and Housing*, pls. 7 and 8.

32. For a description of daily life in tenements, see Elizabeth Bisland, "Co-operative Housekeeping in Tenements," *Cosmopolitan* 8 (November 1889): 35–42.

33. Data from the federal census, 1870.

3. The First Generation of New York Apartments

1. There were 942,292 people, with 419,094 of the population foreign-born, according to the 1870 census; problems with the accuracy of the count have led to estimates of population growth after the Civil War rather than precise numbers. William H. Rideing, "Rapid Transit in New York," *Appleton's Journal* 4 (May 1878).

2. Florence Hartley, *The Ladies' Book of Etiquette and Manual of Politeness* (1872), pp. 29–30, 111–14, 173–76.

3. Mott's building was identified in [Leeds], "Parisian 'Flats,'" p. 562.

4. On the 1850s precedents, see Richardson, "New Homes of New York," 67. Alpern, *Apartments for the Affluent*, 12, mentions the House of Mansions, designed by Alexander Jackson Davis in 1855 as a precedent for later apartment houses because it was articulated as a unified whole. However, its interior arrangements were like a row of party-wall houses; like Dr. Mott's on Bleecker St., it did not contain floors of apartment units. Handlin, *American Home*, p. 520 n. 67, mentions the earlier 1850s Stuyvesant; Paul R. Baker, *Richard Morris Hunt* (1980), p. 499 n. 2, mentions this reference but does not verify the attribution to Hunt nor explain the building any further. In his *Iconography of Manhattan Island*, vol. 6 (1928), Isaac Newton Phelps Stokes called the Stuyvesant Apartments "the first modern apartment house in New York" and mentioned the building in his "Chronology" as an outstanding item for 1869. Hunt's Stuyvesant was given "first" status in Real Estate Record and Builders' Guide, *A History of Real Estate, Buildings, and Architecture in New York*, (1898), p. 600; following this trend, Alpern, in *Apartments for the Affluent*, granted Hunt's Stuyvesant the status of the first apartment house. When Montgomery Schuyler wrote in the 1890s that Hunt's building was the "first of the elevator apartment houses," he apparently used "elevator" to mean dumbwaiter—a common usage of the era (*American Architecture and Other Writings*, 2 vols., ed. William Jordy and Ralph Coe [1961], 2:519). Rentals at the Stuyvesant were from $1,000 to $1,800 per year for each suite, $920 for each studio (Stokes, *Iconography of Manhattan Island*, vol. 5 [1926], p. 1933). Alpern, *Apartments for the Affluent*, p. 1, states that New Yorkers of even modest aspirations would never have lived in anything but a private house until Hunt imported the apartment-house concept from Paris;

however, most modestly aspiring families had in fact been living in less than full private houses for many years. The Real Estate Record's *History*, p. 600, stated that Hunt's Stuyvesant Apartments were really reconstructions of earlier houses. While this is not the case, since the building is clearly recorded in the Buildings Department's "New Buildings Docket" (hereafter cited as NBD) and not in their docket book for renovations, it is interesting to speculate on the mistake: Hunt's building looked so much like four single-family houses, and had been so little rethought in terms of the new building type, that these writers of 1898 mistook it for a renovation.

5. In Boyer, *Manhattan Manners*, 36, a chart assembled from information from the Buildings Department and published in the *Real Estate Record and Builders' Guide* purports to show the number of apartment buildings erected in Manhattan between 1868 and 1880: only 2 before 1874, jumping to 112 in 1875. These figures present a problem in that the Buildings Department invented a category to contain "apartment buildings" only in 1875. The sudden increase in numbers is a direct result of the classifying system.

6. The individual books of the NBD are not paginated; entries are chronologically ordered and identified by plan number. I thank Ann Gordon at the New York Municipal Archives for making the docket books available. The categories of first, second, and third class as used by the Buildings Department do not necessarily mesh with other people's or institutions' uses of these terms. For example, a landlord writing to the *New York Times* in 1864 stated that he owned several second- and third-class rental properties but no tenements; for the Buildings Department, third class *means* tenement.

7. *Annual Report of the Superintendent of Buildings for the Year 1865* (1872), p. 149. In that year 133 second-class dwellings were completed along with 268 first-class dwellings and 142 tenements. In the 1866 *Report*, p. 213, there were only 115 second-class dwellings begun, and the superintendent feared that modest-income people would be forced out of the city to locate housing in the suburbs. In the 1867 *Report* numbers are up again (pp. 280–81). In 1868 many more plans were filed with the Buildings Department: 879 first-class dwellings, 353 second-class dwellings (the majority of which were in the new northern Twelfth, Nineteenth, and Twenty-second wards), and 394 tenements (pp. 420–21).

8. The houses were 60 feet deep and 48 feet high (*Annual Report of the Superintendent of Buildings, 1867*, pp. 287–88). The census for 1880 shows that the occupants of these buildings were families with younger children. The occupations of the male heads of household at 420 West Thirty-fifth St. were listed as carver, machinist, and "produce commission"; at 418 West Thirty-fifth they were silk weaver, engine turner, plumber, and "candy store." The pages for these addresses from the 1870 census are illegible.

9. NBD, 1869, Plan no. 69. Each house measured 20 by 54 feet on a lot of 20 by 81 feet, leaving a generous rear yard for plenty of light and air. Henry J. Burchill was listed as owner, architect, and builder, indicating an entrepreneurial attitude that felt no need of professional architects' advice. The three-unit plan was for a lot 16 feet 8 inches by 100 feet on Fifty-second Street between Second and Third avenues (NBD, 1869, Plan no. 2). In this example too the owner, architect, and builder are the same man, Thomas Judge.

10. Cf. a later report, which stated that shops used to be "considered undignified and undesirable" but that now only the most exclusive apartment buildings insisted on having no shops (S. Fullerton Weaver, "Planning the Modern Apartment Hotel," *Architectural Forum* 41 [November 1924]: 209).

11. Advertisements from *New York Times*, April 4, 1875, p. 5, and April 13, 1871, p. 6. These buildings with flats over shops may not have been built for that use; shops would be more desirable than flats from the landlord's point of view, since they brought in more income than residential uses in this commercial district.

12. NBD, 1869, Plan no. 170; what seems to be a deliberate attempt to cross over the line between a third-class tenement and a second-class dwelling is preserved in this docket book entry. The owner filed plans for a second-class, three-story brick structure. He declared that it was intended for three families, one per floor, on a 25- by 100-foot lot. But the inspector noted, "This plan in my opinion is laid out for two families on each floor." Where the owner claimed a three-family, second-class building, the inspector found a six-family building that he would have categorized as a tenement and that should have conformed with the tenement-house law as regards construction materials, etc. The tenement category could also contain boardinghouses, although that was rare. One 1870 instance was planned for the north side of Forty-first St. between Eighth and Ninth avenues. A four-story structure of 25 by 30 feet on a 90-foot-deep lot, the dwelling was designed to hold eight families. The designation "boardinghouse" was rarely made in the Buildings Department records, however, be-

cause boarding was often a temporary use. Conversions of private houses to boarding did not require structural changes in a building.

13. NBD, 1869, Plan no. 562. The listing of four families was incorrect; perhaps the inspector meant (but forgot) to note four "per floor."

14. "Exhibit A," *Annual Report of the Superintendent of Buildings, 1869*, p. 571.

15. NBD, 1870, Plan no. 811. The Stevens was described as "one of New York's finest French flats" in Ernest Jefferson Williamson, *The American Hotel*, p. 270. It was converted to the Hotel Victoria by the end of its first decade, and was demolished in 1914.

16. NBD, 1870, Plan no. 811. The Stevens was begun September 7, 1870, and completed November 29, 1871. The owner was Paran Stevens; the architect, Richard Morris Hunt; and the builder, William Paul. It was 96 feet high and valued by buildings inspectors at $500,000. Another example of an anomaly in the first-class dwelling category was filed by architect Detlef Lienau in 1871. On Madison Ave. and Twenty-seventh St., this was a mixed-use building with offices in the basement, club rooms on the first and second floors, and one family unit each on the third and fourth floors (NBD, 1871, Plan no. 602). Another type of dwelling that slipped through category boundaries was the apartment over a stable. Such buildings were categorized as "stables," and one knew that they were also dwellings only if inspectors so noted.

17. NBD, 1872, Plan no. 894; George B. Post, architect, designed the Black building for a budget of $150,000.

18. NBD, 1874, Plan no. 8, by the architect F. S. Barus, whose firm is listed in Dennis S. Francis, *Architects in Practice in New York City, 1840–1900* (1979), p. 14. Each building was 25 by 80 feet on a lot 100 feet deep.

19. NBD, 1874, Plan no. 107, by the architect F. S. Barus. Inspectors' names are recorded with the entries, documenting the fact that many inspectors were writing in this new term "French flat"; it was not one inspector's personal quirk.

20. For the continuing cultural nuances of these names, see Speed, "Naming Apartment Houses," p. 283, who mentions "crowded tenements that even the greatest stretch of courtesy would not permit one even to call flats" and nice-looking houses where "tenants insisted they lived in apartments, not flats."

21. NBD, 1880, Plan no. 720. Vaux and Radford are listed as the architects in Francis, *Architects*, p. 78. Views of these buildings are in Bisland, "Co-operative Housekeeping in Tenements," p. 36.

22. "The Building Transactions of the Past Year," *AABN* 7 (February 7, 1880): 47; the author, a buildings inspector, noted that first-class dwellings were for one family and second-class for more than one but that the distinction in the third-class dwellings category between French flats and tenements was inconsistent, although it could be based on plumbing facilities.

23. In a parallel case, Superintendent of Buildings James Macgregor in his *Annual Report, 1867*, pp. 283–88, records his decision to classify some four-unit multiple dwellings as "second class" (no more than three units in the law) rather than "tenement" even though the law clearly says all buildings housing four or more families come under the tenement law. His reason is that the buildings in his opinion "were of a superior class and not intended in the spirit and meaning of the law to come under the classification of tenement houses."

24. C. D. Warner et al., *The American Home Book* (New York: Putnam's, 1872): "The Home," p. 25; *Phillips' Elite Directory* began publication in 1874, coinciding closely with the first wave of French-flat building in New York. The style of listings changes from year to year, but the compilers often use the name of an apartment house as the heading, indenting the list of resident families beneath it. This practice implies that *Phillips' Elite Directory* found nothing socially suspect about apartment living. Later tenants may have found *Phillips' Elite Directory* socially suspect, however, as tenants in the Dakota and other major buildings refused to list their names in the late 1890s editions.

25. These buildings also signify the social acceptability of apartments, evidenced by the fact that many of their occupants were listed in *Phillips' Elite Directory* in the 1870s and 1880s. Phillips listed twenty-six "visitable" Albany tenants in the 1879 directory, including one woman with her own flat, a "Mrs."; in 1880–81 the directory listed two "Drs." at 21 East Twenty-first St., and the following year, four; Mr. and Mrs. Calvert Vaux were included among the residents of the Stuyvesant in 1886–87.

26. Price's plan was published in *AABN* 3 (May 1878), following p. 156. Plans were published for Hunt's Stuyvesant Apartments in Schuyler, *American Architecture*, p. 519 (showing a parlor and a library as the front rooms), and in Alpern, *Apartments for the Affluent*, p. 12 (showing a parlor and a chamber as the front rooms). Plans for the Albany were published in *AABN* 1 (December 23, 1876): following p. 412. Rental units were advertised in the *New York Times* (April 20, 1879): 11–12, where it

was described as an elevator building (meaning dumbwaiter?). Babcock filed plans for the Albany's site originally as NBD, 1874, Plan no. 99, for ten third-class French-flat buildings estimated at $35,000, each with a store on the ground floor.

27. [Leeds], "Parisian 'Flats,'" p. 562.

28. In the *New York Times*, April 1, 1874, p. 7, an apartment was advertised under the heading of "Boarding": "Desirable Third Story suite of apartments to let at Haight House, corner of Fifth Ave., and 15th St., parlor and dining room on 5th Ave. front"; [Leeds], "Parisian 'Flats,'" pp. 561–62.

29. [Leeds], "Parisian 'Flats,'" pp. 561–62.

30. The Albany in London, where Lord Byron had rented rooms after the building was converted to flats in 1804, was described by Sydney Perks, *Residential Flats of All Classes, Including Artisans' Dwellings* (1905), pp. 18–20; illus. p. 19; New York's Albany building was described in *AABN* 1 (December 23, 1876): 413.

31. All advertisements here and later are from various issues of the *New York Times*.

32. *The Plumber and Sanitary Engineer*, in announcing their 1878 competition for an improved tenement design, admitted the drawbacks of the 25-by-100-foot lot; "Urban Housing in New York," pt. 1, *AABN* 3 (March 1878): 90–91, explains the drawbacks of the narrow-lot tradition. Hubert et al., "New York Flats," p. 57, cite the need for land division reform in New York City. A sampling of lot sizes from a single 1874 New Buildings Docket page shows lots of the following sizes: four 25 by 100 feet; others measure 16 feet 8 inches by 102 feet, 20 by 68 feet, 24 feet 9 inches by 125 feet, 26 feet 9 inches by 125 feet, 23 feet by 98 feet 9 inches, and 40 by 100 feet. In the 1860s and 1870s, many of the buildings erected in New York were on lower Manhattan streets, where the map was irregular. In the 1880s and 1890s residential development moved northward, where the street grid was more regular and lot sizes more uniform.

33. Groups of contiguous lots were often subdivided into small, narrow proportions, as in the plans of the developer Benjamin Weber, filed with the Buildings Department in 1869. Weber's property was fifty-four feet wide along West Fifty-fifth St. between Eighth and Ninth avenues. He chose to erect on his frontage four buildings with alternating frontages of 14 and 13 feet, following the long, narrow proportions of local tradition, even though the lot size would have permitted one, two, or three wider buildings. (NBD, 1869, Plan no. 45). Similarly, the new French flats going up in 1876 on a plot 102 by 80 feet could have easily been planned as a single building, but instead were five buildings—called by a single name: the Madison; these French flats were designed by Thom and Wilson at Seventy-second St. and Third Ave., each three stories above a ground-floor store ("Correspondence," *AABN* 1 (April 8, 1876): 118.

34. Israels, "New York Apartment Houses," p. 480; "The Passing of the 25′ by 100′ Lot in New York City," *Architectural Record* 11 (October 1901): 712. After the "New Law" of 1901, which expanded the required courtyard size of tenements, it became next to impossible to erect a multiple dwelling on the old 25-foot narrow lot and still provide the legal requirements of light and air to each unit. Required courtyard sizes were too wide to fit into a single lot. Both the growing popularity of large apartment houses and the legal constraints combined to make the 25-foot-wide apartment building obsolete in new construction by the beginning of the twentieth century.

35. Blackmar, "Housing and Property Relations in New York City, 1785–1850," pp. 260–61, describes, for example, restrictive covenants imposed by Trinity Church on developers of their land at St. John's Park to ensure quality houses.

36. John Niernsee, *Report on the Construction and Embellishment of Private Dwellings in Vienna* (1875). A report on Niernsee's Vienna observations appeared in *AABN* 1 (September 9, 1876): 290–92.

37. Gerrit Forbes, *Report of the New York City Board of Health* (1834); *Annual Report of the Superintendent of Buildings, 1862*, p. 13; Thoms, *Tenant Houses*, compares death-rate tables for London, England, and New York in crowded districts. Beecher, *Treatise on Domestic Economy*, pp. 219–20, recommended a fireplace flue in each bedroom even in country houses, through which fresh air could circulate while residents were sleeping with the doors and windows closed.

38. Richardson, "New Homes of New York," pp. 65–66, 71–72.

39. Howells, *Hazard*, p. 52.

40. "Correspondence—New York," *AABN* 5 (January 11, 1879): 11–12; Lewis Leeds, "Letters—New York Apartment Houses," *New York Times*, July 16, 1882, p. 2, wrote (perhaps exaggerating) that middle-class New York apartment houses had such poor ventilation that they overheated from cooking to the point of raising the mortality rates.

41. Sarah Bradford Landau, "Richard Morris Hunt: Architectural Innovator and Father of a 'Distinctive' American School," in Susan Stein, ed., *The Architecture of Richard Morris Hunt* (Chicago:

University of Chicago Press, 1986), p. 63, shows an abandoned plan for the Stuyvesant Apartments with a large square courtyard.

42. Charles Carroll, "Apartment-Houses," *Appleton's Journal*, n.s. 5 (December 1878): 533; he was not referring to the Stuyvesant in particular but to a generic middle-class French flat.

43. The Albany and other first-generation apartment houses offered themselves as standards for the apartment houses to follow. The Bella, a new apartment house at the southwest corner of Twenty-sixth St. and Fourth Ave., was observed as having the best class of fittings and style, "all the elaboration of the Stevens . . . equally imposing as the Albany." The architect William Schickel designed the Bella of brick with stone trimmings ("The 'Bella' Apartment House," *Real Estate Record and Builders' Guide* 21 [March 23, 1878]: 243).

44. Plans for Holly's family hotel were published in Richardson, "New Homes of New York," pp. 72–74.

45. Described very favorably in "Houses on the European Plan," *Real Estate Record and Builders' Guide* 4 (November 6, 1869): 3.

46. Dreiser, *Sister Carrie*, p. 318.

47. Both public and service circulation were simpler to work out in small buildings than in larger ones. Bigger floor areas seemed to offer more possibilities for consolidation of circulation, but when a centralized circulation system led to five apartments per floor rather than only one or two, the chances for confusion were exaggerated along with chances for economy. Many early buildings seem to have fallen victim to awkward public circulation paths, and the later elevator buildings sometimes had the same kinds of problems.

48. "A New System of Apartment Houses," *AABN* 1 (October 21, 1876): illus. follows p. 340.

49. Tarn, *Five Per Cent Philanthropy*, pp. 100–102; E. T. Potter, "Urban Housing," pt. 5, *AABN* 6 (September 27, 1879): 99; *AABN* 6 (April 1880): 138. The balcony system also gave separate access to each family, enhancing their sense of having an individual home, and reducing contact between tenement families in interior halls and stairs. Too much contact was deemed questionable: not just germs but also ideas could be spread among tenants who saw too much of each other, according to F. van Gashen, *Tenement Houses in Philadelphia* (1895), p. 5.

50. An illustration of pedestrian street-balconies appears in Moshe Safdie, *For Everyone a Garden* (1974), pp. 72–73. Such galleries were seen on other examples of English postwar housing, e.g., James Stirling and Michael Wilford's Southgate, Runcorn New Town, after 1967. See David Mackay, *Multiple Family Housing* (1977), pp. 138–39.

51. Class distinctions among building names are given by Speed in "Naming Apartment Houses," p. 283. *Webster's Third New International Dictionary*, 1963, s.v. "living room," "parlor," "library," still captures some of the differences of meaning important to late nineteenth-century designers and tenants. A "living room" is a room in a residence used for the common social activities of the occupants; a "parlor" is a room in a private dwelling kept chiefly for the reception of visitors rather than for family use and is usually better furnished than the other rooms in the dwelling; a "library" is a room given over to literary and sometimes artistic materials.

52. "French Flats and Apartment Houses in New York," *Carpentry and Building* 2 (January 1880): 2–3.

53. Bisland, "Co-operative Housekeeping in Tenements," pp. 35–42; the illustration of the interior (my fig. 35) shows the room that in plans is labeled "living room" (although on the illustration the artist has written "kitchen"). White, *Sunlighted Tenements*, p. 13; Jackson, *A Place Called Home*, pp. 88–89. See John Kouwenhoven, *Columbia Historical Portrait of New York* (1953); the illustration on p. 460 shows a tenement family doing piecework in their living room; the illustration on p. 384 shows a tenement being used as a factory.

54. Richardson, "New Homes of New York," p. 65. William B. Tuthill, *The City Residence: Its Design and Construction* (1890), pp. 38–41, shows several middle-class plans, so labeled, for 25- and 50-foot-wide lots. See also C. G. Hesselgren, *Apoartments of the Metropolis* (1908) for later plans with middle-class room names.

55. Ford, Morrow, and Thompson, *Slums and Housing*, 2:868. Privies were usual in Manhattan for all classes until water from the Croton Reservoir was brought into city houses in 1842. May Stone, "Plumbing Paradox," *Winterthur Portfolio* 14 (Autumn 1979), gives a survey of fixed indoor plumbing from both a technological and an ideological point of view. Fully developed plans, made as early as 1870, for bathrooms in rural houses appear in Stephen J. Rakeman and Donald Berg, eds., *The 1870 Agriculturist for the Farm, Garden, and Household* (Rockville Centre, N.Y.: Antiquity Reprint, 1980), pp. 38–39, 51, 68, 77. Lack of plumbing fixtures is pointed out by Birmingham, *Life at the Dakota*, p. 37.

56. Teunis J. van der Bent, *Planning of Apartment Houses* (1917), p. 299.

57. Lockwood, *Bricks and Brownstone* (1972), pp. 16, 68, 158, 160, 166, illustrates typical New York row-house plans.

58. See Ernest Flagg, "Planning of Apartment Houses and Tenements," *Architectural Review* 10 (August 1903): 85–90, for a turn-of-the-century reflection on the contrasts perceived between Paris and New York.

59. Vaux, "A.I.A. Address," 218.

60. At first I believed that chambers located near the front door, and often separated from the other chambers in the apartment, might be purposely designed to accommodate boarders, but no census evidence has been found to support this idea. For mid-century house designs where bedrooms are clearly linked with principal social rooms, see Gervase Wheeler, *Homes for the People in Suburb and Country: The Villa, the Mansion, and the Cottage* (1972), pp. 218–22, 341–42.

61. Israels, "New York Apartment Houses," p. 480.

62. "French Flats and Apartment Houses in New York," pp. 2–3, whose portrait of "everybody" I paraphrase here.

63. These numbers are provided in a chart in "Attention, Builders!" *Real Estate Record and Builders' Guide* 27 (April 2, 1881): 299. The source of the figures is not given, but they apparently come from the New Buildings Docket. Although the numbers may not be accurate, the explosion of new apartment buildings is evident. In regard to building private houses, the *Record* cautioned that there had been too much building of houses costing $16,000 to $40,000 (which its editors saw as for middle incomes) when what was needed were real luxury dwellings and housing for the poor and the working populations. As New York became a manufacturing center, the *Record* continued, its mechanics and workmen needed places to live, clean houses, not tenements, in the Twenty-third and Twenty-fourth wards. "The poor should be encouraged to own their own little house and lot in the outlying districts. The dangerous classes in a large city are those who occupy poor and densely populated neighborhoods" (ibid.).

64. "The Bedford Apartment House," *Real Estate Record and Builders' Guide* 25 (January 24, 1880): 81; the architects were O. P. and R. F. Hatfield; the developer was Mr. Cammann.

65. Carroll, "Apartment–Houses," p. 533.

66. "The Florence," *Real Estate Record and Builders' Guide* 21 (April 6, 1878): 287. This Florence, with forty-two suites of apartments, was designed in a symmetrical Florentine Renaissance style with a central pavillion, two wings, a massive dome, and porches supported by four granite columns.

67. "Revolution in Living," *New York Times*, June 3, 1878, p. 4.

68. *New York Times*, September 18, 1880, p. 4.

69. "Attention, Builders!," p. 299.

70. See Boyer, *Manhattan Manners*, pp. 154–65.

4. At Home in the First Apartment Houses

1. For use of the terms "home" and "homelife," see Vaux, "A.I.A. Address," p. 218; "House and Lodging Hunting," *New York Times* (September 25, 1869), p. 4; McCabe, *Paris by Sunlight*, p. 653; Gilman, "The Passing of the Home," pp. 138–40.

2. *New York Times*, November 21, 1865, p. 2; Richardson, "New Homes of New York," p. 64. At the turn of the century the home value of privacy continued to be appealed to: a pamphlet from the New York Land and Warehouse Co. (New York, 1900), p. 32, advertised houses to those newly emerging from the working class with the words "Your own home means room, air, health / Your own bath tub / Your own yard / Your own door step."

3. John Ware, *Home Life: What It Is and What It Needs* (1866), p. 6; *Women's Own Book*. According to Eugene Clarence Gardner, *Home Interiors* (1878), p. 201, to design a house, the architect needs to know little; to design a *home* he must know the client and his family intimately—his whole life style on a level of intimacy that is shocking for strangers to contemplate revealing. "In brief, most men are more intimately affected by the character of their homes than by the potions they absorb, whether doctrinal, legal, or medical. It is true, 'houses' and 'homes' are not identical, but the relationship is very close and peculiar. I confess my inability to draw the line between the material and the spiritual, the economical and the moral, the sanitary and the aesthetic, the useful and the beautiful" (Gardner, *Home Interiors*, pp. 208–9).

4. Ware, *Home Life*, pp. 9, 15.

5. Howells, *Hazard*, pp. 58–59. One 1879 article pointed out the kitchen also as the crucial identifying feature of a middle-class home, but for a different reason: without it, an apartment unit could hardly be more than some kind of hotel suite (Editorial, *American Architect and Building News* 5 [January 11, 1879]: 12).

6. Sopher, "The Landscape of Home," in D. W. Meinig, ed., *The Interpretation of Ordinary Landscapes* (1979), p. 134; William Dean Howells, *April Hopes* (1888), p. 68.

7. May 1 was famous as moving day for many years in New York, but the *New York Times*, April 30, 1880, p. 4, reported that people were giving it up and moving all through April, saving on "inconvenience, nervous friction, endless annoyance, and considerable expense." Before the depression of 1873, it reported, rents were very high and people moved often to try to get cheaper housing. But in the later 1870s rents came down and the supply of housing grew, especially as apartment houses became common.

8. Ware, *Home Life: What It Is and What It Needs*, p.6. This direct equation between a man's home and his status might work in rural settings with detached houses, but contemporaries noticed that among the new buildings of upper Manhattan, a passerby could not tell whether a house was a single-family, a two-family, or a French-flat building from the exterior.

9. This assessment of the house-sized tenement was made in *AABN* 8 (July 31, 1880): 53.

10. The owner was Oswald Ottendorfer; the architect, William Schickel; the site was 50 by 150 feet ("Bella Apartment House," p. 243).

11. Family data from federal census, 1880.

12. *New York Times*, February 14, 1873, p. 4; Halttunen, *Confidence Men and Painted Women*, speculates that by the end of the century, Americans simply had to accept the fact that strangers were not to be taken at face value; even that a certain amount of social deception was necessary to get ahead.

13. "Apartment Houses," pt. 1, *AABN* 29 (September 27, 1890): 194.

14. Beecher, *Treatise on Domestic Economy*, p. 17; Young, *European Modes of Living*, pp. 26–27.

15. Young, "Foreign Modes," p. 474; Hubert et al., "New York Flats," p. 55.

16. Young, "Foreign Modes," p. 474; McCabe, *Paris by Sunlight*, p. 655. Hubert et al., "New York Flats," p. 57.

17. *New York Times*, February 14, 1873, p. 4; "Houses on the European Plan," p. 3. Richardson, "New Homes of New York," p. 68, said that people had to learn from their social betters to feel not at risk of social debasement—which, he said, happened in a short four years from the time the Stuyvesant opened. Richardson's focus on some nervous members of the middle class led him to ignore the huge numbers of people who had shared dwellings before the Stuyvesant opened, but they were not "in society" enough to worry about social debasement.

18. Browne, *Great Metropolis*, p. 548.

19. "Mr. Stewart's Hotel," *Appleton's Journal* 1 (July 3, 1869): 417–19.

20. Williamson, *American Hotel*, pp. 269–70. "Apartment Houses," pt. 4, *AABN* 31 (January 17, 1891): 39, notes that a demand had recently arisen for bachelor-flat buildings to house "lady bachelors."

21. E. T. Littell, "Club Chambers," *AABN* 1 (January 1876): 60; Potter, "Urban Housing," p. 99.

22. In "The Flat," *House Beautiful* 19 (January 1906): 33, a woman gave pointers to other women who wanted to join a "co-operative flat," which meant simply getting together a group of women to rent a flat together. She felt that businesswomen had the best temperaments for "co-flatting." But, as protagonist Lily Bart pointed out in Edith Wharton's *House of Mirth* (1905), pp. 8–9, single, upper-middle-class girls who wanted to make socially successful marriages did not rent their own apartments or even visit bachelors in their flat buildings. Caught by some friends leaving such a flat building after visiting a male friend, Lily had to invent the excuse that she was seeing her seamstress.

23. The adjective "housekeeping" applied to an apartment indicated that a unit had its own kitchen.

24. Young, "Foreign Modes," p. 474.

25. On housework see Susan Strasser, *Never Done: A History of American Housework* (1982), and Ruth Schwartz Cowan, *More Work for Mother* (1983).

26. *New York Times*, November 19, 1874, p. 5.

27. Israels, "New York Apartment Houses," p. 508.

28. Charles Barnard, "Light, Heat, and Power for the Household," *Scribner's Monthly* 19 (November 1879): 145–47, speculated on the future of electric light for the household, not yet available, and on the potentials of a "domestic motor" of some kind.

29. Description from Littell, "Club Chambers," p. 60.

30. On the role of servants see Francis A. Walker, "Our Domestic Service," *Scribner's Monthly* 11 (December 1875): 273–78; Strasser, *Never Done*; David Katzman, *Seven Days a Week* (1978); Dudden, *Serving Women*.

31. *AABN* 91 (January 5, 1907): 6–7, asked designers not to cram servants into garrets; good apartment buildings, it stated, even when their apartments were "non-housekeeping," always had at least one servant's room attached to the main suite.

32. Young, "Foreign Modes," p. 482; Hartley, *Ladies' Book of Etiquette*, p. 242.

33. Beecher, *Treatise on Domestic Economy*, p. 17; Grace Ellis, "Our Household Servants," *Galaxy* 14 (September 1872): 354. Not only were good servants hard to find and keep, but critics complained that the freedom promised to all in the United States tended to lift servants from their social level, reducing their numbers further. While contemporaries asserted that some menial class was necessary to do the drudgery, "the tendency of civilization, culture and education, though good and beautiful, is to advance and elevate so much that we are in danger of being left without any class of persons whose intellect and capacity render them efficient in the humbler duties of life" (Ellis, "Our Household Servants," p. 354). People who had hopes of rising economically, educationally, and culturally could not be expected to be happy as servants or stick to their low-status jobs for any longer than they had to. See Carol Lasser, "The Domestic Balance of Power: Relations Between Mistress and Maid in Nineteenth-Century New England," *Labor History* 28 (Winter 1987): 5–22.

34. Wright, *Moralism and the Model Home*, p. 36.

35. Dreiser, *Sister Carrie*, pp. 307, 342.

36. Siegfried Giedion, *Mechanization Takes Command* (1969), pp. 534–603.

37. Catharine Beecher and Harriet Beecher Stowe, cited by Giedion, *Mechanization Takes Command*, p. 566. Frank R. Stockton and Marian Stockton, *The Home: Where It Should Be and What to Put in It*, pp. 111–13.

38. "Housekeeping," *Cornhill* (London) 29 (1874): 69.

39. "French Apartment Houses," *New York Times*, April 16, 1871, p. 3.

40. [Leeds], "Parisian 'Flats,'" pp. 561–62.

41. Wight, "Apartment Houses Practically Considered," pp. 307–13; Christine Terhune Herrick, "Their Experience in a Flat," *Harper's Weekly* 34 (January 11, 1890): 30–31.

42. Littell, "Club Chambers," p. 60.

43. *New York Times*, September 3, 1876, p. 5.

44. *New York Times*, September 25, 1881, p. 6.

45. Carroll, "Apartment-Houses," pp. 529–35.

46. Advertisement for Sherwood in *New York Times* (April 1, 1875): 11; Carroll, "Apartment-Houses," 531; even the Dakota was called a "family hotel" in the *Real Estate Record and Builders' Guide*, since it had a restaurant–dining room on the ground floor, although most other writers referred to it as an "apartment house." But according to "French Flats and Apartment Houses in New York," p. 3, which described to outsiders just what an apartment house was like, some had a restaurant and served meals in a common dining room, others served meals in private suites, and others had only private kitchens. All variants were still considered apartment houses and not "family hotels."

47. *Webster's Third New International Dictionary*, s.v. "neighbor," "neighborhood." The word "neighbor" has its origins in the Old English *neah*, "near," and *gebur*, "dweller." Two meanings for "neighborhood": "the quality or state of being immediately adjacent or relatively near to something: proximity"; and "a number of people forming a loosely cohesive community . . . living close or fairly close together . . . and usually having some common or fairly common identifying feature (as approximate equality of economic condition, similar social status, similar national origins or religion)" (ibid.).

48. I am indebted to Elizabeth Blackmar for this observation on early nineteenth-century usage from her reading of the Bleecker Diary in New York Public Library, Manuscript Collection.

49. Boyer and Scheer, "Development and Boundaries of Luxury Neighborhoods." They trace the location and character of New York's luxury neighborhoods, using anthropological concepts of taboo and pollution to discuss the relation of luxury to nonluxury uses of land.

50. The Weber buildings (NBD, 1869, Plan no. 45) were to include a stable with one dwelling unit on the second floor; a four-story dwelling for three families—the first and second floors were to be a duplex; a two-story stable and storehouse; a six-story building with basement, to be used as a warehouse; and a five-story building to have five residential units with a store in the basement.

51. Richardson, "New Homes of New York," p. 69.

52. Wight, "Apartment Houses Practically Considered," p. 312.

53. *The Central Park Apartments* (1881): 18–19; according to the authors, exclusivity is usually maintained by applying high rents.

54. An advertisement for the Wellington, at Ninety-second St. and Madison Ave., stated, "high-class . . . adjoining private residences" (*New York Times*, April 10, 1899).

55. Israels, "New York Apartment Houses," pp. 481, 492.

56. Just after the turn of the century, several articles mention geographically specific neighborhoods of similar-quality apartment houses; for example, "Architectural Aberrations No. 17: The New York Family Hotel," *Architectural Record* 11 (October 1901): 700; "Architectural Aberrations No. 20: The Hotel Somerset," *Architectural Record* 13 (March 1903): 293; Franz K. Winkler, "Recent Apartment House Design," *Architectural Record* 11 (January 1902). See also the history of an apartment neighborhood on Central Park South by Christopher Gray, "A Street Most Grand," *Avenue Magazine* (Summer 1983). Advertisers described apartment rentals in terms of additional neighborhood features as well: "convenient to the Park" or "near the Metropolitan Museum of Art" (*New York Times*, April 27, 30, 1890, pp. 15, 7).

57. Editorial, *AABN* 7 (January 10, 1880): 10.

58. "The Problem of Living in New York," *Harper's New Monthly Magazine* 65 (November 1882): 918–19. In one of a series of articles entitled "The City's Growth," the *New York Times*, July 3, 1883, p. 4, noted that the side streets west of Sixth Avenue had long been considered "taboo" for genteel real estate development, since they were filled with cheap old houses, stables, saloons, and tenements. But now apartment houses and French flats were being built there, breaking the taboo and expanding the boundaries of the old respectable districts.

59. *New York Times*, September 18, 1880, p. 4.

5. *The Family Flat Grows Up*

1. Numbers here come from summaries of 1880 and 1890 census data, in George E. Waring, *Report on the Social Statistics of Cities* (1886) and John S. Billings, *Report on the Social Statistics of Cities in the United States at the Eleventh Census, 1890* (1895). Streets counted as "open and accepted" by the city in 1890 amounted to 575 miles, 358 of which were paved.

2. Observations on the vitality of flat construction are in "Correspondence—New York," pp. 12–13; descriptions of regions of development are from Waring, *Report on the Social Statistics of Cities*.

3. "The Growth of the City," *New York Times*, July 2, 1883, p. 8.

4. *The Central Park Apartments* (1881); an advertisement offered large and small suites as well as a three-room fully decorated bachelor apartment (*New York Times*, April 30, 1890, p. 7). An article, "The Growth of the City," *New York Times*, July 2, 1883, p. 8, described the novel Central Park Apartments' appearance, its developer, financing, and rents; it was also described in "Vast Apartment Houses," *Real Estate Record and Builders' Guide* 29 (June 3, 1882): 550.

5. *Central Park Apartments*, p. [3].

6. Descriptions, square footages, and some of these tenants' opinions are from the pamphlet *Central Park Apartments*, pp. 16–17. The cooperative ownership scheme failed because Juan de Navarro engaged in shady financial arrangements over mortgage loans to build the Central Park Apartments, according to an editorial in *AABN* 20 (July 31, 1886): 45. Shareholders found that they did not have clear title to their shares in the building, so it was converted to ordinary rental apartments.

7. For the homogeneous development of Fifty-ninth St., see Gray, "A Street Most Grand." It is true that the streets near the Central Park Apartments endured this kind of mixed use; see fig. 41 for Sixth Ave. mixed uses nearby.

8. NBD, 1880, Plan no. 829. The Dakota's history is recounted in Birmingham, *Life at the Dakota*; a plan and view were published in "Our Special Illustration: The Dakota Apartment House," *Sanitary Engineer* 11 (February 1885): 271, and in Alpern, *Apartments for the Affluent*, pp. 20–21.

9. "Our Special Illustration," p. 271; illus. preceding p. 271; apartment conversions from attic and basement spaces at the Dakota in the 1970s have been documented in Peter Carlsen, "Joe d'Urso," *Design Quarterly*, no. 124 (1984): 1–63.

10. "The 'Berkshire,' New York, N.Y.," *AABN* 14 (August 4, 1883): pl. 397.

11. Schuyler, "Henry Hardenbergh," p. 359. In fig. 48 note how the Berkshire apartments dwarf the church shown next door.

12. Schuyler, "Henry Hardenbergh," p. 338.

13. Ibid.; the Dakota's facade "is attained without any sacrifice of unity, or even of formal symmetry, for each front is laterally, as well as vertically, a triple composition" (ibid.).

14. "New Apartment Houses," *AABN* 5 (May 31, 1879): 175. The idea that architectural style has more serious motivations than simply being "in style" has not been popular as an explanation. I have no contemporary statements explicitly to support my speculations about the performance of architectural details for nineteenth-century apartment dwellers. However, my own experience tells me that people need means to personalize and identify with their homes, and that big buildings with unified exterior compositions frequently defeat this. In modern apartment houses such as Mies van der Rohe's residential tower for the elderly at Lafayette Park, Detroit, the anonymous modernist grid is highly inflected by tenants' additions of varicolored drapes and blinds, differentiating on the exterior one apartment from the next. Tenants in Kelly and Gruzen's concrete Chatham Green apartment towers near City Hall in New York painted the outdoor ceilings of their balconies different colors to achieve personalization of units designed to be subsumed in the whole. A study of an aspect of personalization in suburban houses is Elizabeth Cromley, "Modernizing, or 'You never see a screen door on affluent homes,'" *Journal of American Culture* 5 (Summer 1982): 71–79.

15. Real Estate Record and Builders' Guide, *History of Real Estate*, listed all the apartment buildings the authors thought worth recording, which allows an overview of the names of New York buildings up to that time. In *Life at the Dakota*, p. 48, Birmingham listed western names for apartment houses; Speed, "Naming Apartment Houses," p. 283, poked fun at naming buildings; William Dean Howells, *Hazard*, p. 42. Almost 2,000 named buildings are identified in Norton and Patterson, *Living It Up*; many of these are low budget, even tenement, buildings.

16. One Florence was at Eighteenth St. and Fourth Ave., while another was at the northwest corner of Fifth Ave. and Forty-second St. Duplicate and triplicate names can be discovered from the Sanborn fire insurance maps, which often included a list of the names of the larger apartment houses in each district mapped.

17. Edward Deitch, "A Long Huddle and 'I've Got It': Thus Do Buildings Get Their Names," *New York Times*, November 15, 1981, sec. 8, pp. 1, 14.

18. A letter from Henry Hardenbergh, "The Sub-surface Court-yard of the Dakota Apartment House," *AABN* 31 (January 24, 1891): 63–64, clarifies the use of the two-level courtyard, above for tenants and beneath for services; Birmingham's *Life at the Dakota* has detailed descriptions of the building and its changes over time. Hardenbergh had also designed an earlier rectangular courtyard building for his client Edward Clark, the Van Corlear, published in *AABN* 7 (January 24, 1880): illus. no. 213, descr. p. 28. The Van Corlear's courtyard was notably large at 3,500 square feet. Carroll, "Apartment–Houses," p. 534, says that apartment houses "must be *built round a hollow square*" with its center the courtyard; all other methods of ventilation fail. Later, Walter Kilham, "The Planning of Apartment Houses," pt. 1, *Brickbuilder* 11 (January 1902): 249, prefers indented plans with courtyards that open to the street. He argues that enclosed courts breed stale air and fail to provide the essential view of the street that tenants need. See also Irving K. Pond, "The Architecture of Apartment Buildings," pt. 3, *Brickbuilder* 7 (1898).

19. "Apartment Houses," pt. 2, *AABN* 30 (November 15, 1890): 97.

20. Walter Kilham, "The Planning of Apartment Houses," pt. 3, *Brickbuilder* 12 (December 1903): 244.

21. The St. Honoré was advertised in the *New York Times*, April 14, 1899, p. 12; the Somerset was criticized in "Architectural Aberrations No. 20," p. 297. Lavish fronts were criticized in "The Erection of Co-operative Apartment Houses," *New York Times*, January 3, 1881, p. 10.

22. Porte cocheres were recommended in "Apartment Houses," pt. 2, *AABN* 30, p. 97.

23. The problem of overly fancy decorations in both public spaces and within private units was discussed in *Central Park Apartments*, pp. 17–21. The Central Park's halls and stairways were to be lined with enameled brick instead of plastered like a normal interior ("Vast Apartment Houses," *Real Estate Record and Builders' Guide* 29 [June 3, 1882]: 550). "Tenement Houses," *New York Times*, July 5, 1883, p. 4. Three decades after these first large apartment houses, the New York American, *Renting Guide to High Class Apartments* (New York: Star Co., 1911), explicitly defined the social level of the apartments in its listings by, among other features, the decor of the lobby. In a "high class apartment house" the lobby would be richly decorated in marbles, mosaics, stained glass, rugs and tapestries, handsome chairs, and even palm trees.

24. *New York Times*, April 12, 1885, p. 3.

25. Herrick, "Their Experience in a Flat," p. 31; Carroll, "Apartment–Houses," p. 533.

26. "The 'Berkshire,' New York, N.Y.," p. 54; Birmingham, *Life at the Dakota*, p. 35. O. B. Bunce,

"The City of the Future," *Appleton's Journal* 7 (1872); Handlin, *American Home*, p. 221. For an article on the traditional uses of New York attics and roofs for work and play, see "New York Attics and House Tops," *Scribner's Monthly* 21 (April 1881): 882–91.

27. "The 'Berkshire,' New York, N.Y.," illus. 397. Pond points out in "Architecture of Apartment Buildings," pt. 2, p. 139, that "there is a loss of self-respect to all concerned" when service circulation is not kept completely separated from circulation for guests and tenants building-wide, just as they should be kept separated within the unit. The Berkshire's stair-elevator arrangement was like Parisian apartments, yet critics faulted it because it made a chute through which fire could spread. This kind of fire was reported in an editorial in *AABN* 7 (June 5, 1880): 243.

28. Croly, "Contemporary New York Residence," p. 707. Pond, "Architecture of Apartment Buildings," pt. 3, p. 249, suggests to developers and architects guidelines for when to install an elevator, balancing costs, rentals, and class of intended tenants.

29. George Edward Harding, "Electric Elevators," *AABN* 46 (October 27, 1894): 31, 34. He speculated that just as steam elevators used in the early 1870s had given way to hydraulic, so would hydraulic elevators be replaced everywhere by electric ones. The appeal of elevators spread to proposals for using them in private houses: see "Editor's Table," *Appleton's Journal* 14 (November 13, 1875): 30–31. The writer urged readers to move all home kitchen and laundry facilities and equipment to the attic and roof, where they would expel their smells to the sky. This location was easy to get to with elevators and had the added benefit of freeing the rear yard for pleasure.

30. George Andrews, *Twelve Letters on the Future of New York* (1877), p. 11. Of course, "better" tenants did live on the upper floors of the Stuyvesant.

31. For criticism of awkward circulation, see Littell, "Club Chambers," p. 60; Tuthill, *The City Residence*, p. 40; van der Bent, *Planning of Apartment Houses* (1917): 248. The Prasada, built by the architects Romeyn and Wynne in 1907, had a central square courtyard with a single circulation core on one side of it and enormously long corridors inside the units (Alpern, *Apartments for the Affluent*, pp. 46–47). "Modern apartment planning has abandoned the old 'long hall' type of plan," wrote S. Fullerton Weaver in "Planning the Modern Apartment Hotel," p. 207, cautioning his readers not to use long hall plans; the fact that he needed to warn people against this plan suggests that some were still building long halls at that late date.

32. John Pickering Putnam, "Architecture under Nationalism," pt. 1, *AABN* 29 (July 12, 1890): 24.

33. Hubert et al., "New York Flats," p. 57.

34. "Strange Visitor Took a Bath," *New York Times*, April 2, 1898, p. 6.

35. Carroll, "Apartment–Houses," p. 534.

36. The word "cooperative" was the common expression of the period for shared housing; it usually implies both shared responsibilities and shared expenses, but does not imply the legal ownership characteristics of the modern co-op. Everett N. Blanke, in "The Cliff Dwellers of New York," *Cosmopolitan* 15 (July 1893), p. 355, used "cooperation" to describe the sharing of building-wide costs; in "Editor's Table," the editor of *Appleton's Journal* 15 (February 5, 1876), pp. 182–83, called apartment buildings that have central heating and plumbing systems and centrally hired building staff "cooperative structures."

37. Ernest Flagg, *Prospectus for the Fifth Avenue Plaza Apartments* (1883).

38. Advertisement in the *New York Times*, April 27, 1890, p. 15.

39. Hayden, *Grand Domestic Revolution*; Gilman, "Passing of the Home," pp. 137–47; Helen Campbell, *Household Economics*, p. 59.

40. Explanations by contemporary writers of room-grouping principles can be found in Littell, "Club Chambers," p. 60; Flagg, *Prospectus for the Fifth Avenue Plaza Apartments*, pp. 10–11; Tuthill, *City Residence*, pp. 21–22; Israels, "New York Apartment Houses," pp. 496–97; rules for locating rooms are summarized in Pond, "Architecture of Apartment Buildings," pt. 2, pp. 139–41. Van der Bent confirmed in 1917 that there was a trend in the 1880s toward clarification of uses and spatial zoning in *Planning of Apartment Houses*, p. 291.

41. Israels, "New York Apartment Houses," p. 499.

42. Advertisements in the *New York Times*, April 12, 1885, p. 10, and April 11, 1899, p. 9; *Central Park Apartments*, with statements from the architects Hubert, Pirsson, and Hoddick, p. 21.

43. Hesselgren, *Apartment Houses of the Metropolis*, p. 5, stated that duplex apartments were a New York invention, although earlier Parisian apartments had had rooms on more than one floor. The history of duplex development is told in Elisha Harris Janes, "The Development of Duplex Apartments," pts. 1–3, *Brickbuilder* 21 (June, July, August 1912): 159–61, 183–86, 203–206. Triplexes

were planned for the building described in Flagg, *Prospectus for the Fifth Avenue Plaza Apartments*: 10. Pond, "Architecture of Apartment Buildings," pt. 2, pp. 139–41, considers several kinds of duplexes.

44. Vaux, "Parisian Buildings," pp. 809–810. Henry Hudson Holly designed a duplex "family hotel" (Richardson, "New Homes of New York," p. 75; illus. pp. 64, 72, 74). Another curious split-level duplex in a 50-foot-wide building was published in "New Apartment Houses," *Scribner's Monthly* 21 (April 1881): 964–67, in which the front left suite of rooms and the rear right suite were connected by a stair and formed a single apartment. Each suite had a double-height parlor with the remaining rooms stacked behind in two layers.

45. Flagg, "Planning of Apartment Houses," p. 90. Duplex units were sometimes included in second-class dwellings; e.g., NBD, 1869, Plan no. 2, had a duplex unit on the first and second floors with two single-family units on the third and fourth. Tuthill, *City Residence*, pp. 44–45, gives schematic sections through types of split-level duplexes. In another proposal, in 1890, Hubert, Pirsson, and Hoddick planned a mammoth thirteen-story duplex building for a full block on Madison Ave. to Fourth Ave., Twenty-sixth to Twenty-seventh streets. This scheme was blocked by the 1885 law limiting apartment-house heights (Handlin, *American Home*, p. 226, fig. 82, and Hubert et al., "New York Flats," p. 61).

46. Israels, "New York Apartment Houses," p. 498. In 1917 T. J. van der Bent confirmed this perception when he said that placing bedrooms on a level above living rooms gave only a "sentimental advantage" (*Planning of Apartment Houses*, p. 248). Some examples of expensive duplex apartments, all built after the turn of the century, may be found in Alpern, *Apartments for the Affluent*, pp. 44–45, 68–69, 72–73, and 90–91. A variant, the so-called "studio" apartment, was tried in the first decade of the twentieth century; this type had a double-height artist's studio, facing north to get the most even light for artists to paint by. Remaining rooms with normal ceiling heights on two floors completed the apartment, which characteristically turned out to be too expensive for real artists. See, e.g., A. C. David, "A Co-operative Studio Building," *Architectural Record* 14 (October 1903).

47. Marcou, "Modern House in Paris."

48. *Report on Elevated Dwellings in New York City*, n.p. "Hearing on the Bill to Restrict Height of Buildings," *Sanitary Engineer* 11 (May 21, 1885): 515; the text of a proposed bill was included in *Sanitary Engineer* 11 (April 9, 1885): 398. The law limited non-fireproof apartment houses to 85′; 12-story fireproof apartment houses to 150′ on 80′ wide streets; and 10 story to 125′ high on 60′ wide streets. An average 7 story masonry construction apartment house did not go beyond 75′ usually because the thickening of bearing walls (which was essential to make the building stable above the height) cut down too much on rentable square feet (Israels, "New York Apartment Houses," p. 486).

49. Fire recounted in *New York Times*, April 8, 1884, p. 4.

50. Editorial in *AABN* 20 (July 1886): 74.

6. The Modern Apartment House

1. David Hammack, *Power and Society: Greater New York at the Turn of the Century* (1982), p. 81. Manhattan's population in 1890 was 1,441,216, and in 1900 it was 1,850,093, according to United States Bureau of the Census, *Thirteenth Census . . . 1910* (Washington, D.C.: Government Printing Office, 1913): 2:71.

2. The estimate in 1910 is from Gordon D. MacDonald, *Apartment Building Construction: Manhattan, 1902–1953* (1953), pp. 1, 8. According to MacDonald's table 2, 4,425 apartment buildings were built in Manhattan between 1902 and 1910, comprising 116,950 dwelling units. These estimates are imprecise because of the lack of a definition of "apartment house" at the beginning of the period (it was not a legal term until 1929) and the blurring of the boundaries of apartments into hotels, second-class dwellings, and tenements. Nonetheless, judged by estimated quantity, middle-class multiple dwellings were enormously successful and widely built.

3. Hubert, Pirsson, and Hoddick, "New York Flats," pp. 60–61. From the end of the 1890s until 1901, when the new housing law was enacted, there was a burst of construction in small flats, typically seven stories high. These were undertaken by developers who wanted to take advantage of the current building law that allowed this size of flat to be of nonfireproof construction and feared that the new law would make all new construction prohibitively expensive (see Elisha Harris Janes, "The Development and Financing of Apartment Houses in New York," pt. 1, *Brickbuilder* 17 [December 1908]: 277).

4. Tuthill, *City Residence*, chap. 4.

5. Tuthill, *City Residence*, pp. 38–41; quoted from Hubert, Pirsson, and Hoddick, "New York Flats," pp. 60–61.

6. T. M. Clark, "Apartment-Houses," *AABN* 91 (January 5, 1907): 3–4.

7. Clark, "Apartment-Houses," pp. 6–7. The inclusion of a servant's room within the unit was recommended even for nonhousekeeping units.

8. The building at 520 Park Avenue was illustrated in *AABN* 100 (November 1911), illus. no. 1875. It had both duplex and single-floor units.

9. Handlin, *American Home*, p. 352; Handlin's "primitive" home is the equivalent of James Marston Fitch's term "pre-industrial" for houses with generalized and similar spaces for all rooms, in *American Building: The Historical Forces That Shaped It* (1966), 1:118, 120.

10. Beecher, *Treatise on Domestic Economy*, pp. 276–77, figs. 11, 12; *Appleton's Home Books* (1884), 1:20, 40.

11. Herrick, "Their Experience in a Flat," pp. 30–31.

12. See Diane Douglas, "The Machine in the Parlor," *Journal of American Culture* 5 (Spring 1982), for the tendency to hide work-related machinery like sewing machines inside parlor-style desk or cabinet pieces. An array of multipurpose furniture such as beds that fold up into desks or pianos can be seen in nineteenth-century trade catalogs in Collection of Printed Books, Henry Francis du Pont Winterthur Museum, Winterthur, Del.

13. Ella Louise Taylor, "Rose and Elizabeth in a Flat," *House Beautiful* 11 (February 1902): 163 65. The writer of a letter, "A Small Apartment," to *House Beautiful* 19 (January 1906): 6–7, said she would soon be moving into a small apartment where "the small room opening out of the living room is a bedroom, but [I] will use it as a dining-room, leaving the sliding door open." Another writer of a letter "A Dark Apartment" reported that in her eight-room apartment "room 8 can be used either as a bedroom or dining-room, in which case room 5 would be a library or sitting room" (*House Beautiful* 19 [February 1906]: 7–8).

14. Chapin, *Standard of Living*, found that between 15 percent and 28 percent of a workingman's pay went for rent. A four-room apartment for that class in 1909 went for at least $14 a month in most parts of Manhattan.

15. "City and Suburban Living," *New York Times*, April 1, 1894, p. 18.

16. Frank L. Fisher, *A Complete List of West Side Dwellings*, [1895]. *New York Times*, April 3, 1898, p. 10; April 1, 1899, p. 10.

17. E. Idell Zeisloft, *The New Metropolis* (1899), pp. 274–89.

18. Zeisloft, *New Metropolis*, pp. 279–80; this class often rented a house in New York, paying $2,000 to $5,000 a year, and in summer rented a seaside villa or took the family to a summer hotel. They employed servants and rented a coach instead of buying one.

19. Ibid., p. 280; many of these families also lived in single-family houses on the side streets.

20. Ibid., pp. 280–81.

21. Ibid., pp. 285–87, 289. The biggest class outside the poor (the sixth class) was the fifth class, who had an income of $1,500 to $5,000 per year; they were also the worst off because they could never afford to house, dress, or educate themselves as they felt they deserved. According to Zeisloft, they lived in buildings that they called flats and apartments but in reality were tenements. For these people, he believed the best solution was to get a modest home in the suburbs; for what they could afford there was no nice housing in the city. The sixth class was one-fourth of the whole population—the "contented poor." It included skilled artisans, employees of government agencies, and others with regular incomes of under $1,000 per year. The rent in model tenements for this class was $1.50 per week for two rooms—a kitchen and a bedroom. Working girls made from $3 to $6 a week and spent $1.50 on rent, scrimping on their food and cooking at home. The "submerged poor," the seventh class, were those who lived in squalor.

22. Ibid., pp. 283–84. Also remarking on the rentals available to male and female bachelors is Pond, "Architecture of Apartment Buildings," pt. 3, p. 251.

23. Israels, "New York Apartment Houses."

24. "The Carlyle Chambers," *AABN* 73 (September 21, 1901), pl. 1343; the description of the building focuses entirely on the shopfront windows and appears to take for granted that bachelor apartments belong above commercial activities.

25. Advertisement in *New York Times*, April 3, 1904, p. 18. Israels, "New York Apartment Houses," p. 481. Nonhousekeeping units such as these at the Century and the Carlyle Chambers did not match standard definitions of home, and even fell between legal jurisdictions. Israels, quoting section 9 of the New York City 1899 Building Code, reported that the law governing apartments defined an

apartment as "a home . . . for three or more families, living independently of each other, and in which every such family or household shall have provided for it a kitchen." A hotel, on the other hand, might provide dwelling suites without kitchens but had to have "a general public dining room or cafe or both." When the Buildings Department ruled, c. 1900, that bachelor flats could be excused from the kitchen requirement and still be called apartments, they released bachelor flats from their legal limbo.

26. "An Outbreak of Hotel Building," *Real Estate Record* 48 (October 24, 1891): 500–501.

27. For features of the 1880s family hotels, see *New York Times*, May 17, 1880, p. 4, and "Hotel Life in New York," ibid., April 15, 1883, p. 5. Advertisements in the *New York Times*, September 9, 1894, placed hotels and apartments on the same page, where "family hotels" such as the Gerard, the Hotel Winthrop, and the Hotel Balmoral offered monthly and annual rates and weekly board arrangements, as well as prices for transients.

28. The large number of new apartment-hotel projects is recorded in Buildings Department applications: the department had eleven plans filed in 1900, up from the previous year; in 1901, forty-six plans were filed, and in 1902, forty-four plans had been filed up through October.

29. *King's Photographic Views of New York* (Boston: Moses King, 1895). In 1904 some ninety-five apartment hotels were to be built, averaging seventy-five apartments per building, housing 15,000 people. According to an article in the *Architectural Record*, "three out of four" of these buildings were located south of Fifty-seventh, north of Thirtieth streets—in the heart of entertainment and activity; they were for business "Bohemians" for whom restaurants and theaters played a large part in social life ("Over the Draughting Board: Opinions Official and Unofficial," *The Architectural Record* 13 [January 1903]: 89, 88). The *Architectural Record* also noted that only a few years ago there had been little demand for this residential type, which seems to contradict their observation that many earlier apartment buildings had been converted to the purpose.

30. Reginald Pelham Bolton, "The Apartment Hotel in New York," *Cassier's Magazine* 24 (November 1903): 27–32.

31. *AABN* 91 (January 5, 1907): 10.

32. Ibid., p. 4.

33. Ibid., p. 10.

34. *New York Times*, April 3, 1904, p. 18. There were many listings for rooms and apartments under the category "Apartment Hotels": e.g., Hotel Belmont, 116 West Forty-fifth St.; Touraine, 9 East Thirty-ninth St.; Brunswick, Madison Ave. corner of Eighty-ninth St.; Sevillia, 117 W. Fifty-eighth St. An example of advertising for apartment hotels is this advertisement for the Brayton, 62 Madison Ave. at the corner of Twenty-seventh St.: "High-class fireproof Apartment Hotel. For a few select families. Handsomely furnished and unfurnished, 1, 2, 3 and 4 rooms, baths, private halls. Transients accommodated; week or season. Highest references essential" (*New York Times*, April 3, 1904, p. 18).It had become common to require references.

35. "Over the Draughting Board," pp. 89–91.

36. Ibid., pp. 90–91.

37. Ibid., pp. 90–91; Boyer, *Manhattan Manners*.

38. Robert Grant, "The Art of Living: The Dwelling," *Scribner's Magazine* 17 (February 1895): 144–45.

39. Putnam, "Architecture under Nationalism," pt. 2, pp. 40–42.

40. Ibid., pt. 1, p. 24.

41. "The Problem of Living in New York," *Harper's New Monthly Magazine* 65 (November 1882): 922; Editorial, *AABN* 91 (January 5, 1907): 2.

42. Editorial, *AABN* 91 (January 5, 1907): 1–2.

43. Dudden, *Serving Women*, p. 73; Katzman, *Seven Days a Week*, p. 286, table.

44. Israels, "New York Apartment Houses," p. 496. Plumbing improvements required building-wide systems combined with individual apartment installations, which became an attraction to renters. In the first decade of the twentieth century, advertisements for both single and multiple dwellings made a special feature of multiple bathrooms and toilets.

45. Cowan, *More Work for Mother: The Ironies of Household Technology from the Open Hearth to the Microwave*, discusses aspects of this change and makes the analysis that the more effective housework machinery became, the higher standards rose. Now, the modern household worker with much better machinery has to work just as hard to meet current standards as the machineless household worker of the nineteenth century did to meet the standards of her day.

46. The features of these various apartments are listed in rental advertisements in the *New York*

Times, April 3, 1904, p. 18. Israels, "New York Apartment Houses," p. 496, expressed his concern for apartment plans that would be sensitive to new technological additions. Katherine Busbey, reporting on American dwelling habits in 1910 for an English audience (*Home Life in America*), noted that advertisements in Washington, D.C., used the code "A.M.I.," which meant "all modern improvements." Busbey's list of typical "A.M.I." in flats included a gas range, steam or hot-water heating, warm and cold water in bath and kitchen, and a freight lift to the basement. Usually supplied in an American flat also, Busbey reported, was a large bathroom with porcelain-lined tub and exposed nickel plumbing, which must have impressed her English readers.

47. Clark, "Apartment Houses," p. 4; the large collection of trade catalogs in the Winterthur Museum Library gives a sampling of the new inventions available to housekeepers in the late nineteenth and early twentieth centuries. Some of these items, particular models of ranges and refrigerators, are designated as especially for apartments, usually because they are smaller than the usual size.

48. Israels, "New York Apartment Houses," p. 502.

49. Ibid., pp. 499, 502. Cf. Israels's "co-operative character of the age" with Alan Trachtenberg, *The Incorporation of America* (1982), which examines the trend toward business incorporation from 1880 to 1920. Helen Campbell, "Is Woman Embodied Obstruction?" *Arena* 15 (February 1896): 373. Christine Herrick observed that the line between true "co-operative housekeeping" as theorized by feminists and familiar forms of urban domestic arrangements was blurred, passing over into a variety of apartment hotels and family hotels to the ordinary apartment house ("Co-operative Housekeeping," p. 188). A cooperative apartment house proposed by Professor Fick of Copenhagen was published in "The Apartment House Up to Date," *Architectural Record* 22 (July 1907): 68–71.

50. *AABN* 91 (January 5, 1907): pl. 1619 and p. 21; "The Casa Alameda, New York, N.Y.," *AABN* 40 (May 1893): pl. 909.

51. Janes, "Development and Financing of Apartment Houses," pt. 1, p. 277; "Architectural Aberrations No. 19: The Dorilton," *Architectural Record* 12 (June 1902): 221; "Architectural Aberrations No. 17"; "Architectural Aberrations No. 20: The Hotel Somerset," *Architectural Record* 13 (March 1903): 292, 296; Thorstein Veblen, *Theory of the Leisure Class* (1899; New York: Macmillan, 1912), p. 154.

52. *AABN* 31 (February 21, 1891): pl. 791; Israels, "New York Apartment Houses," pp. 507–8.

53. Israels, "New York Apartment Houses," p. 508; classical detailing was described in Real Estate Record and Builders' Guide, *History of Real Estate*, p. 607, as a "labor saving device for the pressed and hurried architect."

54. Editorial in *AABN* 75 (January 11, 1902): 9; Croly, "Contemporary New York Residence," p. 705.

55. *American Architect and Building News* 91 (January 5, 1907): 1; this writer suggests that more could be done to develop privacy-giving devices such as Chambord-type spiral stairs where those going up use a separate flight from those coming down.

56. Cowan, *More Work for Mother*, has explored this paradox and concludes that the ideology of family privacy with the housewife inside the house lay behind manufacturers' choices to develop and press on the market individualized household conveniences. Examples of refrigerator catalogs from the Winterthur Museum collection include *McCray Refrigerators for Residences* (Chicago, 1911), the McCray Co., p. 15, "No. 438 Designed Particularly for Apartment Houses"; the McCray Co. publication "How to Use a Refrigerator" (Chicago, 1903); *McCray Refrigerators for the Residence* (Kendallville, Ind., and Chicago, 1906), no. 81 in catalog; *Monroe Porcelain Refrigerators* (Lockland, Ohio, n.d.[1906?]); *Eddy's Refrigerators* (Boston, Mass., 1903).

57. "The Duplex Apartment House," *Architectural Record* 29 (April 1911): 327.

58. Editorial in *AABN* 91 (January 5, 1907): 1.

BIBLIOGRAPHY

"The Albany." *American Architect and Building News* 1 (December 23, 1876): pl. following p. 412.

Allain, Albert. "Architectural Design as It Is in France." *Architectural Record* 11 (January 1902): 37–59.

Alpern, Andrew. *Apartments for the Affluent: A Historical Survey of Buildings in New York.* New York: McGraw-Hill, 1975. Reissued as *New York's Fabulous Luxury Apartments.* New York: Dover, 1987.

Andrews, George. *Twelve Letters on the Future of New York.* New York: Martin Brown, 1877.

Andrews, Wayne. *Architecture in New York.* New York: Atheneum, 1969.

Annual Report of the Superintendent of Buildings. Reports for 1862–69. New York: Poole and MacLauchlan, 1872.

"Apartment-hotel at Numbers 204–206 West 72nd Street, New York, N.Y." *American Architect and Building News* 78 (November 1902): pl. 1045.

"Apartment Hotels in New York City." *Architectural Record* 13 (January 1903): 85–91.

"Apartment House in Central Park West, New York, N.Y." *American Architect and Building News* 70 (December 1900): 96, pl. 1304.

"Apartment House on Clark Street near Fulton." *American Architect and Building News* 28 (May 1890): 138, pl. 753.

"Apartment House on East 21st Street by Bruce Price." *American Architect and Building News* 3 (May 1878): pl. following p. 156.

"Apartment House Up to Date." *Architectural Record* 22 (July 1907): 68–71.

"Apartment Houses." Parts 1–4. *American Architect and Building News* 29 (September 27, 1890): 194–95; 30 (November 15, 1890): 97–100; 31 (January 10 and 17, 1891): 20–23, 37–39.

"Apartment Houses." *American Architect and Building News* 91 (January 5, 1907): 1–21. Special issue.

"Apartment Houses." *Real Estate Record and Builders' Guide* 3 (July 17, 1869): 3.

"Apartment Life." *Independent* 54 (January 1902): 110–11.

Appleton's Home Books. 3 vols. New York: Appleton, 1884.

"The Apthorp Apartments—The Largest in the World." *Architecture* 18 (1908): 129–31.

"Architectural Aberrations No. 17: The New York Family Hotel." *Architectural Record* 11 (October 1901): 700–704.

"Architectural Aberrations No. 19: The Dorilton." *Architectural Record* 12 (June 1902): 221–26.

"Architectural Aberrations No. 20: The Hotel Somerset." *Architectural Record* 13 (March 1903): 293–96.

Architecture de Paris: Maisons les plus remarquables de Paris. London: Asher, 1871.

Associated Architects. *Artistic Modern Homes.* New York: Associated Architects, 1902.

The Astral Apartments (pamphlet). Brooklyn, [1895].

"Attention, Builders!" *Real Estate Record and Builders' Guide* 27 (April 2, 1881): 299.

Bachelard, Gaston. *The Poetics of Space.* Boston: Beacon Press, 1969.

Baker, Paul R. *Richard Morris Hunt.* Cambridge, Mass.: MIT Press, 1980.

Barnard, Charles. "Home and Society: Light, Heat, and Power for the Household." *Scribner's Monthly* 19 (November 1879): 145–47.

Barth, Gunther. *City People: The Rise of Modern City Culture in Nineteenth-Century America.* New York: Oxford University Press, 1980.

Bauer, Catherine. *Modern Housing.* Boston: Houghton Mifflin, 1934.

Becherer, Richard. *Science plus Sentiment: César Daly's Formula for Modern Architecture.* Ann Arbor, Mich.: UMI Research Press, 1984.

Beecher, Catharine. *A Treatise on Domestic Economy.* New York: Marsh, Capen, Lyon, and Webb, 1841. Reprint ed., New York: Schocken, 1977.

Beecher, Catharine, and Stowe, Harriet Beecher. *The American Woman's Home.* New York: J. B. Ford, 1869.

"The Bella Apartment House." *Real Estate Record and Builders' Guide* 21 (March 23, 1878): 243.

"The 'Berkshire,' New York, N.Y." *American Architect and Building News* 14 (August 4, 1883): 53, pl. 397.

Billings, John S. M. D. *Report on the Social Statistics of Cities in the United States at the Eleventh Census: 1890.* Washington, D.C.: Government Printing Office, 1895.

Birmingham, Stephen. *Life at the Dakota: New York's Most Unusual Address.* New York: Random House, 1979.

Bisland, Elizabeth. "Co-operative Housekeeping in Tenements." *Cosmopolitan* 8 (November 1889): 35–42.

Blackall, C. "The Housing of the Poor." Parts 1, 2. *American Architect and Building News* 52 (April, May 1896): 23–26, 63–69.

Blackmar, Elizabeth S. "Housing and Property Relations in New York City, 1785–1850." Ph.D. diss., Harvard University, 1980.

———. *Manhattan for Rent, 1785–1850.* Ithaca: Cornell University Press, 1989.

———. "Re-walking the 'Walking City': Housing and Property Relations in New York City, 1780–1840." *Radical History Review* 21 (Fall 1979): 131–48. Reprinted in *Material Life in America, 1600–1869,* ed. Robert St. George, pp. 371–84. Boston: Northeastern University Press, 1987.

Blanke, Everett N. "The Cliff Dwellers of New York." *Cosmopolitan* 15 (July 1893): 354–62.

Blumin, Stuart M. "The Hypothesis of Middle-Class Formation in Nineteenth-Century America: A Critique and Some Proposals." *American Historical Review* 90 (April 1985): 299–338.

"Boarding Out." *Harper's Weekly* 1 (March 7, 1857): 146.

Bolton, Reginald Pelham. "The Apartment Hotel in New York." *Cassier's Magazine* (London) 24 (November 1903): 27–32.

Bourne, Larry S., ed. *Internal Structure of the City: Readings on Space and Environment.* New York: Oxford University Press, 1971.

Bowker, R. R. "Working Men's Homes." *Harper's New Monthly Magazine* 68 (April 1884): 769–84.

Boyer, M. Christine. *Manhattan Manners*. New York: Rizzoli, 1985.

Boyer, M. Christine, and Scheer, Jessica. "The Development and Boundaries of Luxury Neighborhoods in New York, 1625–1890." Draft of Working Paper No. 1. New York: Columbia University Center for Preservation Planning, 1980.

Boyer, Paul. *Urban Masses and Moral Order in America, 1820–1920*. Cambridge, Mass.: Harvard University Press, 1978.

Branca, Patricia. "Image and Reality: The Myth of the Idle Victorian Woman." In *Clio's Consciousness Raised*, ed. Mary Hartman and Lois Banner, pp. 179–91. New York: Harper and Row, 1974.

Browne, Junius Henri. *The Great Metropolis: A Mirror of New York*. Hartford: American Publishing, 1869.

Buckham, Charles W. "Duplex Co-operative Apartment Houses." *American Architect* 96, no. 1774 (July–December 1909): 266–71.

_____. "The Present and Future Development of the Apartment House." *American Architect and Building News* 100 (November 1911): 224–27.

Bunce, O. B. "The City of the Future." *Appleton's Journal* 7 (1872): 156–58.

Bunner, H. C. *The Story of a New York House*. New York: Scribner's, 1887.

Busbey, Katherine G. *Home Life in America*. London: Methuen, and New York: Macmillan, 1910.

Campbell, Helen. "A Comfortable House." *Cosmopolitan* 3 (May 1887): 195–97.

_____. *Household Economics*. New York: Putnam's, 1896.

_____. "Household Furnishings." *Architectural Record* 6 (October–December 1896): 97–104.

"The Carlyle Chambers." *American Architect and Building News* 73 (September 21, 1901): 96, pl. 1343.

Carroll, Charles. "Apartment-Houses." *Appleton's Journal* n.s. 5 (December 1878): 529–35.

"The Casa Alameda, New York, N.Y." *American Architect and Building News* 40 (May 1893): 139, pl. 909.

"The Central Park Apartment." *Building* 2 (December 1883): 32.

The Central Park Apartments on 7th Avenue . . . Facing the Park. Pamphlet. New York: American Banknote, 1881.

Chamberlin, Helen M. "A Small City Apartment." *House Beautiful* 4 (June 1898): 18–21.

Chandler, Charles Frederick. Scrapbooks, 1873–83. Avery Library Collection, Columbia University, New York.

Chapin, Robert Coit. *Standard of Living among Workingmen's Families in New York City*. New York: Charities Publication Committee (Russell Sage Foundation), 1909.

Church, Ella Rodman. *How to Furnish a Home*. Vol. 1 of *Appleton's Home Books*. New York: Appleton, 1884.

Clark, Clifford. "Domestic Architecture as an Index to Social History." *Journal of Interdisciplinary History* 7 (Summer 1976): 33–56.

Clark, T. J. *The Painting of Modern Life*. New York: Knopf, 1985.

Clark, T. M. "Apartment-Houses." *American Architect and Building News* 91 (January 5, 1907): 3–11.

Cohen, Lizabeth. "Embellishing a Life of Labor: An Interpretation of the Material Culture of American Working-Class Homes, 1885–1915." *Journal of American Culture* 3 (Winter 1980): 752–75.

Cohn, Jan. *The Palace or the Poorhouse: The American House as Cultural Symbol.* East Lansing: Michigan State University Press, 1979.

Coolidge, John. *Mill and Mansion.* New York: Columbia University Press, 1942.

"A Co-operative Apartment House in New York." *Architectural Record* 24 (July 1908): 1–18.

"Correspondence: New Apartment Houses." *American Architect and Building News* 5 (May 31, 1879): 175.

"Cost of a Home." *Harper's New Monthly Magazine* 33 (October 1866): 660–63.

Cowan, Ruth Schwartz. "The Industrial Revolution in the Home: Household Technology and Social Change in the United States." *Technology and Culture* 17 (January 1976): 1–26.

———. *More Work for Mother: The Ironies of Household Technology from the Open Hearth to the Microwave.* New York: Basic Books, 1983.

Croly, Herbert. "The Contemporary New York Residence." *Architectural Record* 12 (December 1902): 704–22.

"The Dakota Apartment House." *Sanitary Engineer* 11 (1885): 271.

David, A. C. "A Co-operative Studio Building." *Architectural Record* 14 (October 1903): 233–54.

DeBow, J. D. B. *The Seventh Census of the United States, 1850.* Washington, D.C., 1853.

De Forest, Robert W., and Lawrence Veiller, eds. *The Tenement House Problem.* 2 vols. New York: Macmillan, 1903.

Department of Buildings of the City of New York. "New Buildings Docket." 1866–1880.

Department of the Interior. *Compendium of the Tenth Census* (June 1880). Washington, D.C.: Government Printing Office, 1883.

"Designing a Modern House." *Scribner's Magazine* 28 (July 1900): 125–28.

Disturnell, John. *New York as It Was and as It Is.* New York: Van Nostrand, 1876.

Douglas, Ann. *The Feminization of American Culture.* New York: Avon, 1977.

Douglas, Diane. "The Machine in the Parlor." *Journal of American Culture* 5 (Spring 1982): 20–29.

Douglas, Mary, and Baron Isherwood. *The World of Goods.* New York: Norton, 1979.

Dow, Joy Wheeler. *American Renaissance: A Review of Domestic Architecture.* New York: W. T. Comstock, 1904.

Dreiser, Theodore. *Sister Carrie.* New York: Penguin, 1981.

Dudden, Faye. *Serving Women: Household Service in Nineteenth-Century America.* Middletown, Conn.: Wesleyan University Press, 1983.

Dunlap, George Arthur. *The City in the American Novel, 1789–1900.* New York: Russell and Russell, 1965.

"The Duplex Apartment House." *Architectural Record* 29 (April 1911): 326–34.

Dwelling Reform Association: Its Origins, Plans, Purposes, Endorsements, Constitution, and Officers. New York: Dwelling Reform Assoc., 1874.

Edgell, George Harold. *The American Architecture of Today.* New York: Scribner's, 1928.

Editorial. *American Architect and Building News* 20 (July 3, 1886): 2; 3 (February 9, 1878): 45; 7 (January 10, 1880): 10; 75 (January 11, 1902): 9; 76 (June 28, 1902): 97; 91 (January 5, 1907): 1–2.

"Editor's Table." *Appleton's Journal* 14 (November 1875): 631–32; 15 (February 1876): 182–83; n.s. 3 (December 1877): 570–71; n.s. 9, no. 52 (October 1880): 382–83; n.s. 11 (December 1881): 568–69.

Ellington, George. *The Women of New York.* New York: New York Book, 1869. Reprint ed., New York: Arno, 1972.

Epstein, Amy Kallman. "Multifamily Dwellings and the Search for Respectability: Origins of the New York Apartment House." *Urbanism Past and Present* 5 (Summer 1980): 29–39.

Evenson, Norma. *Paris: A Century of Change.* New Haven: Yale University Press, 1979.

Fisher, Frank L. *A Complete List of West Side Dwellings.* New York, [1895].

Fitch, James Marston. *American Building: The Historical Forces That Shaped It.* vol. 1. 2d ed. Boston, Mass.: Houghton Mifflin, 1966.

Flagg, Ernest. "The New York Tenement House Evil and Its Cure." *Scribner's Magazine* 16 (July 1894): 108–17.

———. "Planning of Apartment Houses and Tenements." *Architectural Review* (Boston) 10 (August 1903): 85–90.

———. *Prospectus for the Fifth Avenue Plaza Apartments.* New York, 1883.

"The Flat." *House Beautiful* 19 (January 1906): 33.

Follett, Jean. "The Hotel Pelham: A New Building Type for America." *American Art Journal* 15 (Autumn 1983): 58–73.

Forbes, Gerrit. *Report of the New York City Board of Health.* New York: Board of Health, 1834.

Ford, George B. "The Housing Problem." Parts 1–5 *Brickbuilder* 18 (February, April, May, July, September 1909): 26–29, 76–79, 100–104, 144–47, 185–89.

———. "A Modern Paris Apartment House." *Brickbuilder* 17 (January–December 1908): 101–02.

Ford, James, Katherine Morrow, and George N. Thompson. *Slums and Housing.* 2 vols. Cambridge, Mass.: Harvard University Press, 1936.

Francis, Dennis S. *Architects in Practice in New York City, 1840–1900.* New York: Committee for the Preservation of Architectural Records, 1979.

"French Flats and Apartment Houses in New York." *Carpentry and Building* 2 (January 1880): 2–3.

Frohne, H. W. "The Apartment House." *Architectural Record* 27 (March 1910): 205–17.

———. "Contemporary Apartment Building in New York City." *Architectural Record* 28 (July 1910): 61–70.

Fryer, William. *Laws and Ordinances Relating to Buildings in Greater New York.* Boston: Franklin Press, 1881.

Furniss, Louise E. "New York Boarding Houses." *Appleton's Journal* 5 (March 1871): 259–61.

Gallatin, James. *Tenement House Reform in the City of New York.* Boston: Franklin Press, 1881.

Garczynski, Rodolphe E. "Some Old Houses." *Appleton's Journal* 8 (December 1872): 696–99.

Gardner, Eugene Clarence. *Home Interiors.* Boston: J. R. Osgood, 1878.

———. "Model Homes for Model Housekeeping." *Good Housekeeping* 1 (July 25, 1885): 1–4.

Gay, Peter. *The Bourgeois Experience.* Vol. 1: *Education of the Senses.* New York: Oxford University Press, 1984.

Giddens, Anthony, and David Held, eds. *Classes, Power, and Conflict.* Berkeley: University of California Press, 1982.

Giedion, Siegfried. *Mechanization Takes Command.* New York: Norton, 1969.

———. *Space, Time, and Architecture.* 3d ed. Cambridge, Mass.: Harvard University Press, 1956.

Gilman, Charlotte Perkins. "The Passing of the Home in Great American Cities." *Cosmopolitan* 38 (December 1904): 137–47.

Godwin, George. "Houses in Flats for London." *Builder* 3. (January 1875): 25.

Goldstone, Harmon, and Martha Dalrymple. *History Preserved: A Guide to New York City Landmarks and Historic Districts.* New York: Simon and Schuster, 1974.

Goode, James. *Best Addresses: A Century of Washington's Distinguished Apartment Houses.* Washington, D.C.: Smithsonian Institution Press, 1988.

Goodholme, Todd S., ed. *A Domestic Cyclopedia of Practical Information.* New York: Henry Holt, 1878.

Goodman, Paul, and Percival Goodman. *Communitas: Means of Livelihood and Ways of Life.* 1947. Reprint ed., New York: Random House, Vintage Books, 1960.

Gould, Elgin R. L. *The Housing of the Working People.* Eighth special report of the Commission of Labor. Washington, D.C., 1895.

Grant, Robert. "The Art of Living: The Dwelling." *Scribner's Magazine* 17 (February 1895): 135–49.

Gray, Christopher. "A Street Most Grand." *Avenue,* Summer 1983, pp. 50–58.

Gray, George Herbert. *Housing and Citizenship.* New York: Reinhold, 1946.

Halfield, Ethel Glover. "Flatland." *House Beautiful* 12 (August 1902): 189–91.

Hall, Susan. "Apartments to Let." *Galaxy* 14 (1872): 672–76.

Halttunen, Karen. *Confidence Men and Painted Women.* New Haven: Yale University Press, 1982.

Hamilton, Gail. "The Hotel of the Future." *Scribner's Monthly* 11 (November 1875): 108–12.

Hammack, David. *Power and Society: Greater New York at the Turn of the Century.* New York: Russell Sage Foundation, 1982.

Hancock, John. "The Apartment House in Urban America." In *Buildings and Society,* ed. Anthony King, pp. 151–89. London: Routledge and Kegan Paul, 1980.

Handlin, David P. *The American Home: Architecture and Society, 1815–1915.* Boston: Little, Brown, 1979.

Harding, George Edward. "Electric Elevators." *American Architect and Building News* 46 (October 27, 1894): 31.

Hareven, Tamara K. "Family Time and Historical Time." *Daedalus* 106 (Spring 1977): 57–70.

Hartley, Florence. *The Ladies' Book of Etiquette and Manual of Politeness.* Boston: Lee and Shephard, 1872.

Hastings, C. W. "The Passing of the Interior Tenement Stair." *Architects and Builders Magazine* 44 (February 1912): 46–51.

Hayden, Dolores. "Charlotte Perkins Gilman and the Kitchenless House." *Radical History Review* 21 (Fall 1979): 225–47.

———. *A Grand Domestic Revolution: American Visions of Household Liberation.* Cambridge, Mass.: MIT Press, 1980.

———. *Redesigning the American Dream.* New York: Norton, 1984.

Hayward, D. Geoffrey. "Home as an Environmental and Psychological Concept." *Landscape* 20 (October 1975): 2–9.

Healthy Homes for Rich and Poor. New York: Sanitary Engineer, 1880. Reprinted from the *Sanitary Engineer,* "Tenement House Reform—History of the Competition for a Model House for Workingmen and Its Results, 1878–79."

"Hearing on the Bill to Restrict Height of Buildings." *Sanitary Engineer* 11 (May–June 1885): 515.

Herrick, Christine Terhune. "Co-operative Housekeeping." *Munsey's Magazine* 31 (May 1904): 185–88.

———. "Their Experience in a Flat." *Harper's Weekly* 34 (January 11, 1890): 30–31.

Herts, Benjamin Russel. *The Decoration and Furnishings of Apartments.* New York: Putnam's, 1915.

Hesselgren, C. G. *Apartment Houses of the Metropolis.* New York: C. G. Hesselgren, 1908.

Higham, John. *Strangers in the Land: Patterns of American Nativism, 1860–1925*. New York: Atheneum, 1965.

Historic American Buildings Survey. *New York City Architecture: Selections*. Washington, D.C.: National Park Service, 1969.

Holt, Glen E. "The Changing Perception of Urban Pathology: An Essay on the Development of Mass Transit . . ." In *Cities in American History*, ed. Kenneth Jackson and Stanley Schulz, pp. 324–43. New York: Knopf, 1972.

Hooper, Lucy H. "French Society and Parisianized Americans." *Appleton's Journal* 12 (September 1874): 395–98.

Hornung, Clarence. *New York the Way It Was, 1850–1890*. New York: Schocken, 1977.

Horowitz, Daniel. "Frugality or Comfort: Middle-Class Styles of Life in the Early Twentieth Century." *American Quarterly* 37 (Summer 1985): 239–59.

"Hotel Morals." "Man about Town" column. *Harper's Weekly* 1 (September 5, 1857): 563.

"Housekeeping." *Cornhill Magazine* (London) 29 (1874): 69–79.

"Houseless." *Harper's New Monthly Magazine* 26 (May 1863): 789–91.

"Houses on the European Plan." *Real Estate Record and Builders' Guide* 4 (November 6, 1869): 3.

Housing Reform in New York City: Report of the Tenement House Committee. New York: Charities Organization Society, 1914.

Howells, William Dean. *April Hopes*. New York: Harper, 1888.

_____. *A Hazard of New Fortunes*. New York: Harper, 1890. Reprint ed., New York: Signet Classic, New American Library, 1965.

Hubert, Pirsson, and Hoddick. "New York Flats and French Flats." *Architectural Record* 2 (July 1892): 55–64.

Hutchins, William. "New York Hotels." Parts 1 and 2. *Architectural Record* 12 (October, November 1902): 459–71, 621–35.

Improved Housing Council. *Conditions of Competition for Plans of Model Apartment Houses*. New York: Improved Housing Council, 1896.

Israels, Charles. "The Metropolitan Apartment House and Hotel." *Real Estate Record and Builders' Guide* 73 (June 1904): 1464–73.

_____. "New York Apartment Houses." *Architectural Record* 11 (July 1901): 476–508.

Jackson, Anthony. *A Place Called Home: A History of Low-Cost Housing in Manhattan*. Cambridge, Mass.: MIT Press, 1976.

Jackson, John Brinckerhof. *American Space: The Centennial Years, 1865–1876*. New York: Norton, 1972.

Janes, Elisha Harris. "The Development and Financing of Apartment Houses in New York." Parts 1 and 2. *Brickbuilder* 17 (December 1908): 276–78; 18 (January 1909): 10–13.

_____. "The Development of Duplex Apartments." Parts 1–3. *Brickbuilder* 21 (June, July, August 1912): 159–61, 183–86, 203–206.

Kasson, John F. *Civilizing the Machine: Technology and Republican Values in America, 1776–1900*. New York: Viking Press, 1976.

Katz, Michael B. "Social Class in North American Urban History." *Journal of Interdisciplinary History* 11 (Spring 1981): 579–605.

Katzman, David M. *Seven Days a Week: Women and Domestic Service*. New York: Oxford University Press, 1978.

Kaufmann, Edgar, ed. *Rise of an American Architecture*. New York: Praeger and the Metropolitan Museum of Art, 1970.

Keller, Suzanne. *The Urban Neighborhood: A Sociological Perspective*. New York: Random House, 1968.

Kennedy, Joseph C. G. *Preliminary Report on the Eighth Census, 1860*. Washington, D.C.: Government Printing Office, 1862.

Kilham, Walter. "The Planning of Apartment Houses." Parts 1–4. *Brickbuilder* 11 (January 1902): 245–52; 12 (January 1903): 3–6; 12 (December 1903): 244–49; 13 (January 1904): 2–8.

King's Photographic Views of New York. Boston: Moses King, 1895.

Kouwenhoven, John. *Columbia Historical Portrait of New York*. New York: Doubleday, 1953.

Landau, Sarah Bradford. "The Row Houses of New York's West Side." *Journal of the Society of Architectural Historians* 34 (March 1975): 19–36.

Lears, T. J. Jackson. *No Place of Grace: Antimodernism and the Transformation of American Culture, 1880–1920*. New York: Pantheon, 1981.

[Leeds, Lewis]. "Parisian Flats." *Appleton's Journal* 6 (1871): 561–62.

Leeds, Lewis W. "A Modern Paris House." *Plumber and Sanitary Engineer* 21 (1879): 268–69.

Lipstadt, Helene. "Housing the Bourgeoisie: César Daly and the Ideal Home." *Oppositions* 8 (Spring 1977): 33–47.

Littell, E. T. "Club Chambers and Apartment Houses." *American Architect and Building News* 1 (January 1876): 59–60.

Lockwood, Charles. *Bricks and Brownstone: The New York Row House*. New York: McGraw-Hill, 1972.

———. *Manhattan Moves Uptown: An Illustrated History*. New York: Houghton Mifflin, 1976.

Logan, Olive. "At Home in Paris." *Putnam's Magazine*, n.s. 3 (March 1869): 352–57.

"London Residence Flats." *American Architect and Building News* 91 (January 1907): 15–17.

Longstreet, Abby Buchanan. *Social Etiquette of New York*. New York: Appleton, 1879.

Lubitz, Edward. "The Tenement Problem in New York City and the Movement for Its Reform, 1856–1867." Ph.D. diss., New York University, 1970.

Lubove, Roy. "I. N. Phelps Stokes: Tenement Architect, Economist, Planner." *Journal of the Society of Architectural Historians* 23 (May 1964): 75–87.

———. *The Progressives and the Slums: Tenement House Reform in New York City, 1890–1917*. Pittsburgh: University of Pittsburgh Press, 1962.

McCabe, James. *Lights and Shadows of New York Life: The Sights and Sensations of the Great City*. Philadelphia: National Publishing, 1872.

———. *New York by Sunlight and Gaslight*. N.p.: Edgewood, 1882.

———. *Paris by Sunlight and Gaslight*. Philadelphia: National Publishing, 1869.

MacDonald, Gordon. *Apartment Building Construction: Manhattan, 1902–1953*. New York: Real Estate Board of New York [1953].

Mackay, David. *Multiple Family Housing*. New York: Architectural Book, 1977.

Marcou, Paul F. "The Modern House in Paris." *Architectural Record* 2 (January–March 1893): 324–31.

Marcuse, Peter. "Housing in Early City Planning." *Journal of Urban History* 6 (February 1980): 153–73.

Mazade, Fernand. "Living in Paris on an income of $3000 a Year." Parts 1–3. *Architectural Record* 13 (April, May, June 1903): 349–57, 423–32, 549–54.

"Model Tenement Houses." *Carpentry and Building* 2 (October 1880): 191.

"Modernized Existence." *Harper's Weekly* 47 (April 1903): 639–40.

"Modern Plumbing." *Architectural Record* 8 (July 1898): 111–13.

"Mr. Stewart's Hotel for Working People." *Appleton's Journal* 1 (July 3, 1869): 417–19.

"Mr. Stuyvesant's Experiment." *Real Estate Record and Builders' Guide* 4 (November 13, 1869): 3.

"New Apartment, 57th Street and Madison Avenue, New York City." *American Architect and Building News* 15 (May 1884): 234, pl. 438.

"A New Apartment House Design." *American Architect and Building News* 3 (April 6, 1878): 123.

"New Apartment Houses." *Scribner's Monthly* 21 (April 1881): 964–67.

"The New Fifth Avenue." *Critic* 2 (July 1882): 171–72.

"A New System of Apartment Houses." *American Architect and Building News* 1 (October 21, 1876): illus. following p. 340.

New York American. *Renting Guide to High Class Apartments*. New York: Star, 1911.

"New York Attics and House Tops." *Scribner's Monthly* 21 (April 1881): 882–91.

New York City Tenement House Department. *Second Report*. New York, 1903–1905.

"New York Daguerreotyped—Business and Wall Street." *Putnam's Magazine* 1 (February 1853): 121–36.

"New York Daguerreotyped   Hotels, Stores, and Banks." *Putnam's Magazine* 1 (April 1853): 353–68.

"New York Daguerreotyped—Private Residences." *Putnam's Magazine* 3 (March 1854): 233–48.

"New York Daguerreotyped—Public Buildings." *Putnam's Magazine* 3 (February 1854): 141–52.

New York Tenement Houses. Pamphlet no. 4. New York: Citizens' Union, 1897.

New York Times. 1860–1910.

Niernsee, John R. *Report on the Construction and Embellishment of Private Dwellings in Vienna*. Washington, D.C.: Government Printing Office, 1875.

Norton, Thomas E., and Jerry E. Patterson. *Living It Up: A Guide to the Named Apartment Houses of New York*. New York: Atheneum, 1984.

"Notes and Clippings—Apartment Houses Not Tenements." *American Architect and Building News* 76 (April 5, 1902): 8.

Osborne, Charles F. *Notes on the Art of House Planning*. New York: W. T. Comstock, 1888.

"An Outbreak of Hotel Building." *Real Estate Record and Builders' Guide* 48 (October 24, 1891): 500–501.

"Over the Draughting Board." *Architectural Record* 13 (January 1903): 85–91.

"Parisian 'Flats.'" *Appleton's Journal* 6 (November 18, 1871): 561–62.

"Passing of the Parlor." *Atlantic* 91 (May 1903): 712–14.

Paul, Samuel. *Apartments: Their Design and Development*. New York: Reinhold, [1967].

Pease and Elliman. *Pease & Elliman's Catalog of East Side New York Apartment Plans*. New York: A. G. Blaisdell, [1929].

Perin, Constance. *Everything in Its Place: Social Order and Land Use in America*. Princeton: Princeton University Press, 1977.

Perks, Sydney. *Residential Flats of All Classes, Including Artisans' Dwellings*. London: B. T. Batsford, 1905.

Phillips' Elite Directory of Private Families and Ladies' Visiting and Shopping Guide for New York City. Annual. New York: Phillips, 1874–1903.

Pink, Louis H. *Old Tenements and the New Law*. New York, 1907.

Pinkney, David H. *Napoleon III and the Rebuilding of Paris.* Princeton: Princeton University Press, 1958.

Platt, Frederick. *America's Gilded Age: Its Architecture and Decoration.* South Brunswick: A.S. Barnes, [1976].

Plunz, Richard. *A History of Housing in New York City.* New York: Columbia University Press, 1989.

Pond, Irving K. "The Architecture of Apartment Buildings." Parts 1–3. *Brickbuilder* 7 (June, July, December 1898): 116–18, 139–40, 249–52.

The Poor in Great Cities. New York: Scribner's, 1895.

Porteous, J. Douglas. "Home: The Territorial Core." *Geographical Review* 66 (October 1976): 383–90.

Potter, Edward Tuckerman. "Comparative Table Illustrating E. T. Potter's System for Concentrated Residences." *American Architect and Building News* 26 (August 10, 1889): 65.

———. "The Problems of Concentrated Residence." *American Architect and Building News* 26 (October 5, 1889): 156–57.

———. "A System of Concentrated Residence." *American Architect and Building News* 26 (December 7, 1889): 266–67.

———. "Tenement Houses." *American Architect and Building News* 70 (November 24, 1900): 59–62.

———. "Urban Housing." Part 5. *American Architect and Building News* 6 (September 27, 1879): 98–99.

———. "Urban Housing in New York." Parts 1–3. *American Architect and Building News* 3 (March 16, April 20, May 18, 1878): 90–91, 137–38, 171–73.

Price, G. Matlack. "A Pioneer in Apartment House Architecture: Philip G. Hubert." *Architectural Record* 36 (July 1914): 74–76.

"The Problem of Living in New York." *Harper's New Monthly Magazine* 65 (November 1882): 918–24.

Przeworski, Adam. *Capitalism and Social Democracy.* Cambridge: Cambridge University Press, 1985.

Putnam, John Pickering. *Architecture under Nationalism.* Boston: Ticknor and the Nationalist Educational Association, 1890.

———. "Architecture under Nationalism." Parts 1–6 *American Architect and Building News* 29 (July 12, 19; August 16, 30; September 13, 27, 1890): 21–25, 40–42, 98–99, 134–35, 168–70, 199–202.

"The Randolph Apartment House, New York, N.Y." *American Architect and Building News* 19 (January 1886): 43.

Real Estate Record Association. *A History of Real Estate, Building, and Architecture in New York.* New York: Record and Guide, 1898.

———. *A Review of Thirty Years' Work.* New York: Record and Guide, 1899.

Reed, Samuel B. *House Plans for Everybody.* 2d ed. New York: Orange Judd, 1878.

Report of the Superintendent of Buildings for the Years 1870 and 1871. New York: William A. Speaight, 1872.

Report on Elevated Dwellings in New York City. New York: New York Evening Post, 1883.

Reynolds, Marcus. *The Housing of the Poor in American Cities.* Publications of the American Economic Association, vol. 8, nos. 2 and 3. Baltimore: American Economic Assoc., 1892.

Richardson, B. W. "Health at Home." Parts 1–4. *Appleton's Journal,* n.s. 8 (April, June 1880): 311, 521–26; n.s. 9 (August, October 1880): 114–19, 376–79.

Richardson, James. "The New Homes of New York." *Scribner's Monthly* 8 (1874): 63–76.

Rideing, William H. "Rapid Transit in New York." *Appleton's Journal* 4 (May 1878): 393–408.

Riis, Jacob August. *A Ten Years' War: An Account of the Battle with the Slum in New York.* New York: Houghton Mifflin, 1900.

Roberts, Henry. *The Dwellings of the Labouring Classes.* London: Seeleys, [1855].

Rosenwaike, Ira. *Population History of New York City.* Syracuse, N.Y.: Syracuse University Press, 1972.

Ryan, Mary. *Cradle of the Middle Class: The Family in Oneida County, New York, 1790–1865.* Cambridge: Cambridge University Press, 1981.

Saegert, Susan. "Masculine Cities and Feminine Suburbs: Polarized Ideas, Contradictory Realities" *Signs* 5 (Spring 1980): S96–S111. Supplementary issue: *Women and the American City.*

Safdie, Moshe. *For Everyone a Garden.* Cambridge: MIT Press, 1974.

Saglio, Maurice. "City Apartment Houses in Paris." *Architectural Record* 5 (June 1896): 347–61.

Saint, Andrew. *Richard Norman Shaw.* New Haven: Yale University Press, 1976.

Schneider, Donald D. "The Works and Doctrine of Jacques I. Hittorff." Ph.D. diss., Princeton University, 1971.

Schopfer, Jean. "City Apartments in Paris." *Architectural Review* (Boston) 10 (July 1903): 91–97.

Schuyler, Montgomery. *American Architecture and Other Writings.* 2 vols. Ed. William Jordy and Ralph Coe. Cambridge, Mass.: Harvard University Press, Belknap Press, 1961.

———. "Henry Janeway Hardenbergh." *Architectural Record* 6 (January–March 1897): 335–75.

———. "The New New York House." *Architectural Record* 19 (February 1906): 83–103.

Sennett, Richard. *The Fall of Public Man.* New York: Random House, Vintage Books, 1978.

Sherwood, Roger. *Modern Housing Prototypes.* Cambridge, Mass.: Harvard University Press, 1978.

Siegal, Adrienne. *The Image of the American City in Popular Literature, 1820–1870.* Port Washington, N.Y.: Kennikat Press, and London: National University Publications, 1981.

Silver, Nathan. *Lost New York.* Boston: Houghton Mifflin, 1967.

Sklar, Kathryn Kish. *Catharine Beecher: A Study in American Domesticity.* New Haven: Yale University Press, 1973.

"A Small Apartment" (letter). *House Beautiful* 19 (January 1906): 6–7.

Smith, Henry Nash. *Popular Culture and Industrialism, 1865–1890.* New York: Doubleday, Anchor Books, 1967.

Sopher, David E. "The Landscape of Home." In *Interpretation of Ordinary Landscapes,* ed. D. W. Meinig, pp. 129–49. New York: Oxford University Press, 1979.

Sparrow, W. Shaw, ed. *Flats, Urban Houses, and Cottage Homes.* London: Hodder and Stoughton, 1907.

Speed, Jno. Gilmer. "Naming Apartment Houses." *Harper's Weekly* 38 (March 24, 1894): 283.

Stansell, Christine. *City of Women: Sex and Class in New York 1789—1860.* New York: Knopf, 1986.

Stern, Robert A. M. "With Rhetoric: The New York Apartment House." *Via* 4 (1980): 78–111.

Stockton, Frank R., and Marian Stockton. *The Home: Where It Should Be and What to Put in It.* New York: Putnam's, 1873.

Stokes, Isaac Newton Phelps. *Inconography of Manhattan Island.* 6 vols. New York: R. H. Dodd, 1915–28.

Stone, May. "Plumbing Paradox." *Winterthur Portfolio* 14 (Autumn 1979): 283–304.

Strasser, Susan. *Never Done: A History of American Housework.* New York: Pantheon, 1982.

Sturgis, Russell. "Interior Decoration of the City House." *Harper's Monthly* 99 (July 1899): 208–21.

Superintendent of Buildings of New York. "The Building Transactions of the Past Year." *American Architect and Building News* 7 (February 7, 1880): 47.

Sutcliffe, Anthony, ed. *Multi-Storey Living: The British Working Class Experience.* London: Croom Helm, and New York: Cambridge University Press, 1974.

Tarn, John Nelson. *Five Per Cent Philanthropy: An Account of Housing in Urban Areas between 1840 and 1914.* New York: Cambridge University Press, 1973.

"Tenement House Competition." Parts 1–3. *Plumber and Sanitary Engineer* 2 (March, April, May 1879): 103–106, 131–32, 158–59.

"The Tenement House Movement." *American Architect and Building News* 5 (May 1879): 146.

"The Tenement House Problem." *American Architect and Building News* 8 (July 1880): 39–40, 53–54.

Tenement House Reform: Final Report. New York: Committee of Nine, 1879.

Thoms, William F. *Tenant Houses: Their Ground Area, Cubic Feet of Air Space, and Ventilation.* Albany, N.Y., 1867.

Tomes, Robert. "The Houses We Live In." *Harper's New Monthly Magazine* 30 (May 1865): 735–41.

Torré, Susana, Cynthia Rock, and Gwendolyn Wright. "Rethinking Closets, Kitchens, and Other Forgotten Spaces." *Ms.* 6 (December 1977): 54–55.

Trachtenberg, Alan. *The Incorporation of America: Culture and Society in the Gilded Age.* New York: Hill and Wang, 1982.

Trescott, Martha Moore, ed. *Dynamos and Virgins Revisited: Women and Technological Change.* Methuen, N.J.: Scarecrow Press, 1979.

Turnure, Arthur B. "Co-operative Public Laundries." *Cosmopolitan* 9 (August 1890): 423.

Tuthill, William B. *The City Residence: Its Design and Construction.* New York: W. T. Comstock, 1890.

United States Bureau of the Census. *Thirteenth Census of the United States Taken in the Year 1910.* Abstract of the Census. Washington, D.C.: Government Printing Office, 1912.

Van der Bent, Teunis J. *Planning of Apartment Houses, Tenements, and Country Homes.* New York: Brentano's, [1917].

Van Gashen, F. *Tenement Houses in Philadelphia.* Philadelphia: Civic Club of Phila., 1895.

"Vast Apartment Houses." *Real Estate Record and Builders' Guide* 29 (June 3, 1882): 550.

Vaux, Calvert. "American Institute of Architects Address." *Crayon* 4 (July 1857): 218.

———. "Parisian Buildings for City Residents." *Harper's Weekly* 1 (December 19, 1857): 809–10.

———. *Villas and Cottages.* New York: Harper, 1867.

Veiller, Lawrence. "The Charity Organization Society's Tenement House Competition." *American Architect and Building News* 67 (March 1900): 77–79.

———. *Tenement House Legislation in New York, 1852–1900.* Albany, N.Y., 1900.

"The Venerable Dakota in New York." *Architectural Forum* 110 (March 1959): 122–29.

Walker, Francis A. "Our Domestic Service." *Scribner's Monthly* 11 (December 1875): 273–78.

Ware, James E. "New York's Great Movement of Housing Reform." *Review of Reviews,* December 1896, pp. 693–701.

Ware, John F. *Home Life: What It Is and What It Needs.* Boston: Wm. V. Spencer, 1866.

Waring, George E., Jr. *Report on the Social Statistics of Cities.* Washington, D.C.: Government Printing Office, 1886. Reprint ed., New York: Arno, 1970.

_____. "The Sanitary 'Scare.'" *American Architect and Building News* 4 (November 1878): 180.

"The Washington Apartments on 29 Washington Square West, New York City." *Building* 4 (January 1886): 42.

Weaver, S. Fullerton. "Planning the Modern Apartment Hotel." *Architectural Forum* 41 (November 1924): 205–12 (a special issue on apartment hotels).

Westfall, Carroll William. "From Homes to Towers: A Century of Chicago's Best Hotels and Tall Apartment Buildings." In John Zukowsky, ed., *Chicago Architecture, 1872–1922: Birth of a Metropolis.* Chicago: Art Institute of Chicago, 1987.

Wharton, Edith. *The Age of Innocence.* New York: Scribner's, 1968.

_____. *The Custom of the Country.* New York: Scribner's, 1913.

_____. *House of Mirth.* New York: Scribner's, 1905.

Wheeler, Candace, ed. *Household Art.* New York: Harper, 1893.

Wheeler, Gervase. *Homes for the People in Suburb and Country: The Villa, the Mansion, and the Cottage.* New York: Scribner's, 1855. Reprint ed., New York: Arno, 1972.

White, Alfred Treadway. *Better Homes for Working Men.* New York, 1885.

_____. *Improved Dwellings for the Laboring Classes.* New York: Putnam's, 1879.

_____. *The Riverside Buildings of the Improved Dwellings Co.* [Brooklyn, N.Y.], 1890.

_____. *Sunlighted Tenements: Thirty-five Years' Experience as an Owner.* National Housing Association Publication, no. 12. New York, 1912.

White, Richard Grant. "Old New York and Its Houses." *Century* 26, n.s. 4 (May–October 1883): 845–59.

Wight, Peter B. "Apartment Houses Practically Considered." *Putnam's Magazine* 16 (September 1870): 306–13.

Williamson, Ernest Jefferson. *The American Hotel.* New York: Knopf, 1930.

Wilson, Margaret Gibbons. *The American Woman in Transition: The Urban Influence, 1870–1920.* Westport, Conn.: Greenwood Press, 1979.

Winkler, Franz K. "Recent Apartment House Design: Central Park West, New York." *Architectural Record* 11 (January 1902): 98–109.

Women's Own Book. Jewett City, Conn.: Reade Publishing, 1873.

Wood, Edith Elmer. *The Homes the Public Builds.* New York: Public Affairs Committee, 1940.

"Works of Ernest Flagg." *Architectural Record* 11 (April 1902): 38–47.

World's Loose-Leaf Album of Apartment Houses. New York: New York World, 1910.

Wright, Gwendolyn. *Building the Dream: A History of American Housing.* New York: Pantheon, 1981.

_____. *Moralism and the Model Home: Domestic Architecture and Cultural Conflict in Chicago, 1873–1913.* Chicago: University of Chicago Press, 1980.

Wright, Julia McNair. *The Complete Home: An Encyclopedia of Domestic Life and Affairs.* Philadelphia: J. Garrettson, 1885.

Wright, Lawrence. *Clean and Decent: The Fascinating History of the Bathroom and the Water Closet.* Toronto and Buffalo: University of Toronto Press, 1967.

Young, Sarah Gilman. *European Modes of Living, or the Question of Apartment Houses.* New York: Putnam's, 1881.

_____. "Foreign Modes of Living." *Galaxy* 14 (1872): 474–82.

Zeisloft, E. Idell. *The New Metropolis.* New York: Appleton, 1899.

INDEX

Library of Congress Cataloging-in-Publication Data

Cromley, Elizabeth C.
  Alone together : a history of New York's early apartments /
Elizabeth Collins Cromley.
       p. cm.
    Bibliography: p.
    Includes index.
    ISBN 0–8014–2324–4
    1. Apartment buildings—New York (N.Y.)   2. Architecture,
Modern—19th century—New York (N.Y.)   3. Architecture, Modern—20th
century—New York (N.Y.)   4. Architecture and society—New York
(N.Y.)   I. Title.
  NA7860.C76   1989
  728'.314'09747109034—dc20   89-42869